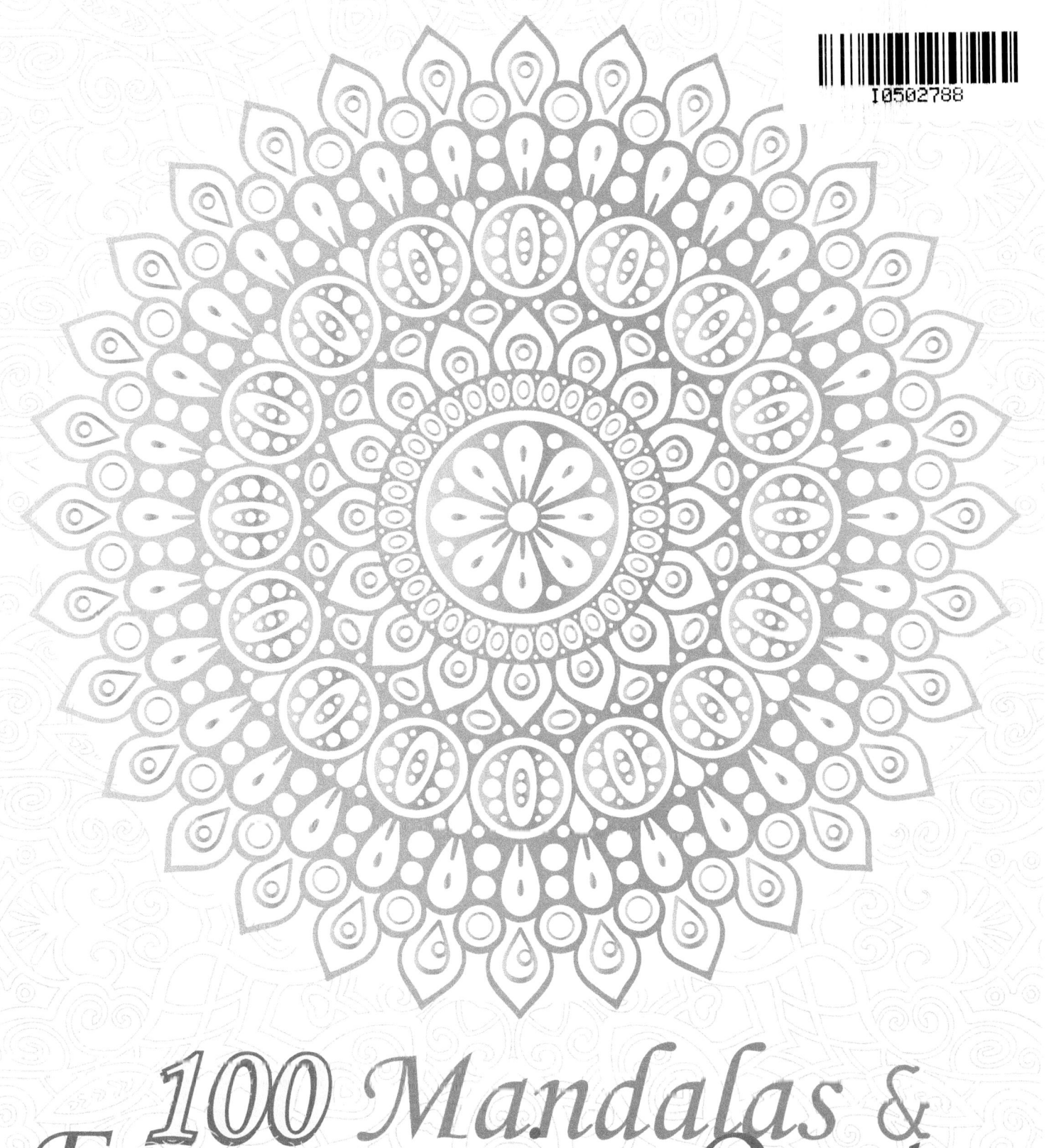

100 Mandalas & Empowering Quotes
Just Add Color

Philip F. Ambrosio

For all those who
revel in the tranquility
of coloring ...

This is for you

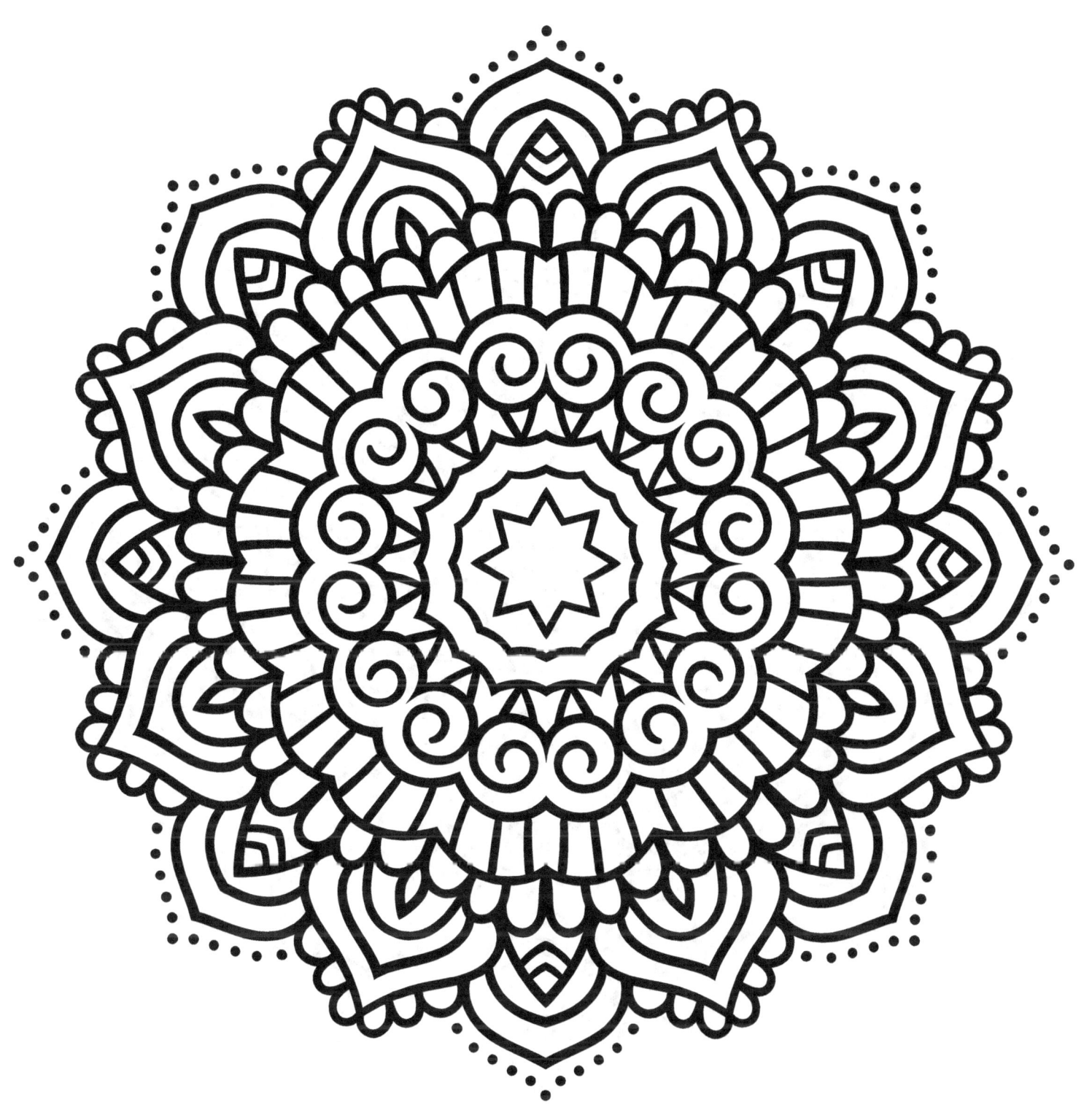

Perfection is not attainable,
but if we chase perfection we can catch excellence.
—Vince Lombardi

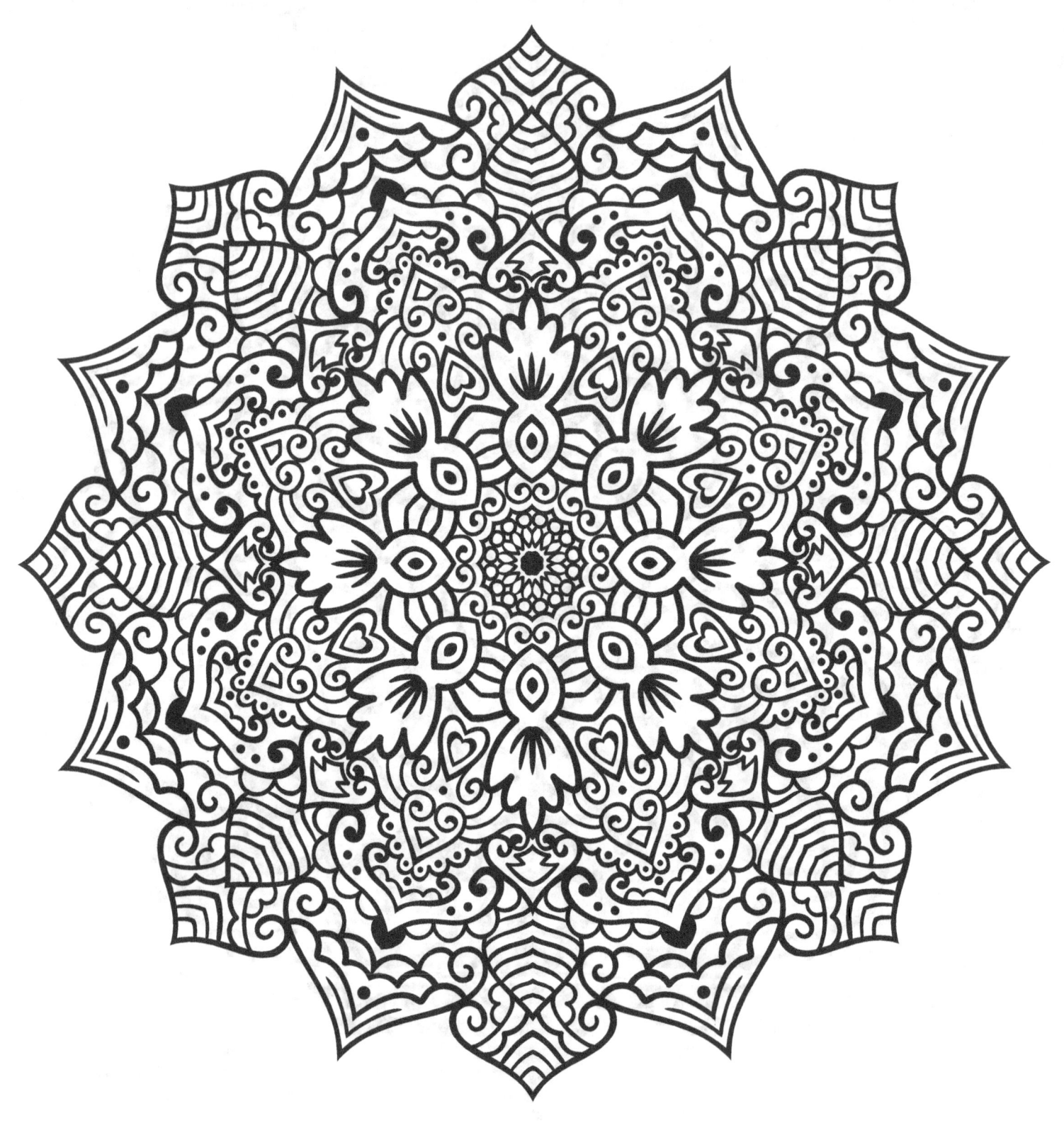

*I can't change the direction of the wind,
but I can adjust my sails to always reach
my destination.*
—Jimmy Dean

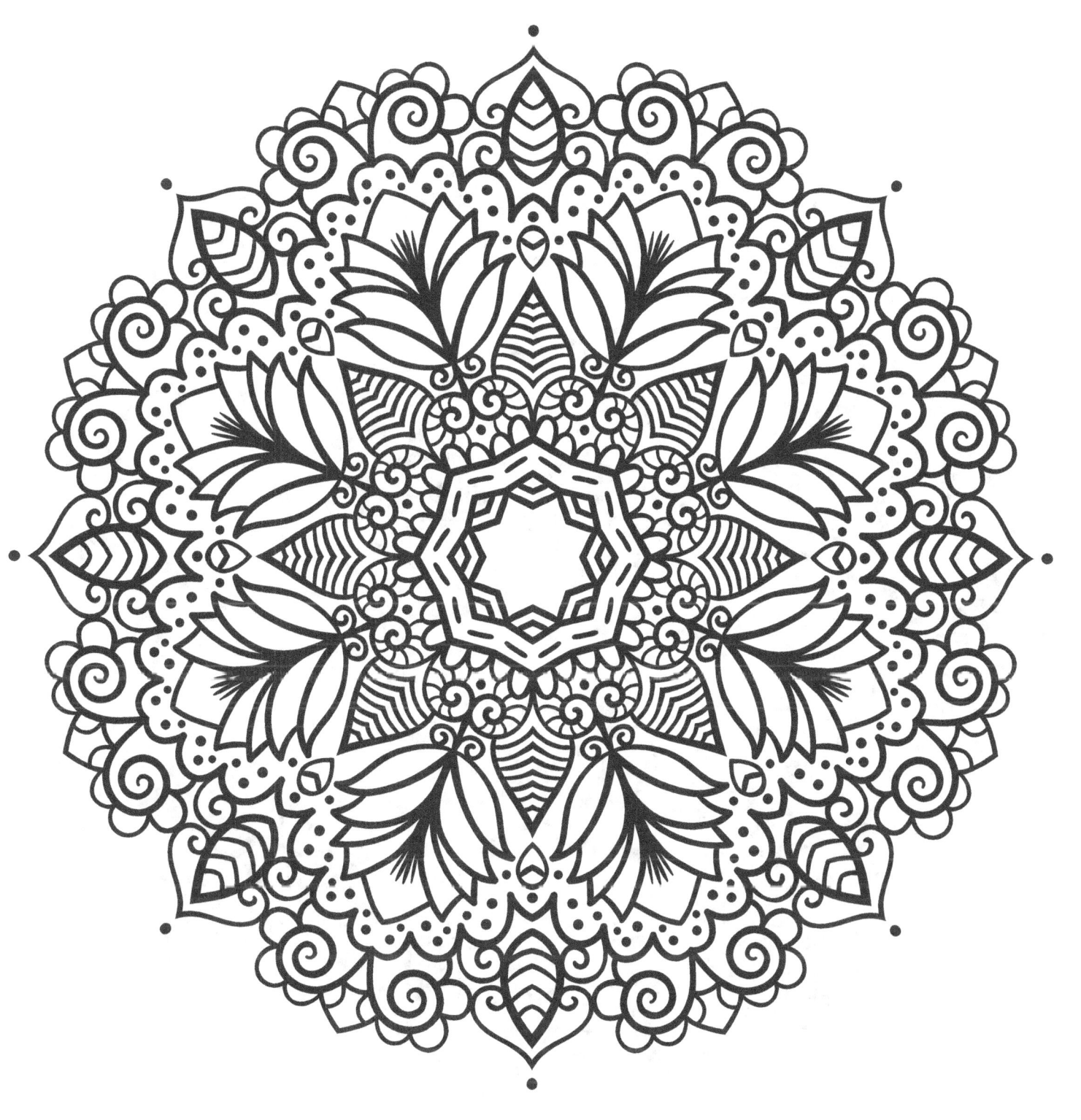

*Too many of us are not living our dreams
because we are living our fears.
—Les Brown*

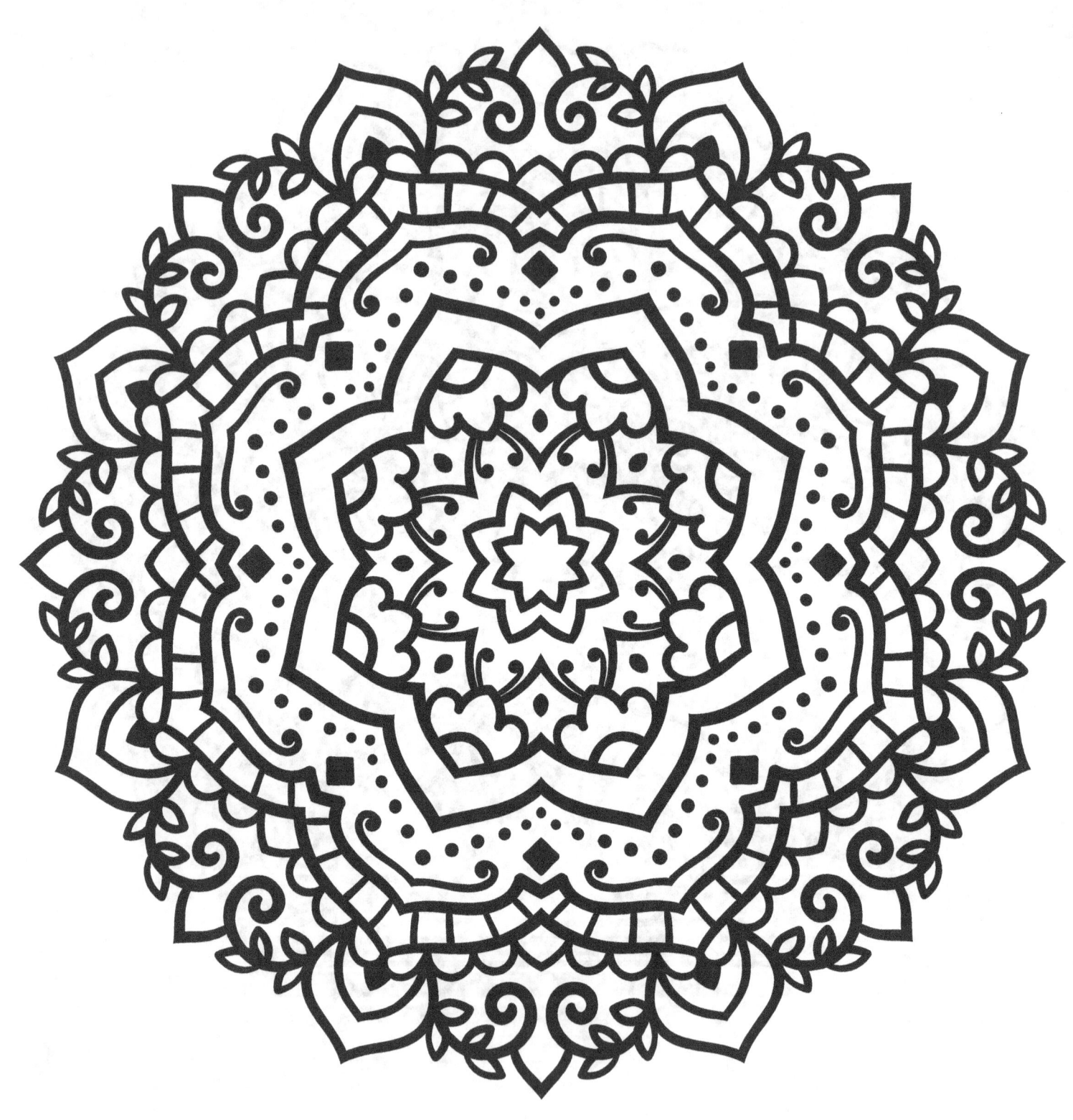

*To handle yourself, use your head;
to handle others, use your heart.
—Eleanor Roos*

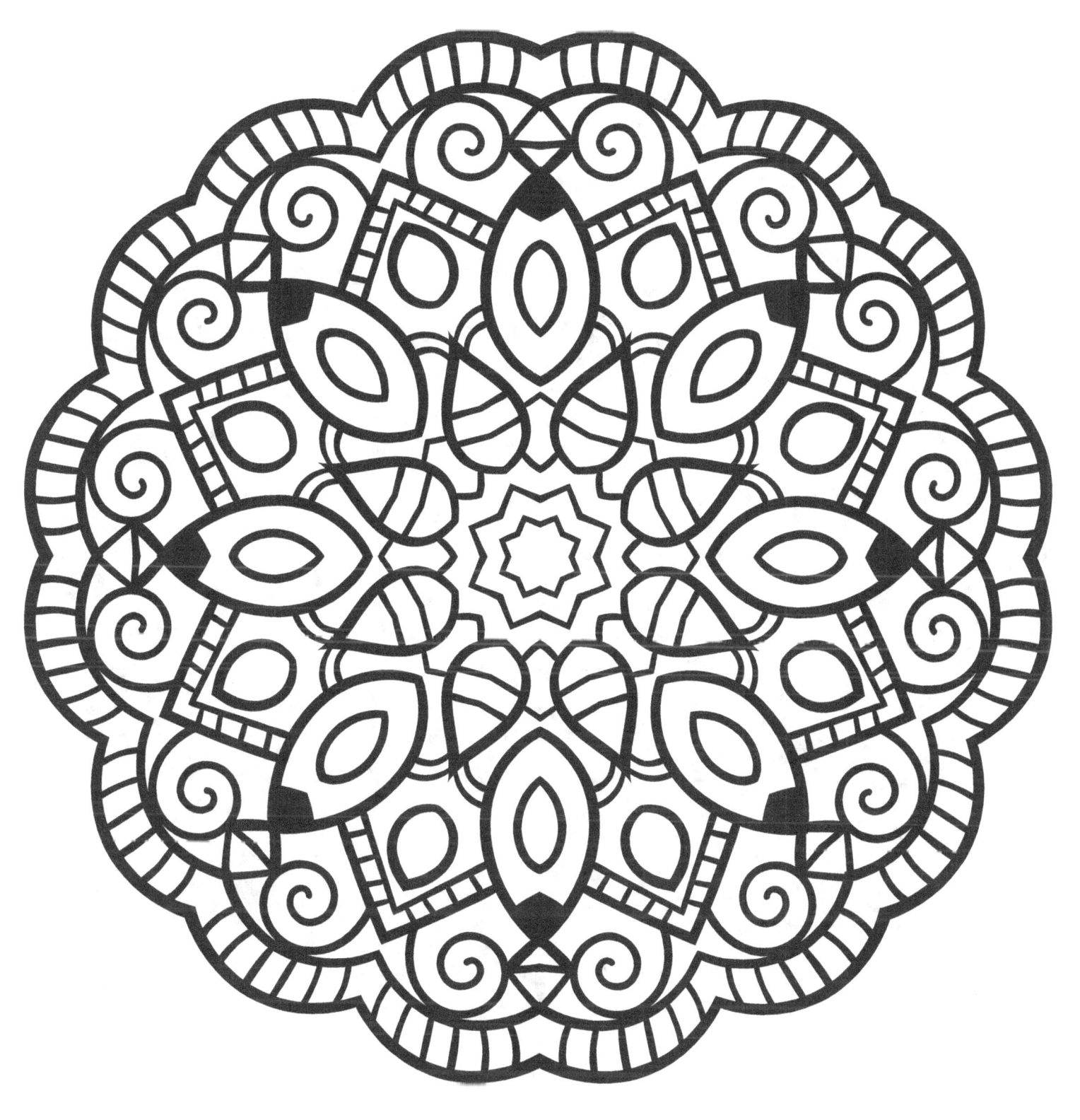

Do or do not. There is no try.
—Yoda

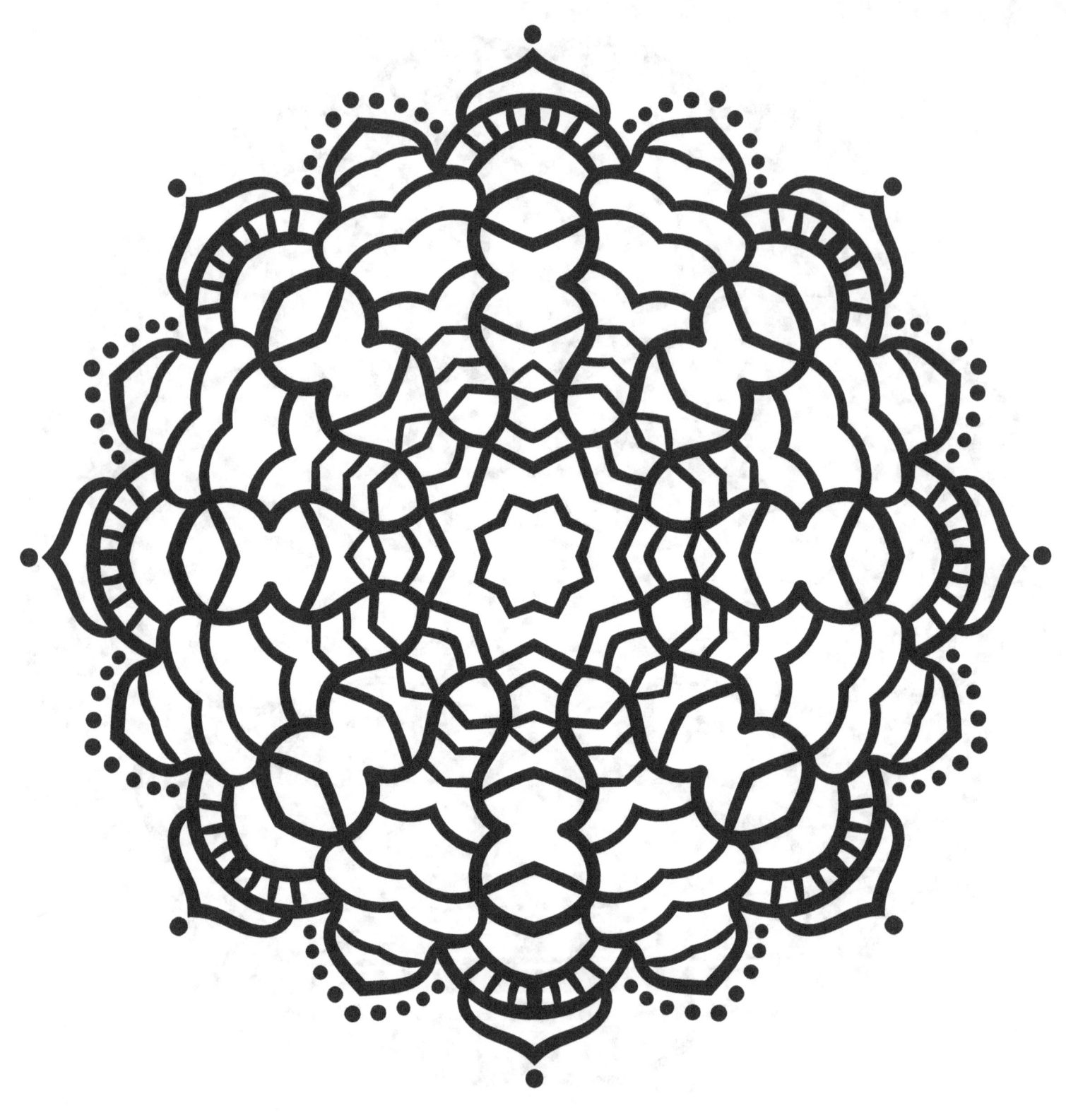

Believe you can and you're halfway there.
—Theodore Roosevelt

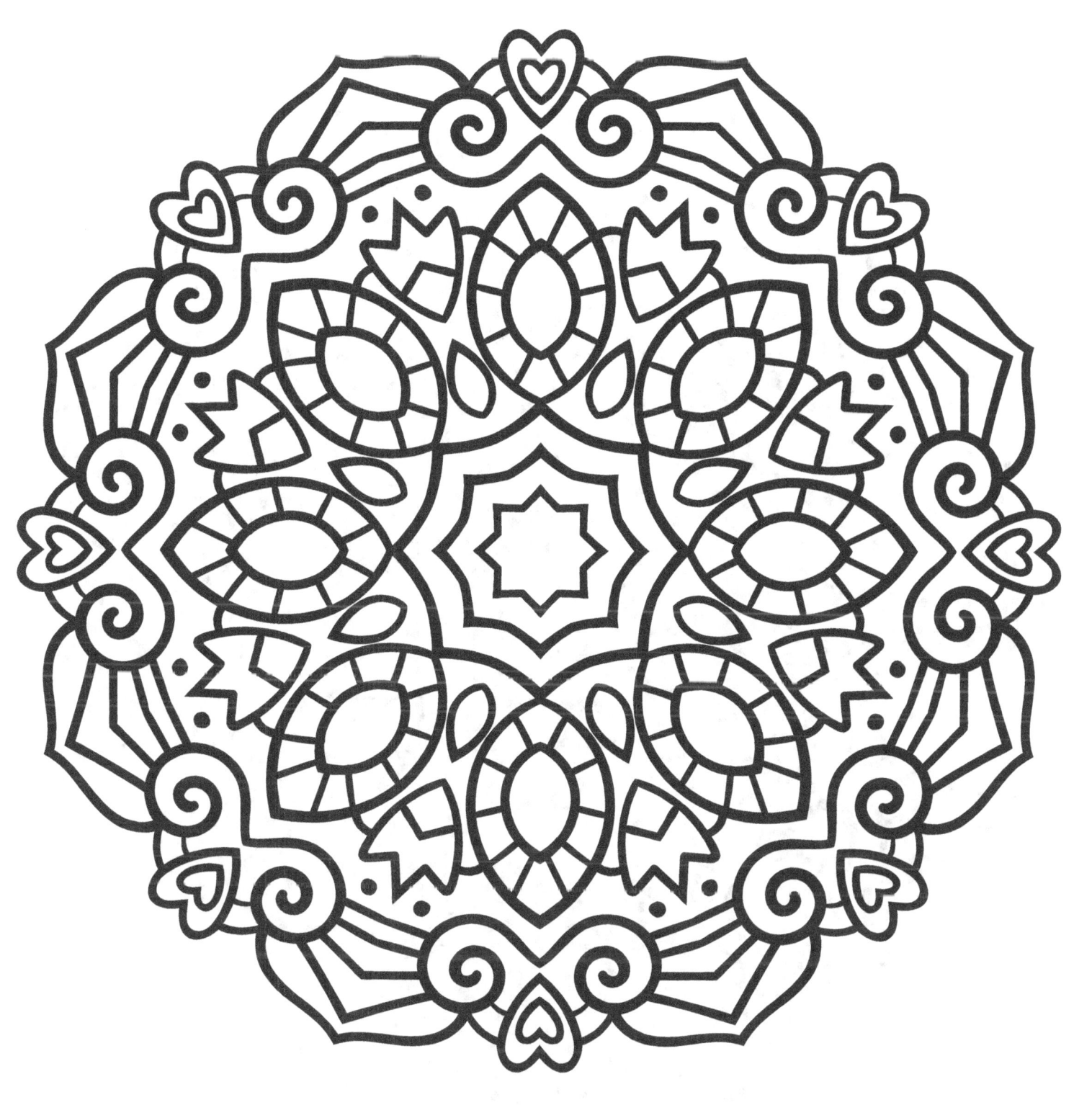

I am not a product of my circumstances.
I am a product of my decisions.
—Stephen Covey

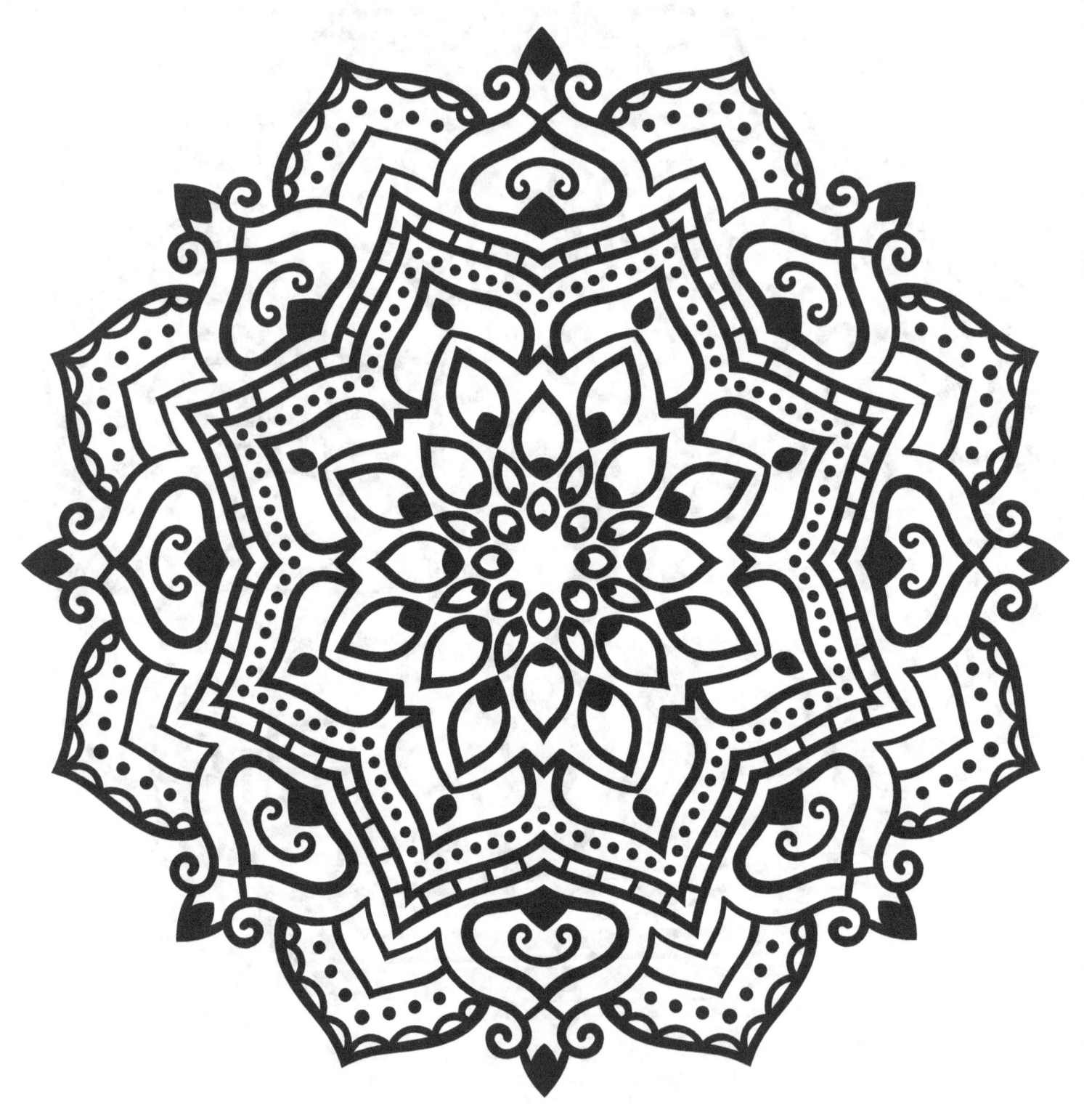

*It is during our darkest moments
that we must focus to see the light.
—Aristotle Onassis*

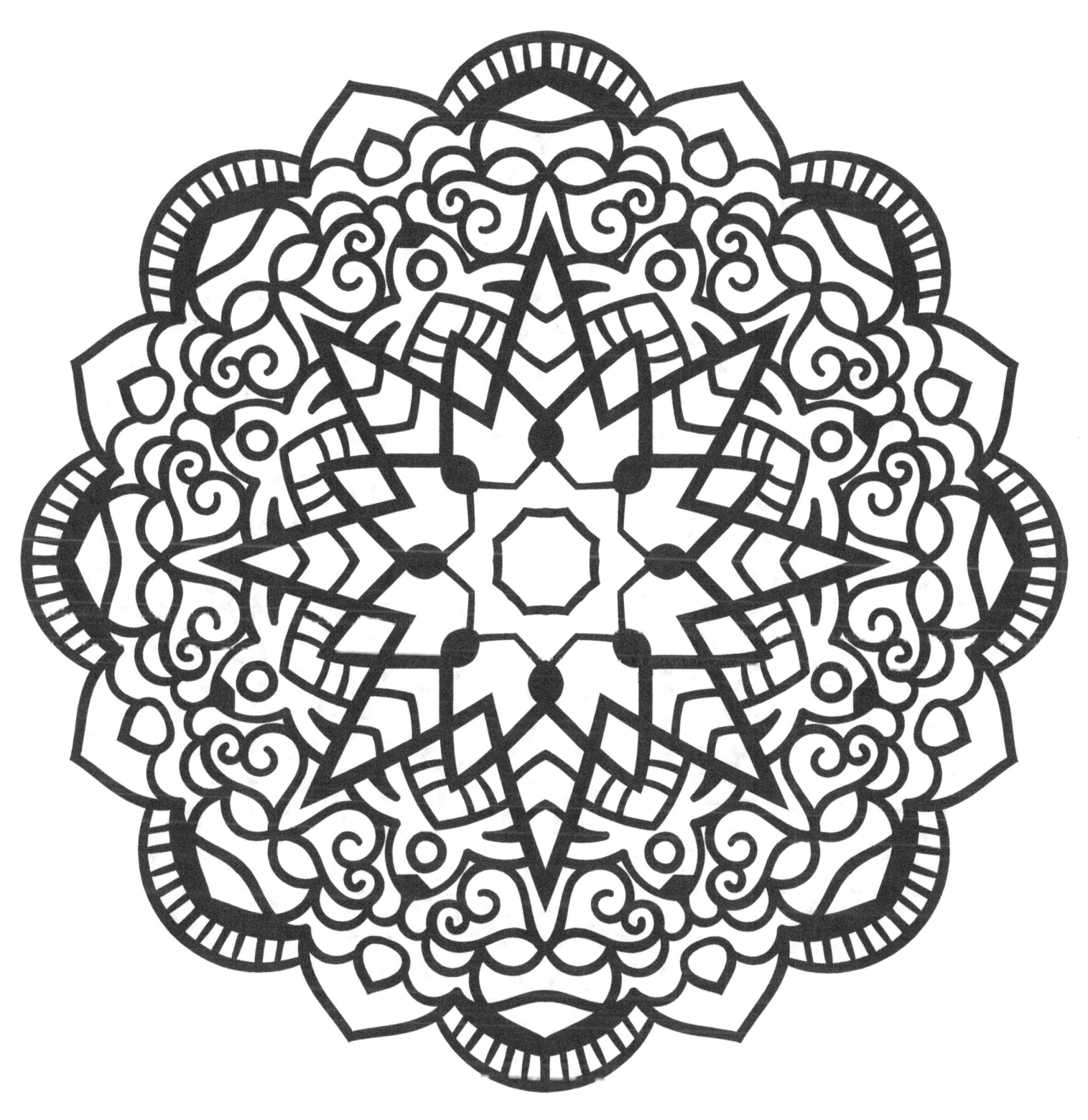

The only way to do great work
is to love what you do.
—Steve Jobs

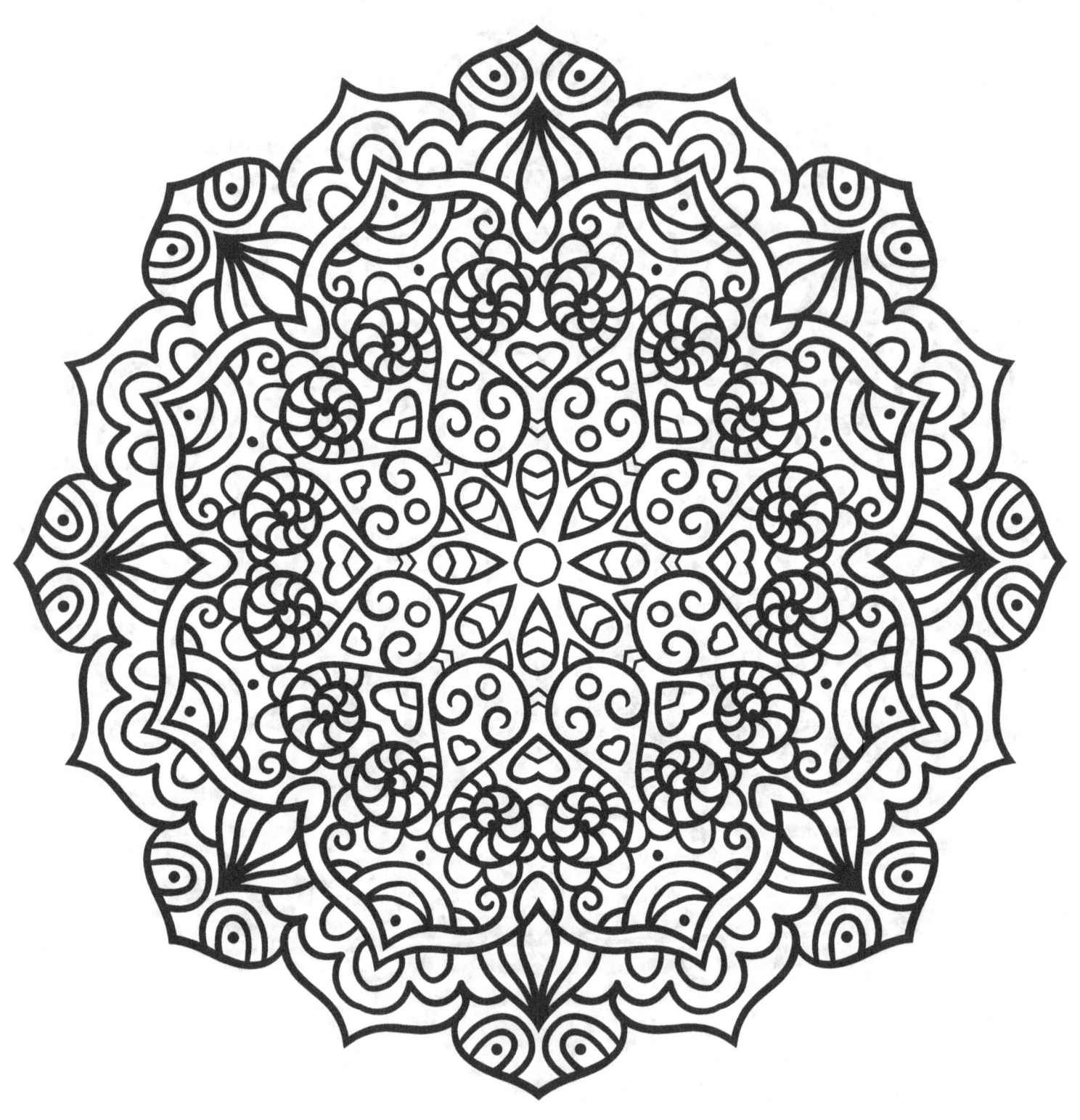

*Don't judge each day by the harvest you reap
but by the seeds that you plant.*
—Robert Louis Stevenson

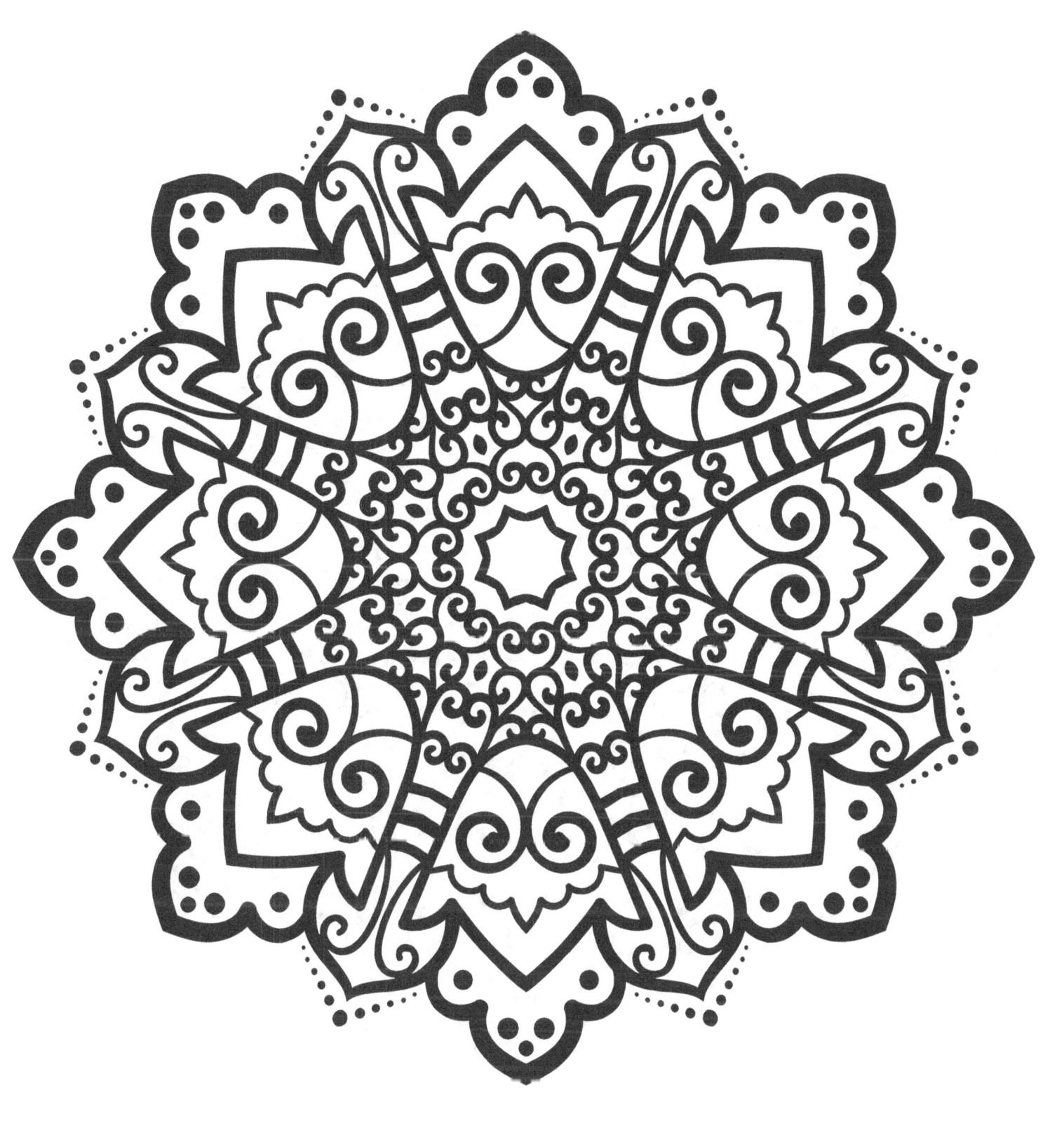

If you hear a voice within you say
"you cannot paint," then by all means paint and that voice
will be silenced.
—Vincent Van Gogh

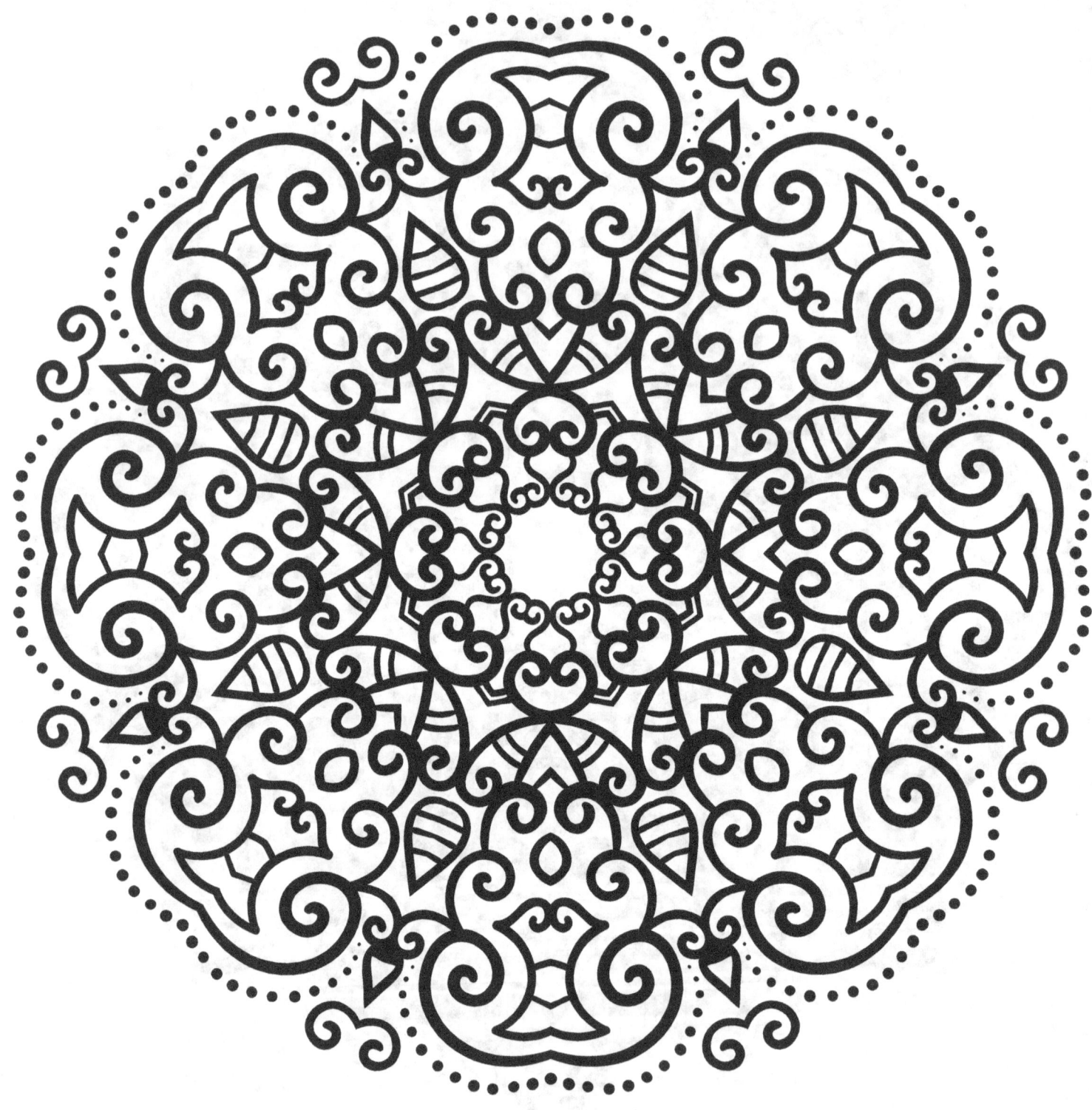

*Remember that not getting what you want
is sometimes a wonderful stroke of luck.*
—Dalai Lama

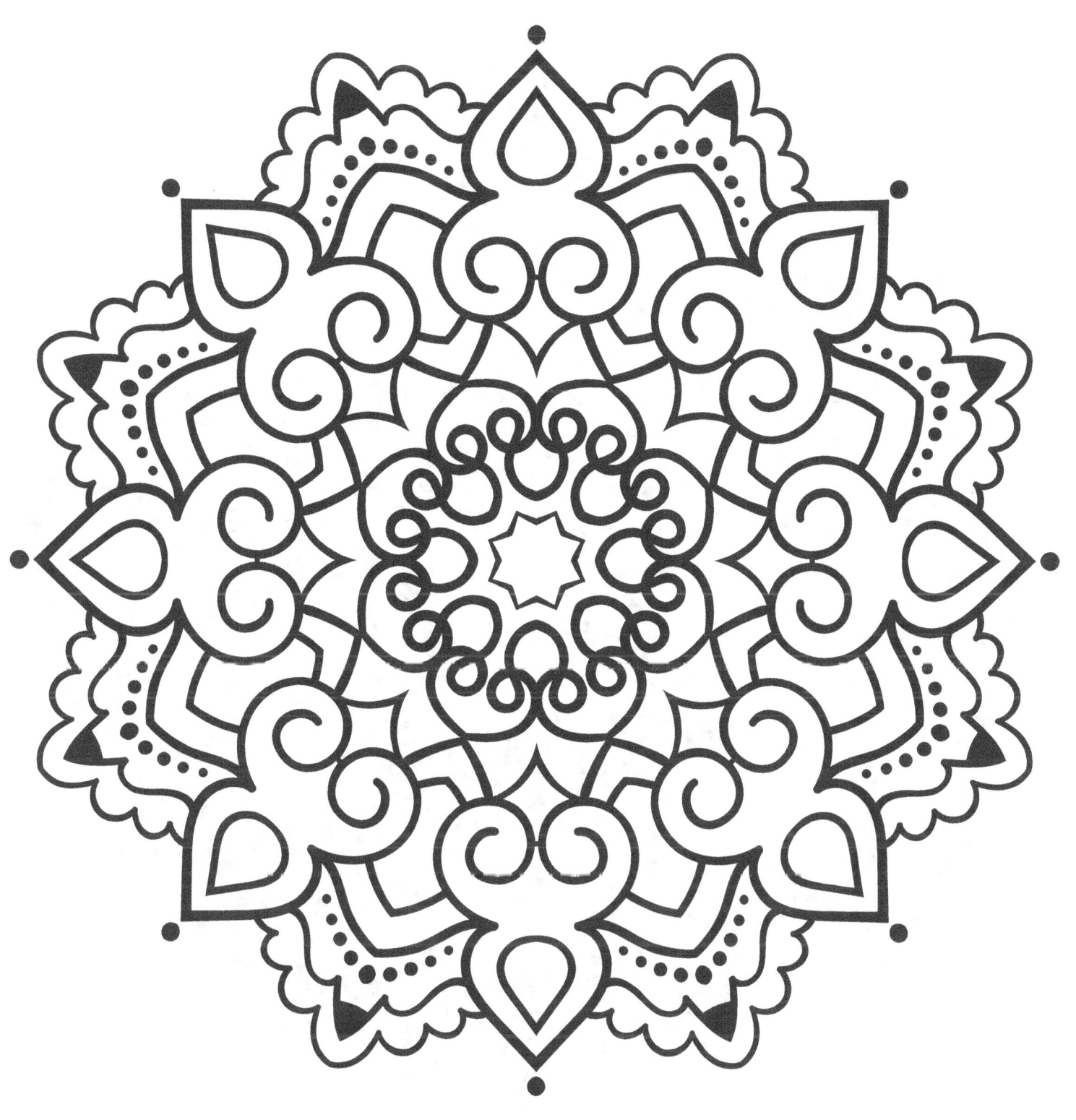

I have learned over the years that when one's mind is made up, this diminishes fear.
—Rosa Parks

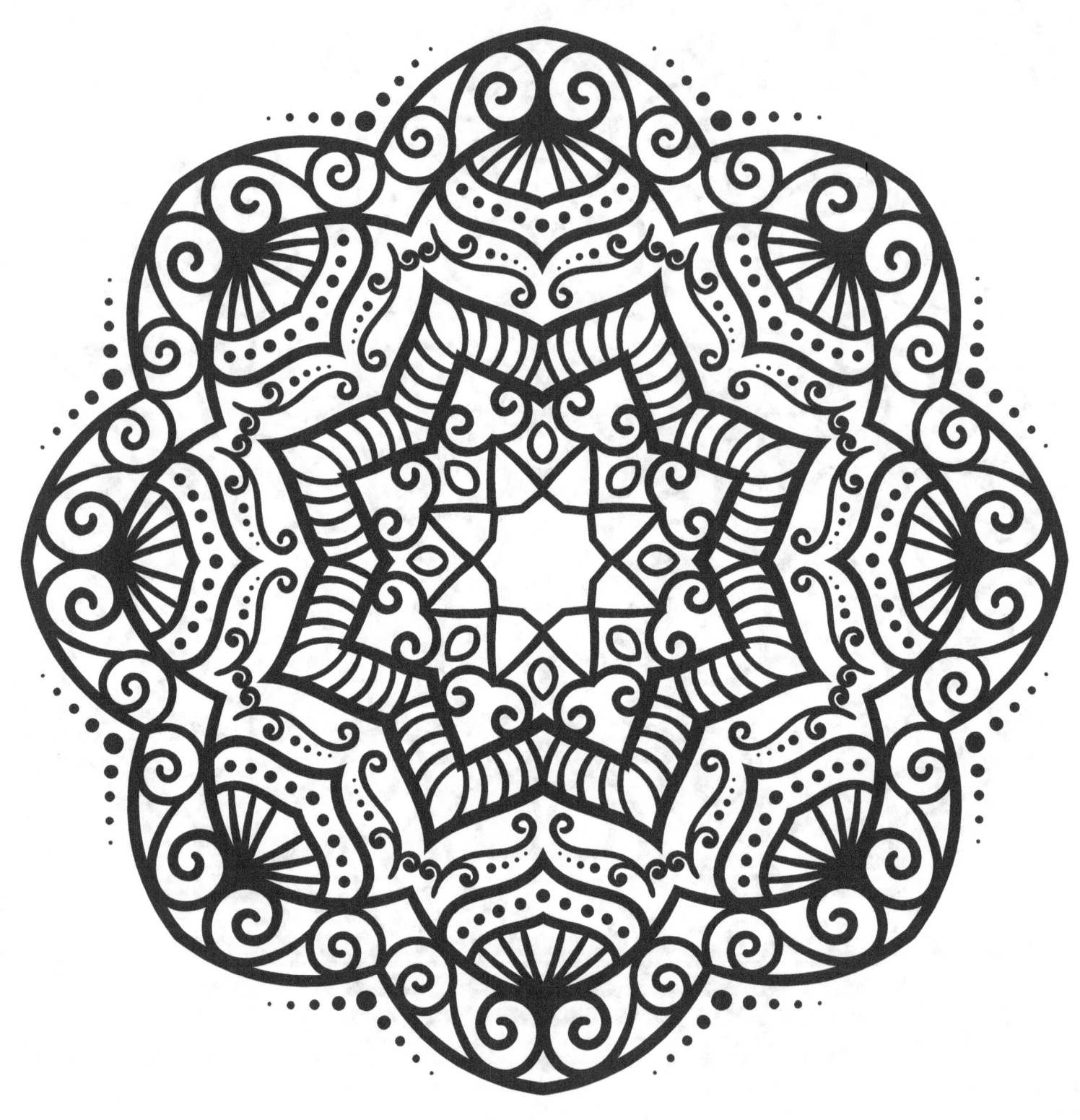

The question isn't who is going to let me;
it's who is going to stop me.
—Ayn Rand

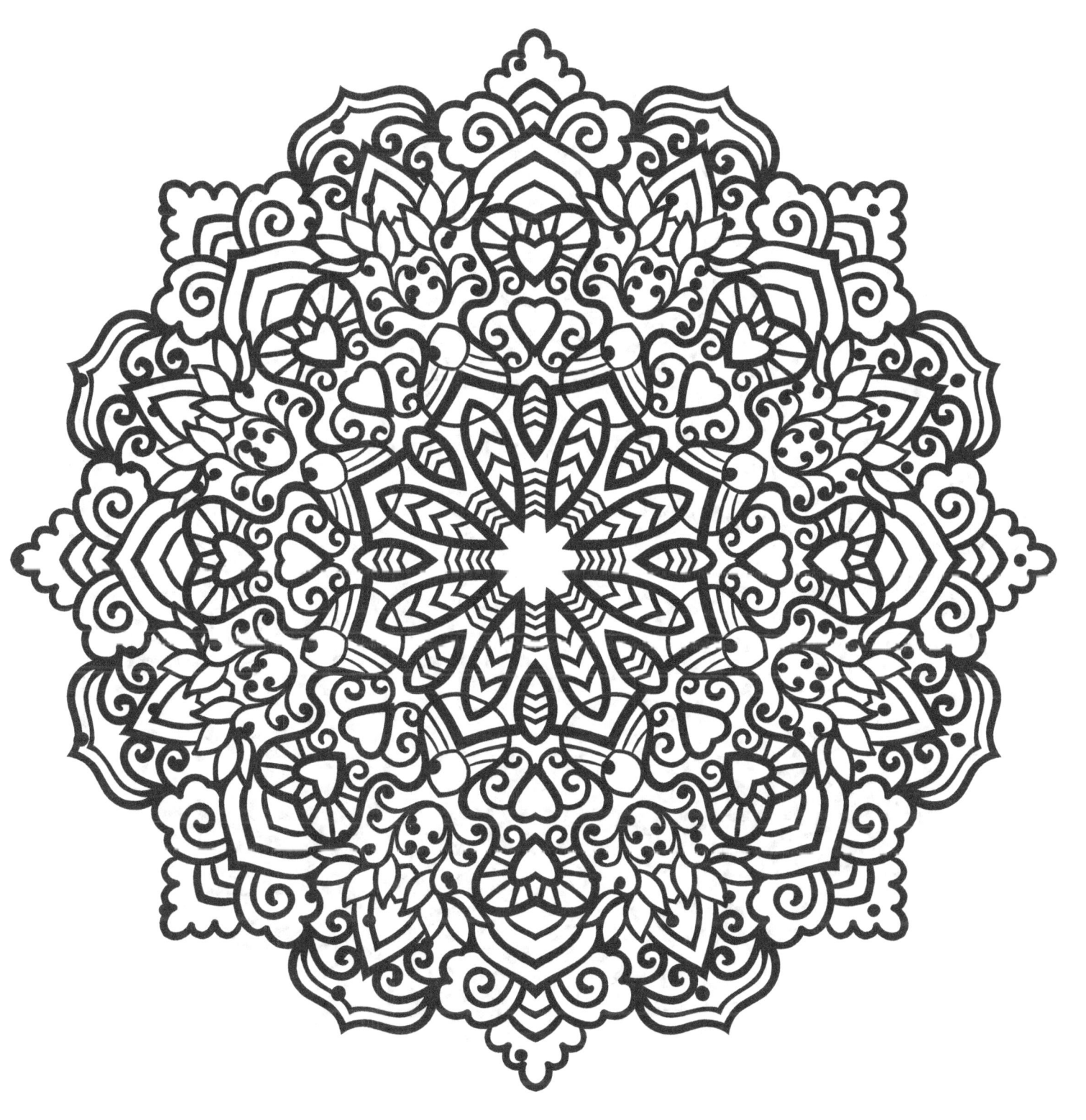

A person who never made a mistake
never tried anything new.
—Albert Einstein

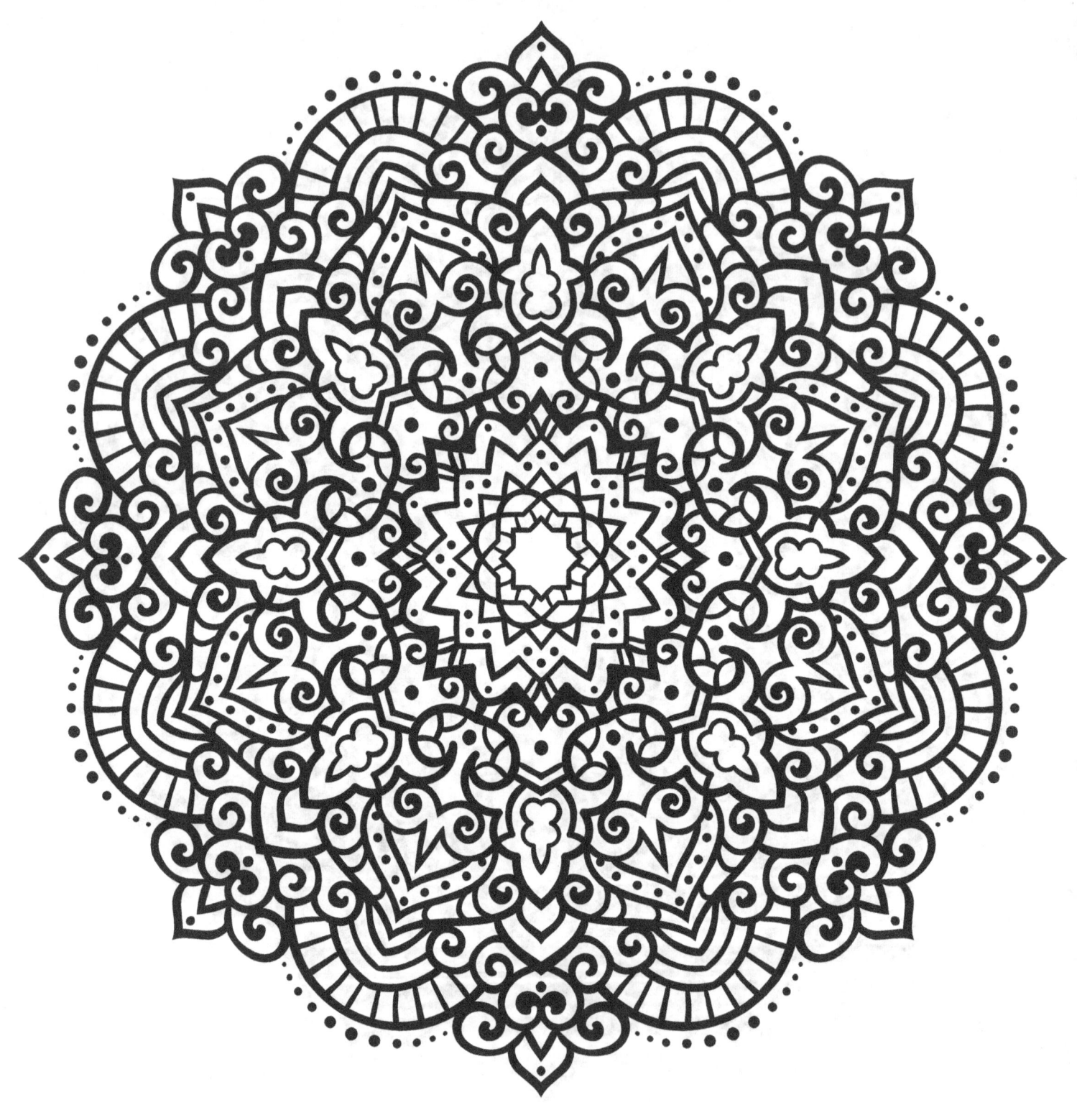

If you're offered a seat on a rocket ship,
don't ask what seat! Just get on.
—Sheryl Sandberg

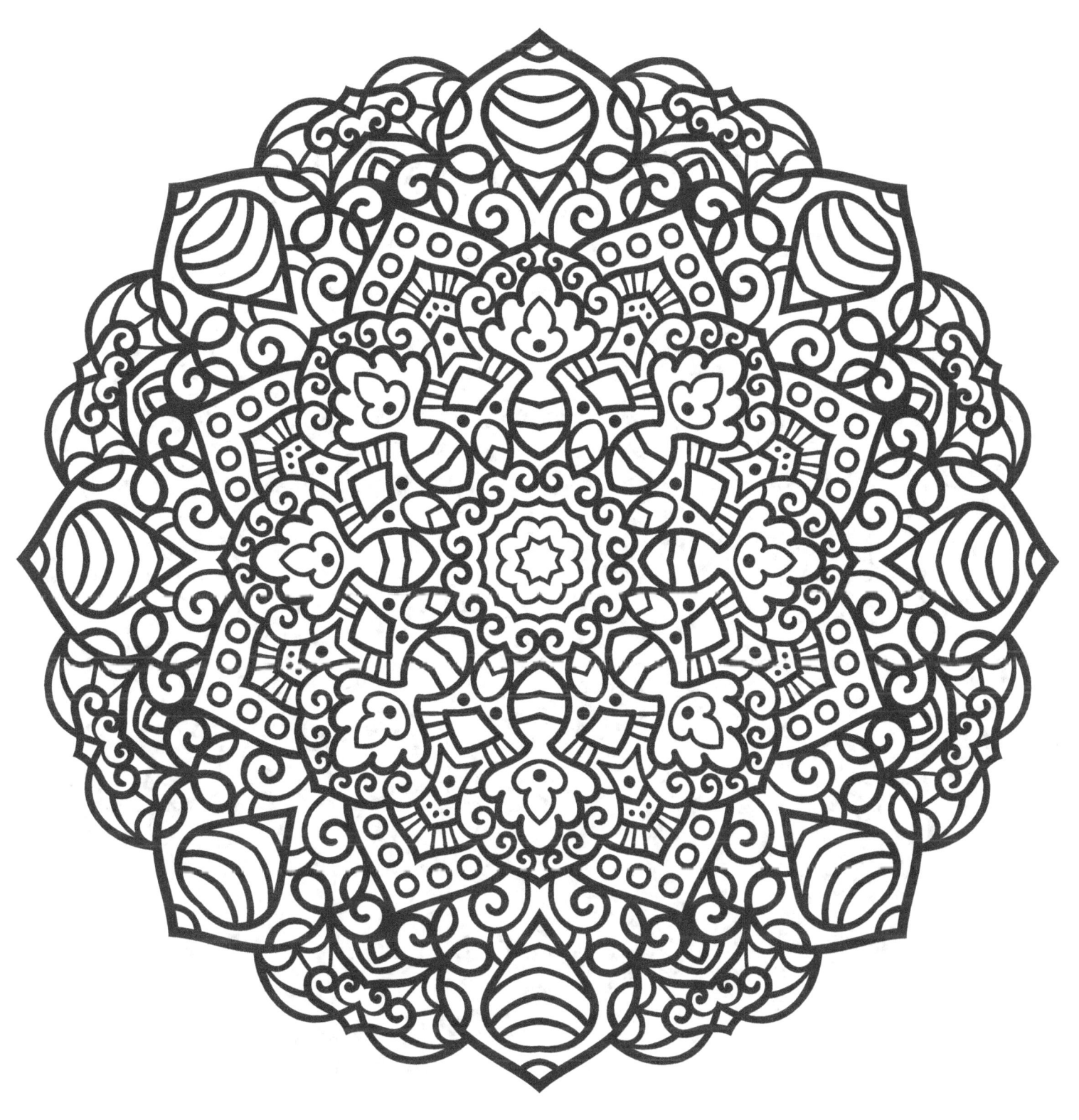

Everything has beauty,
but not everyone can see.
—Confucius

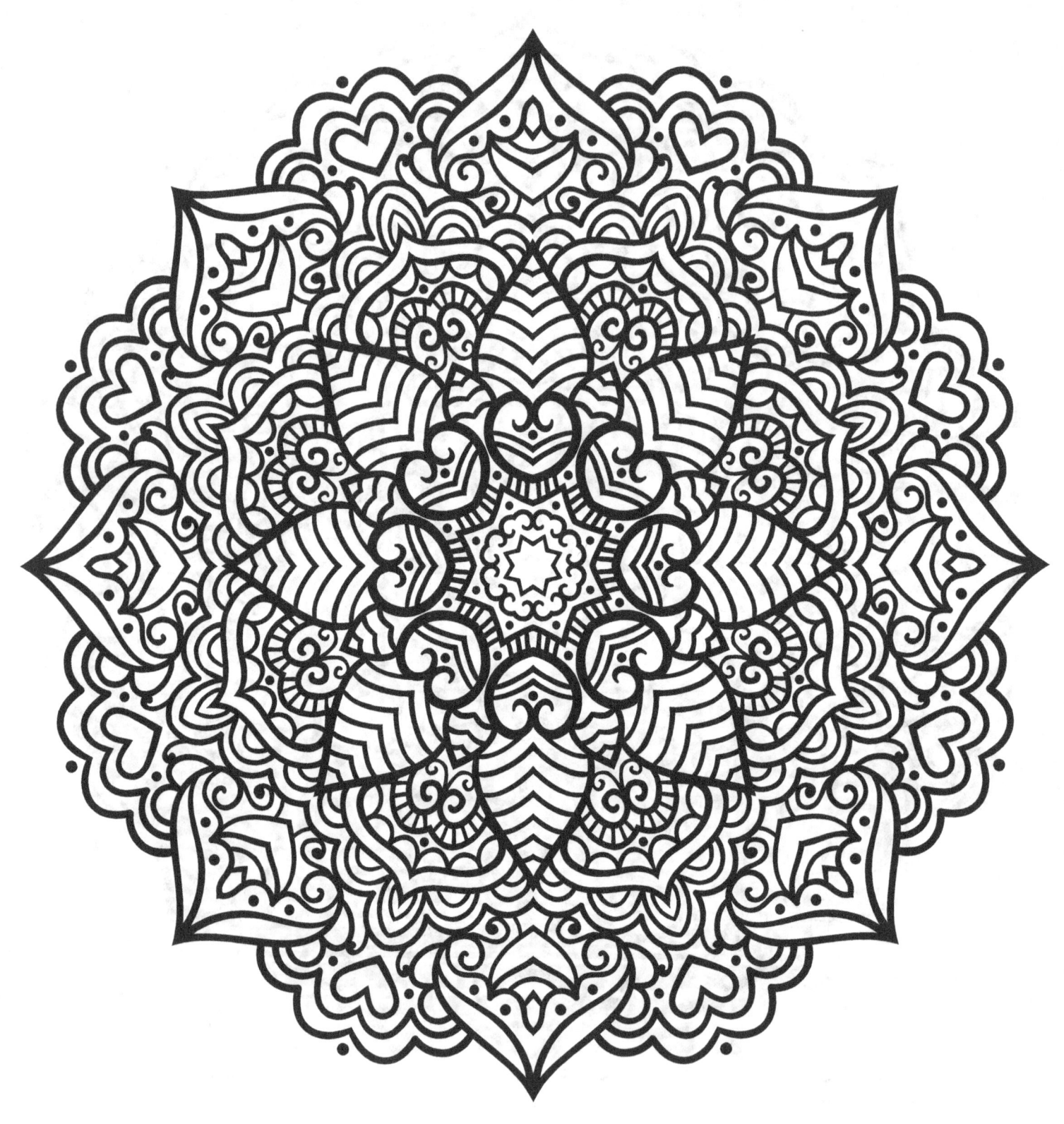

We can't help everyone,
but everyone can help someone.
—Ronald Reagan

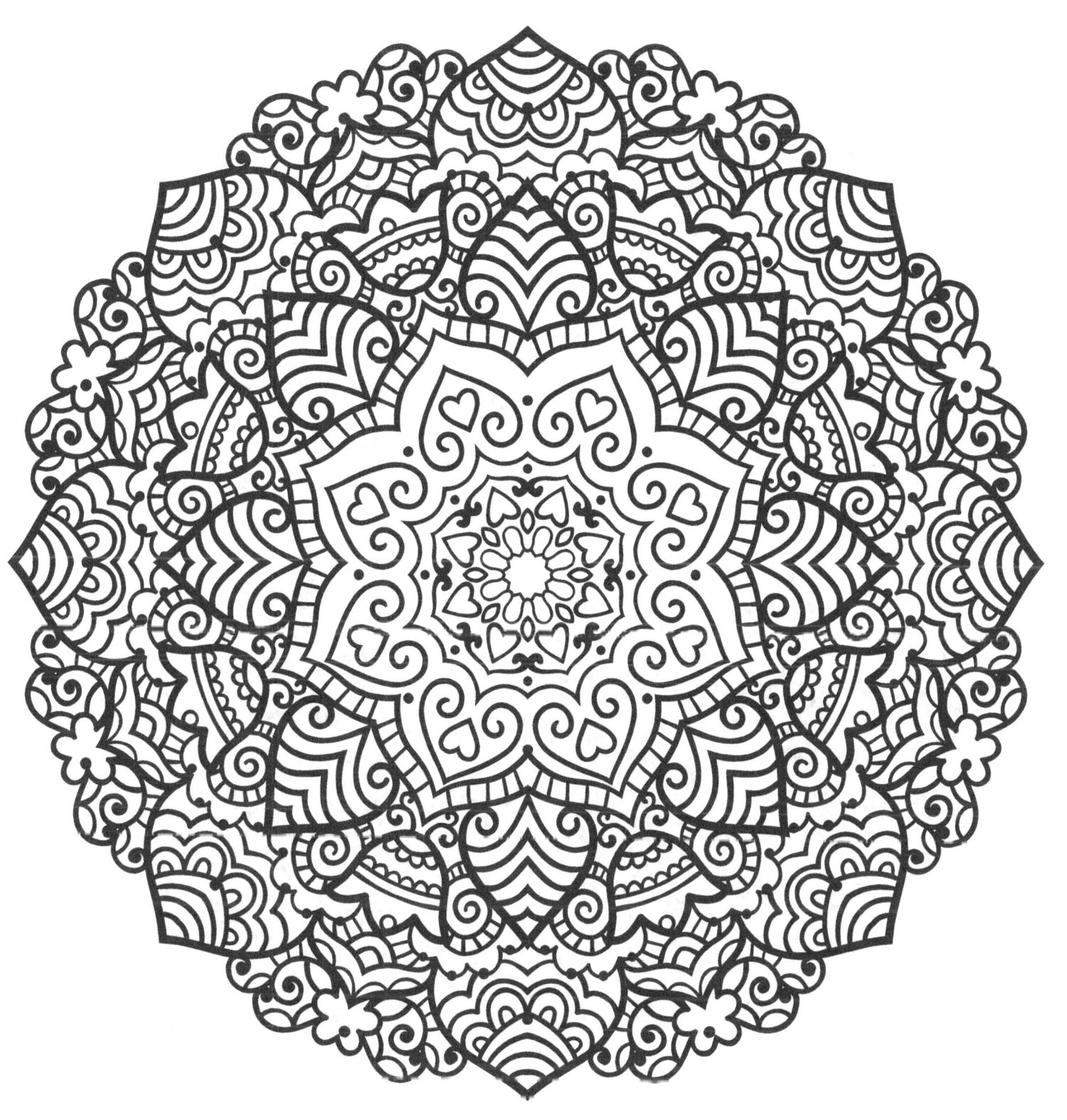

We can easily forgive a child who is afraid of the dark;
the real tragedy of life is when men are afraid
of the light.
—Plato

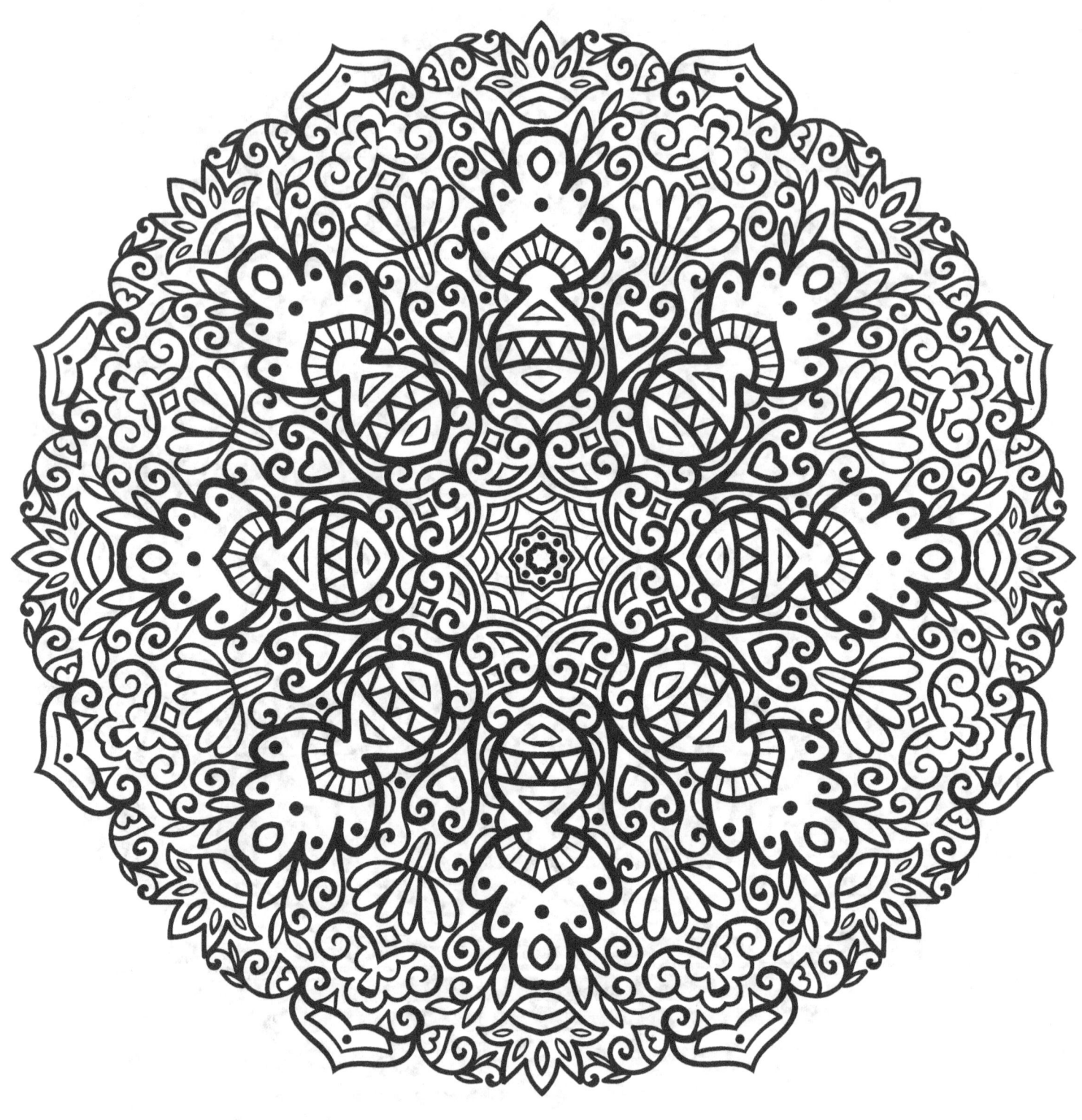

Certain things catch your eye, but pursue only those that capture the heart.
—Ancient Indian Proverb

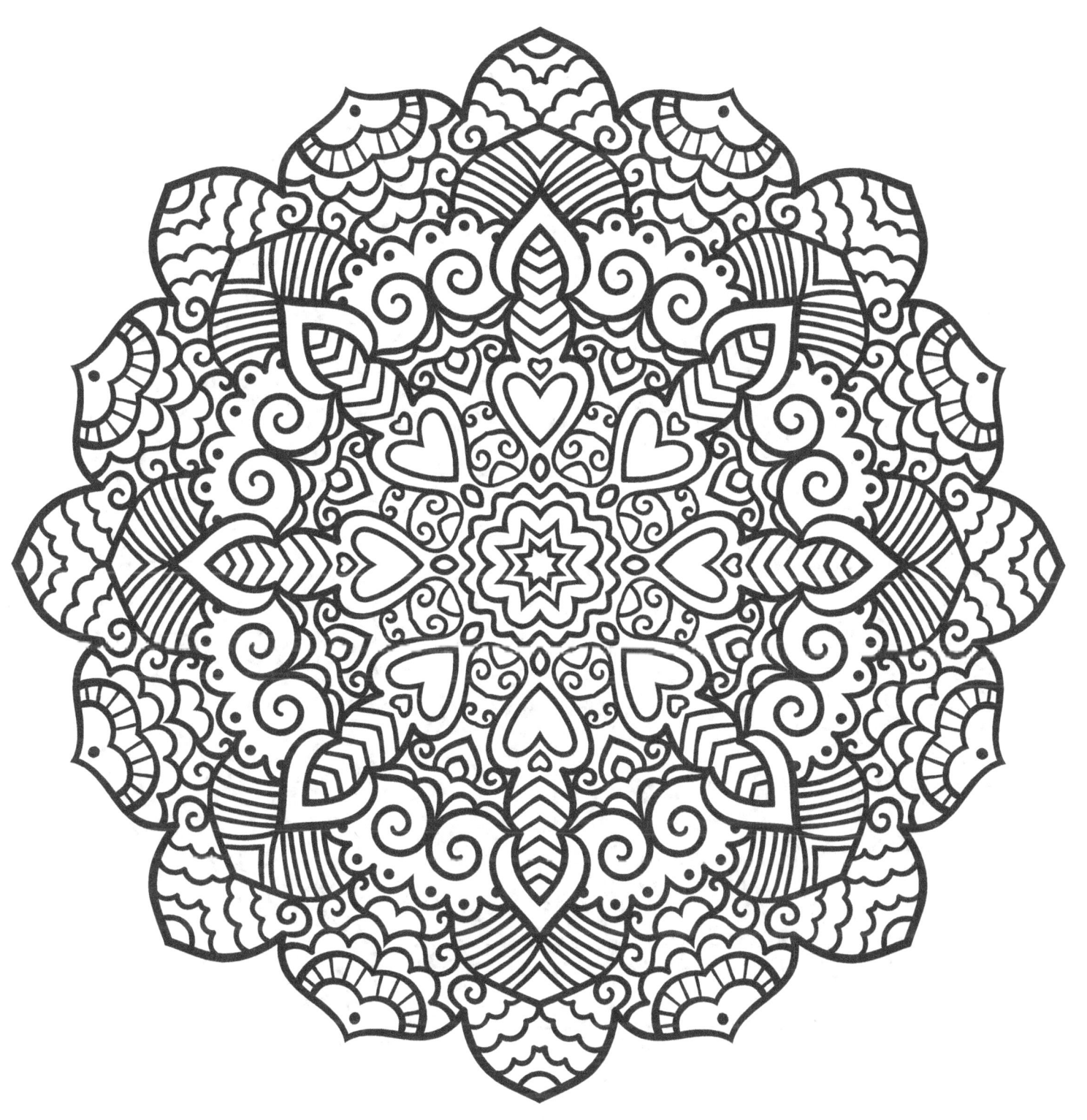

How wonderful it is that nobody need wait a single moment before starting to improve the world.
—Anne Frank

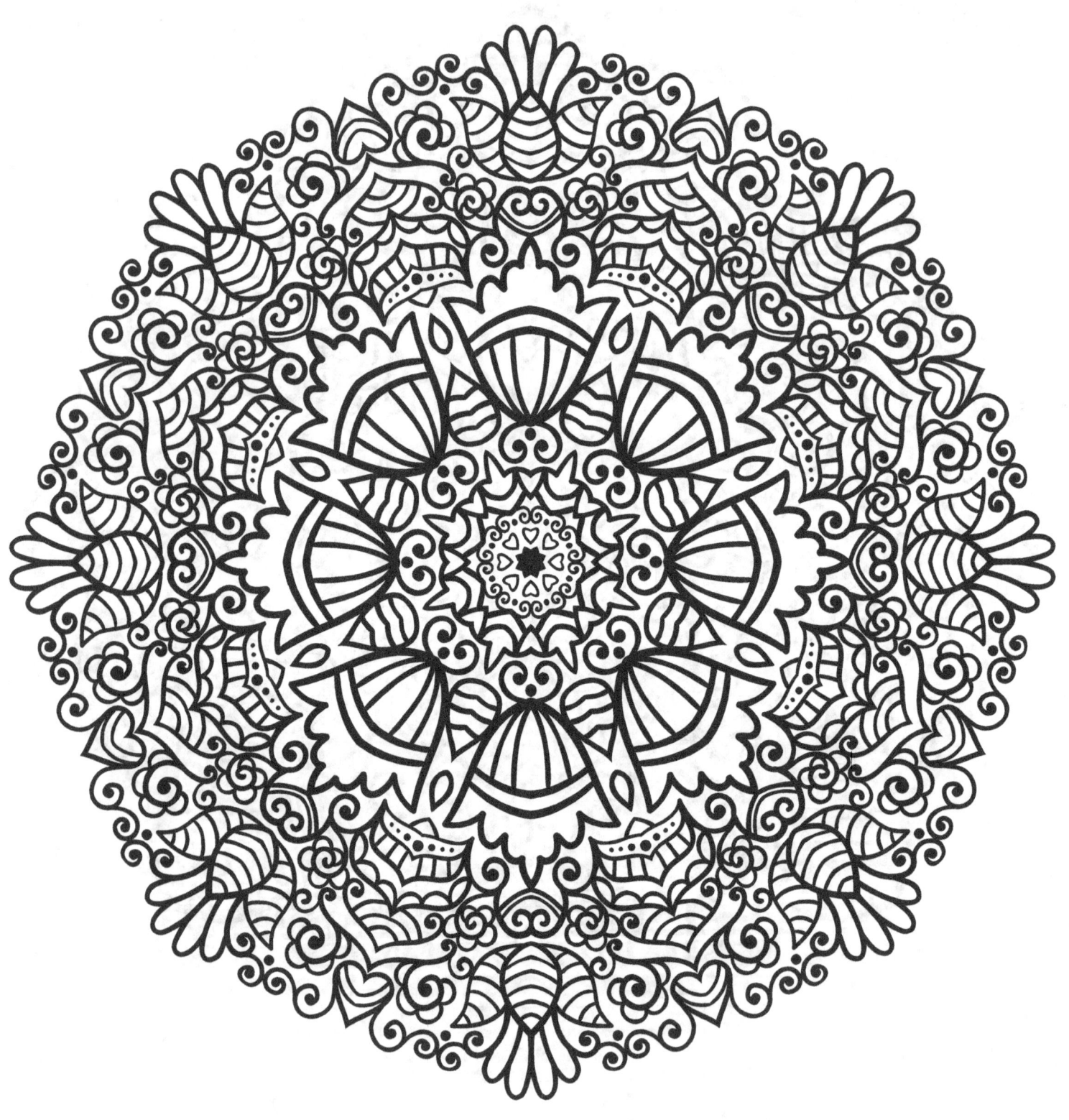

Limitations live only in our minds. But if we use our imaginations, our possibilities become limitless.
—Jamie Paolinetti

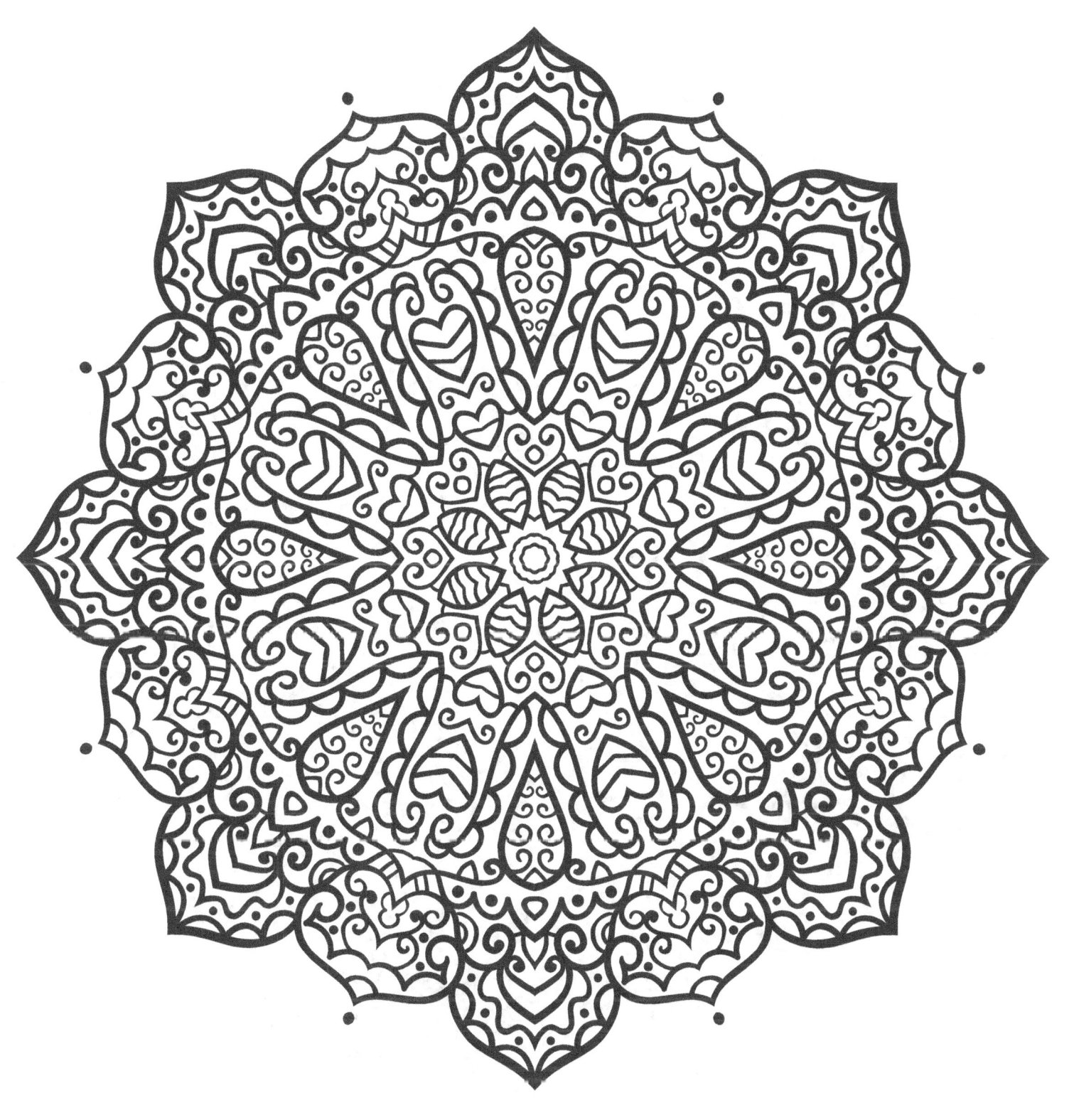

I have been impressed with the urgency of doing. Knowing is not enough; we must apply. Being willing is not enough; we must do.
—*Leonardo da Vinci*

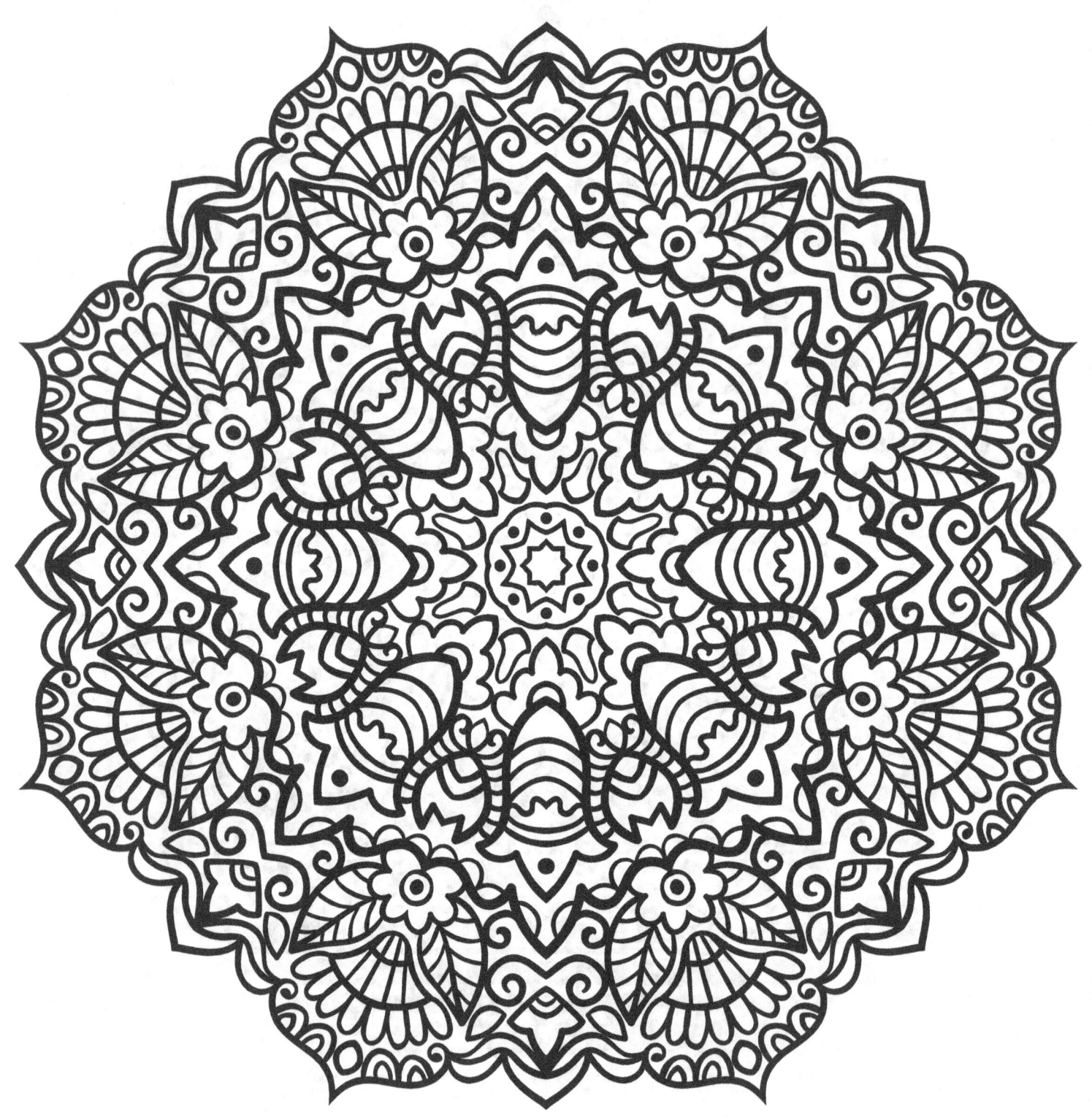

The only person you are destined to become is the person you decide to be.
—Ralph Waldo Emerson

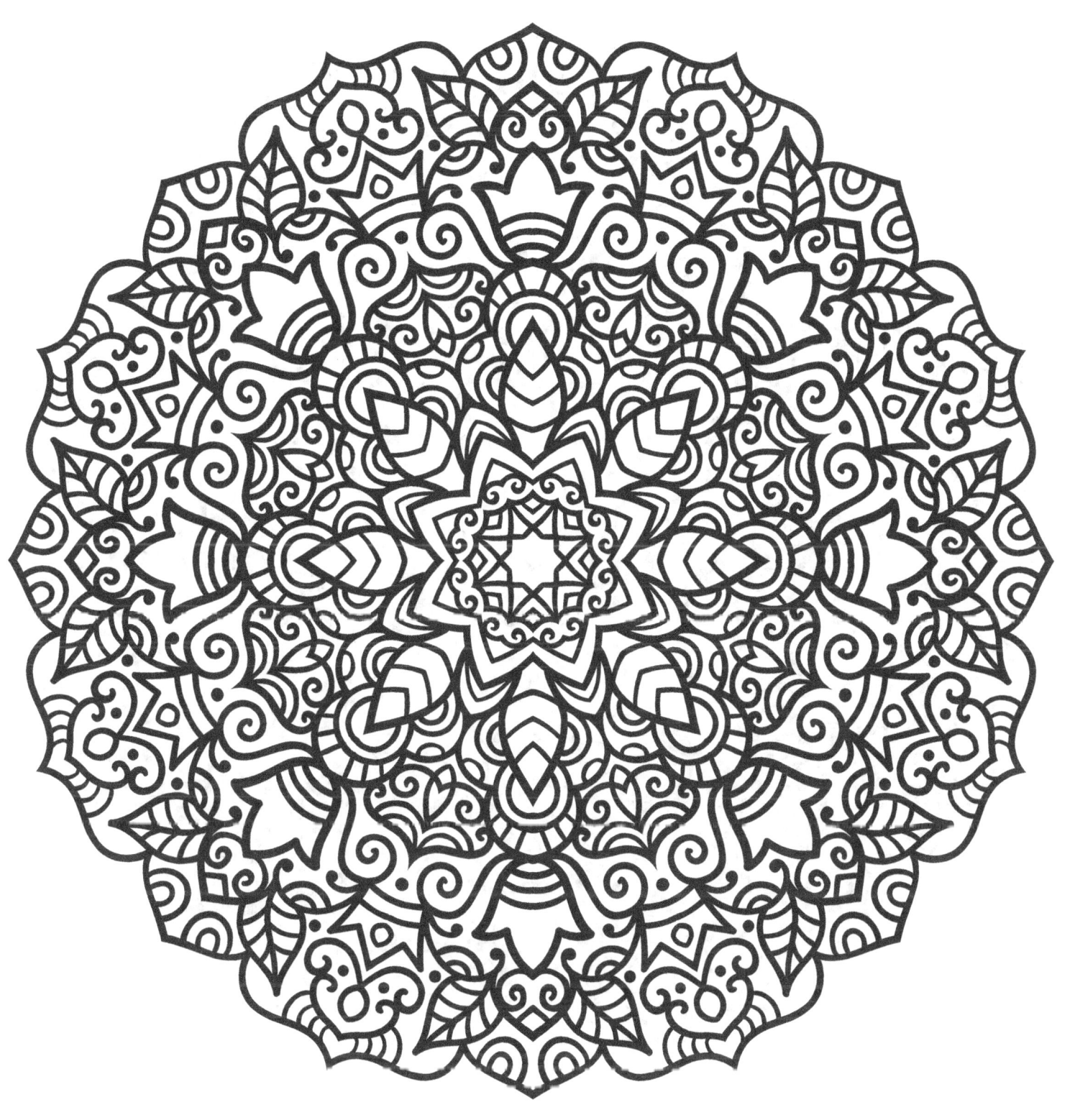

What we achieve inwardly will change outer reality.
—Plutarch

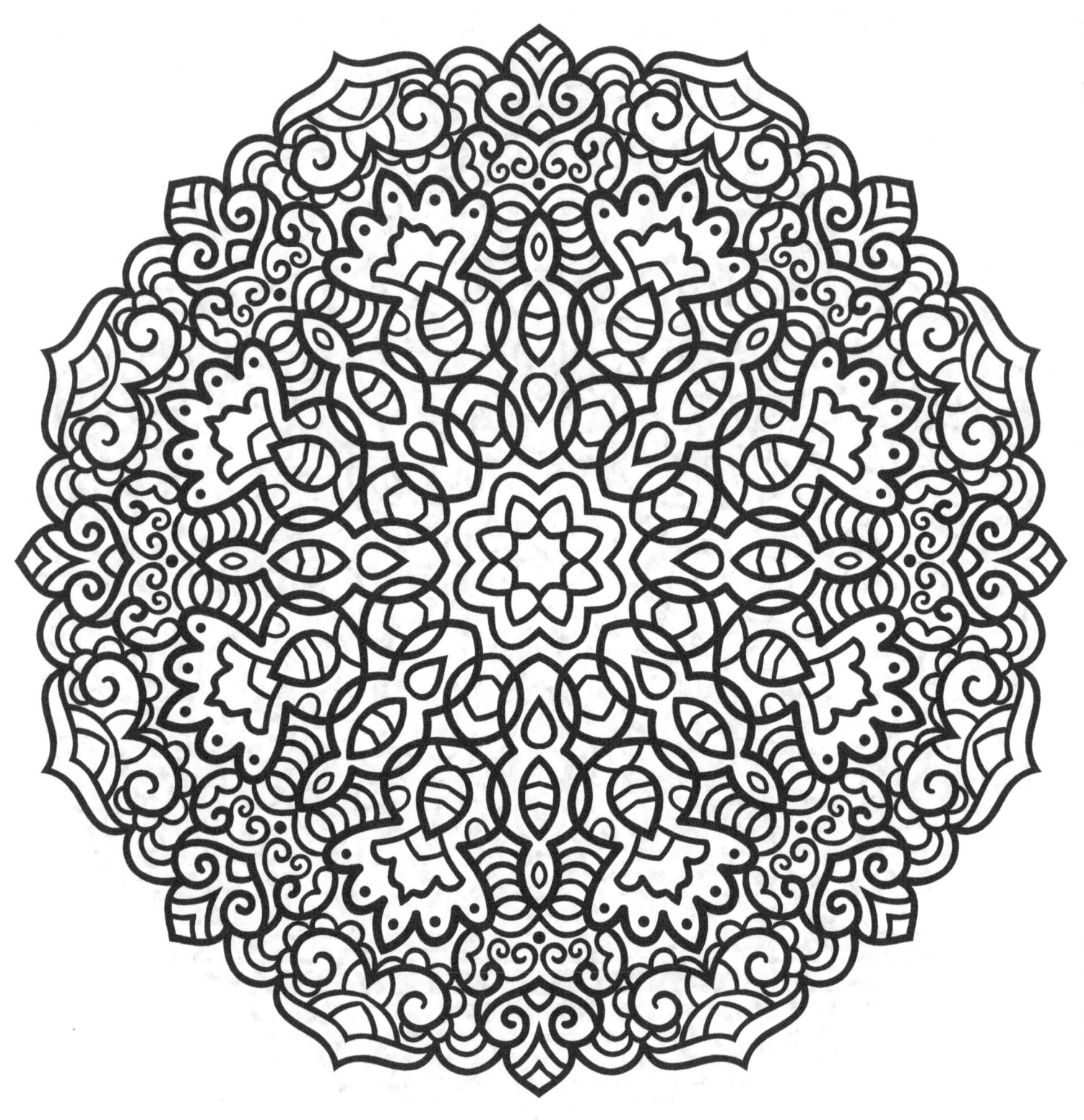

Nothing will work unless you do.
—Maya Angelou

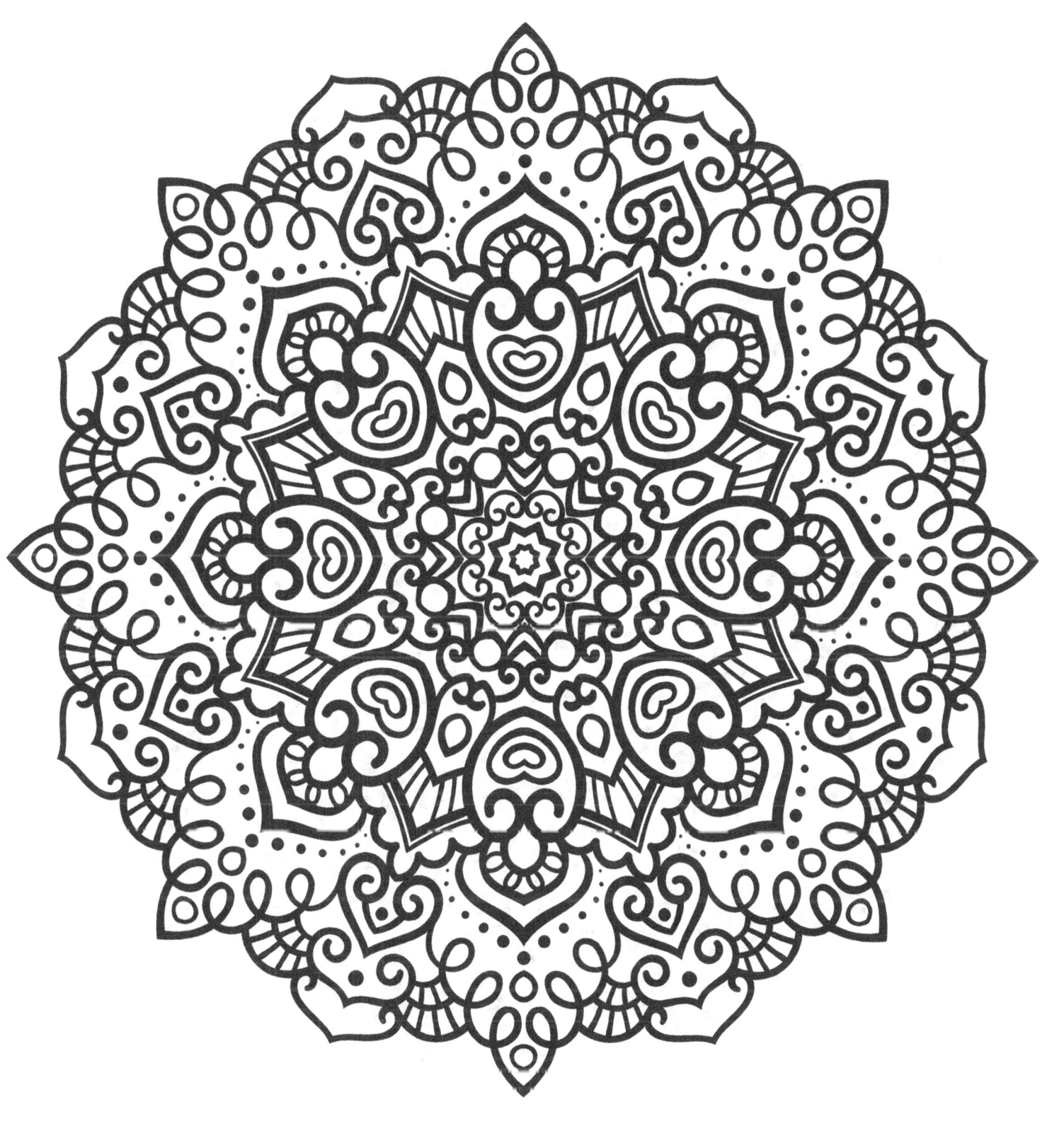

Everything you've ever wanted is on the other side of fear.
—George Addair

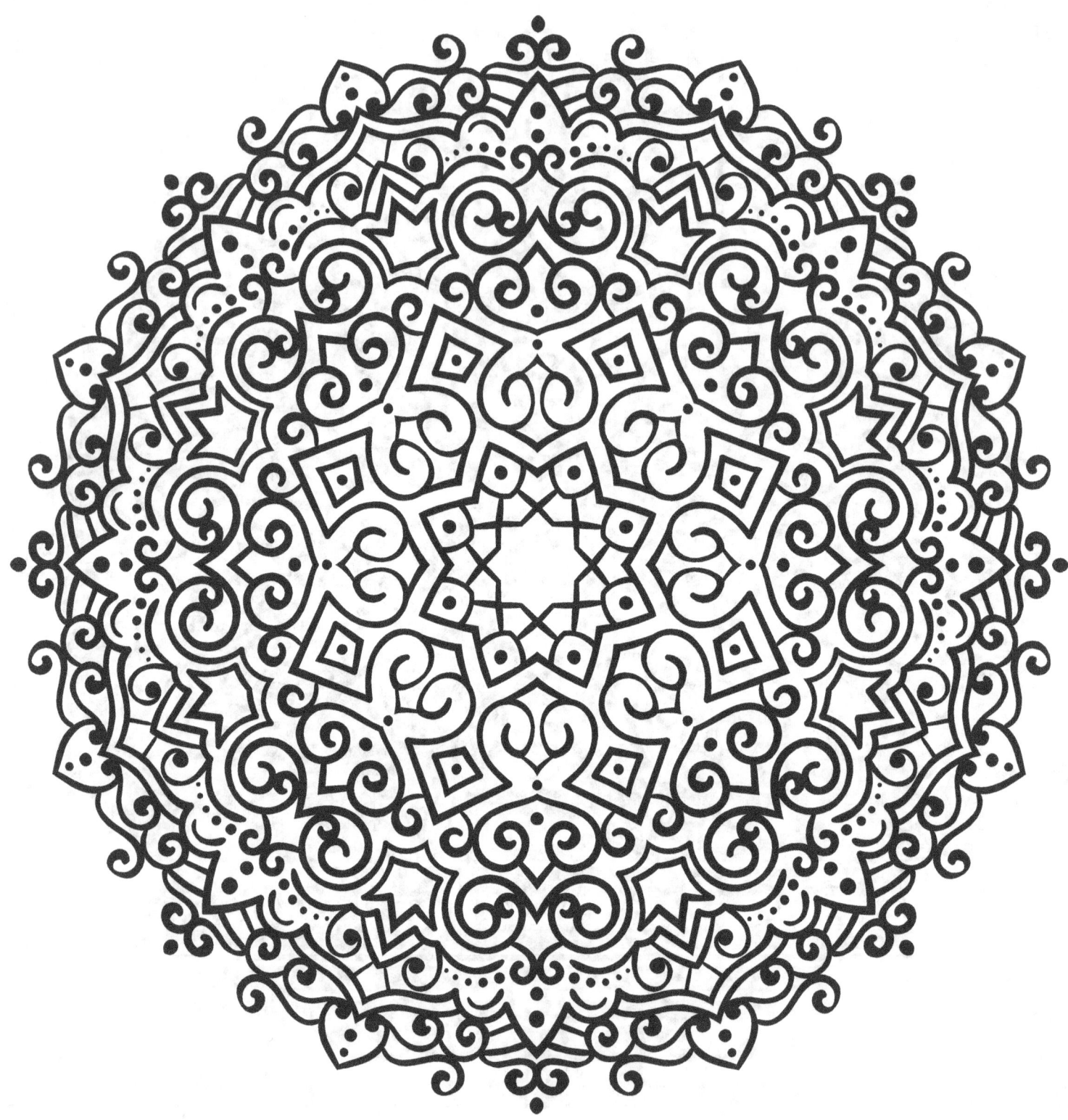

I alone cannot change the world, but I can cast a stone across the water to create many ripples.
—Mother Teresa

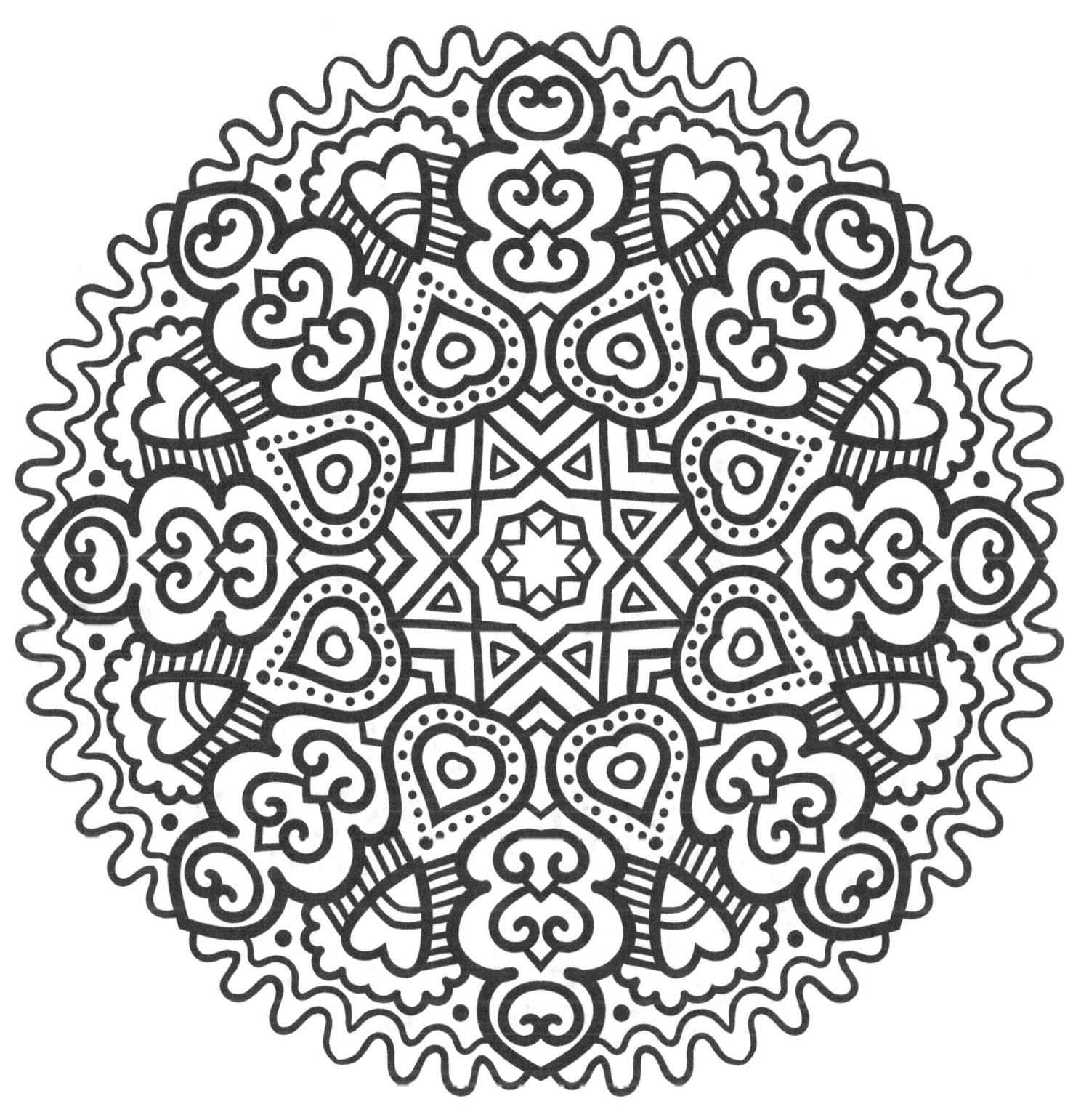

If you want to lift yourself up, lift up someone else.
—Booker T. Washington

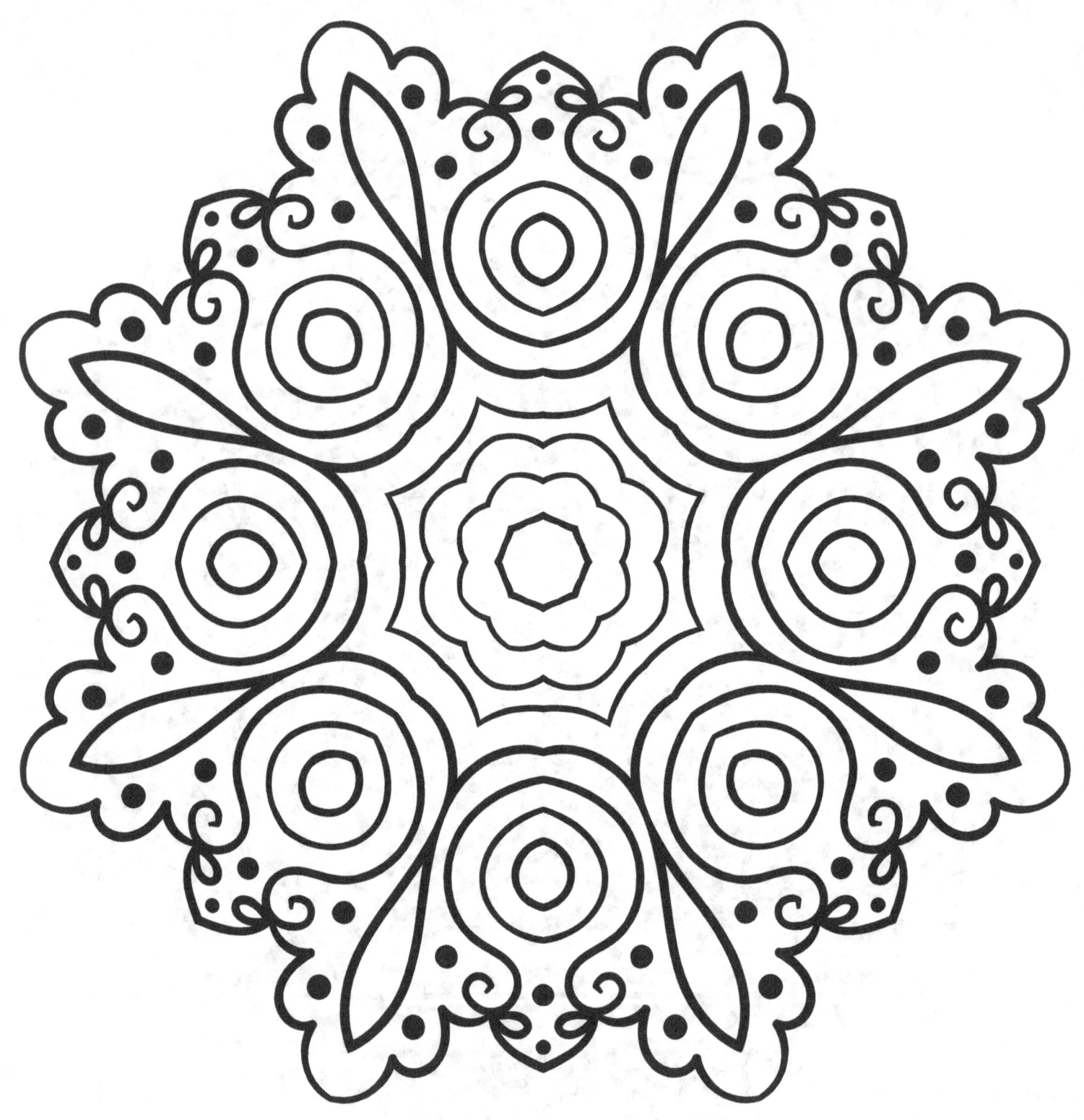

When one door of happiness closes, another opens, but ften we look so long at the closed door that we do not see the one that has been opened for us.
—Helen Keller

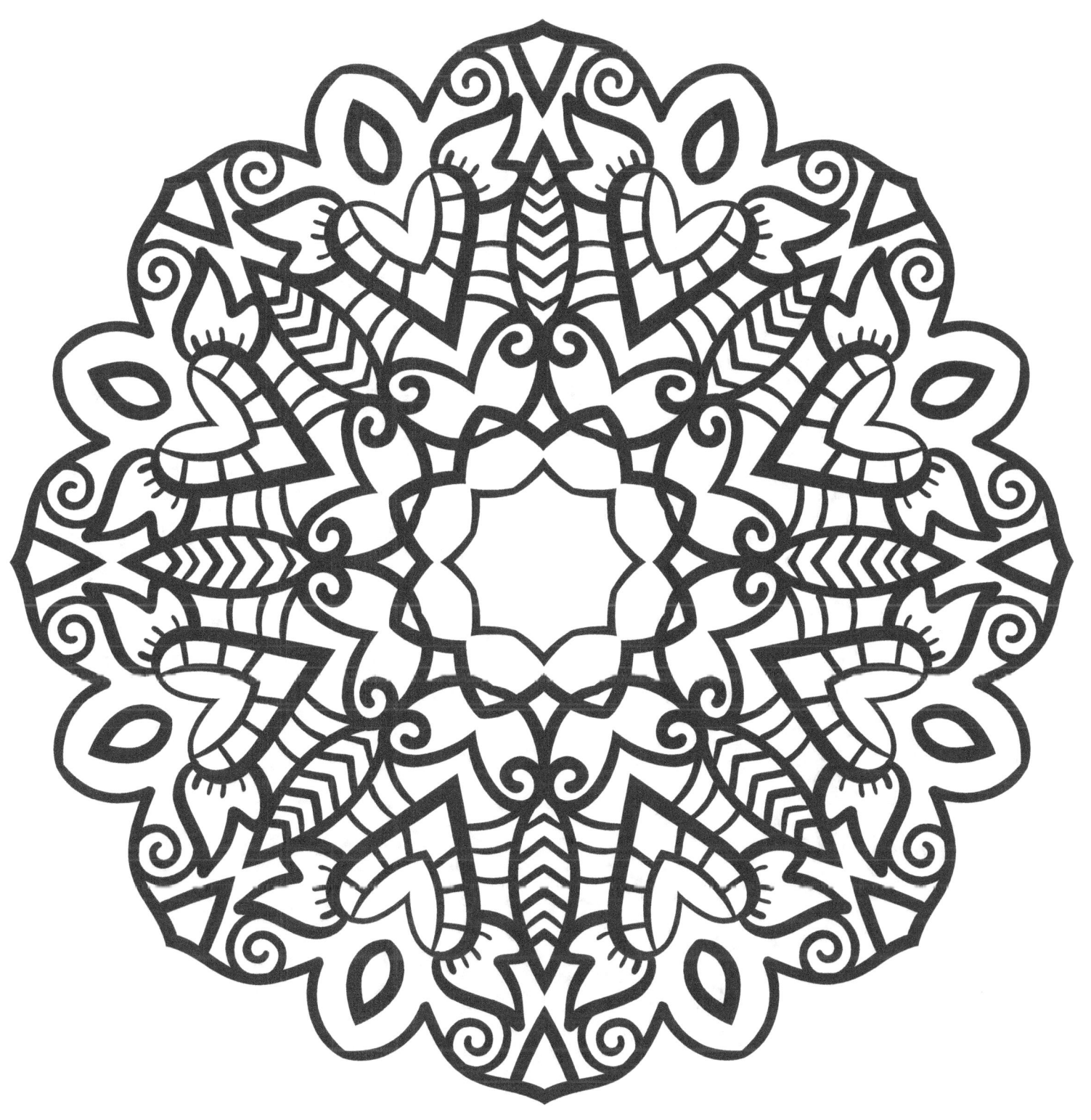

When I was 5 years old, my mother always told me that happiness was the key to life. When I went to school, they asked me what I wanted to be when I grew up. I wrote down "happy". They told me I didn't understand the assignment, and I told them they didn't understand life.
—John Lennon

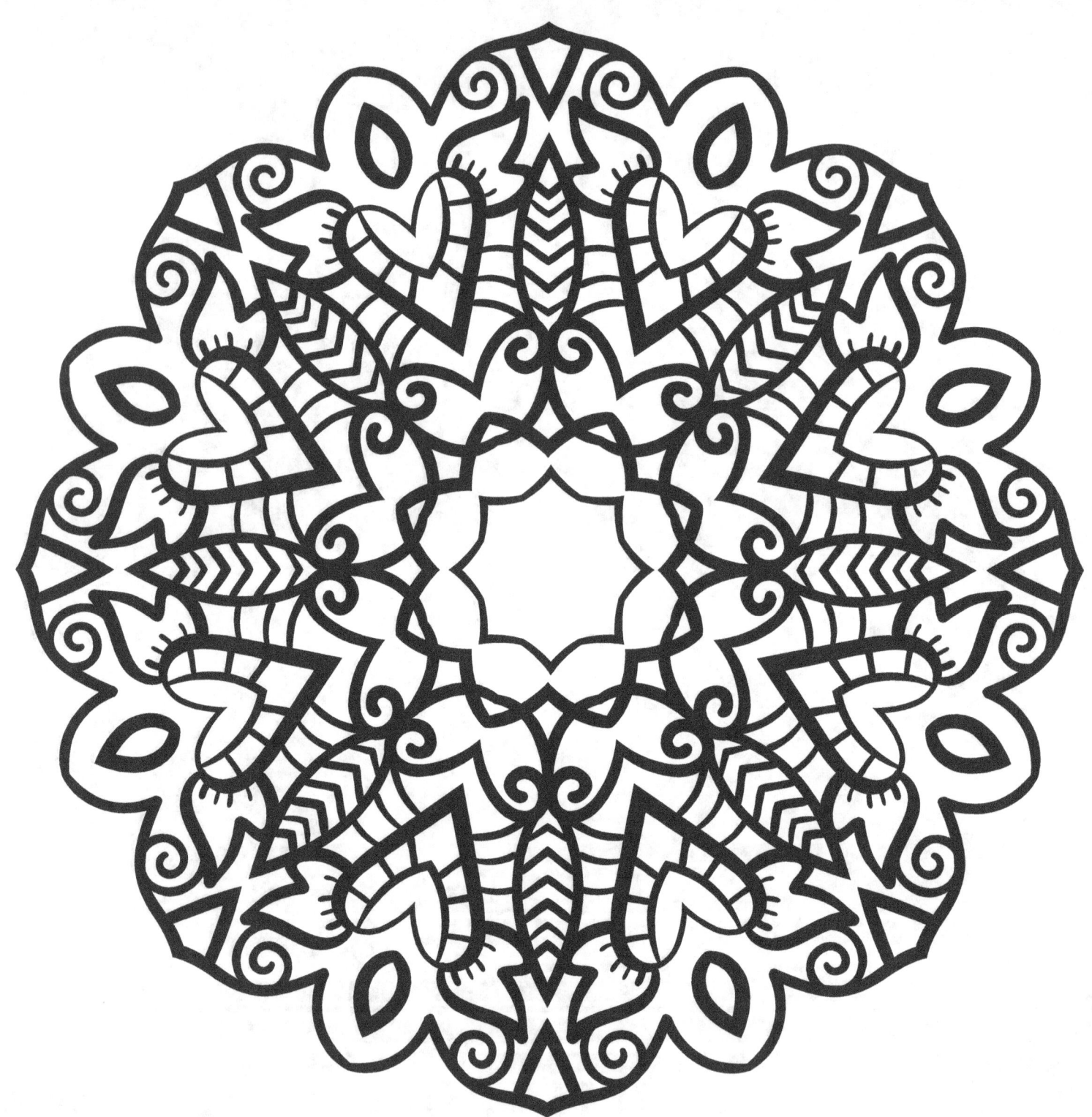

When I was 5 years old, my mother always told me that happiness was the key to life. When I went to school, they asked me what I wanted to be when I grew up. I wrote down "happy". They told me I didn't understand the assignment, and I told them they didn't understand life.
—John Lennon

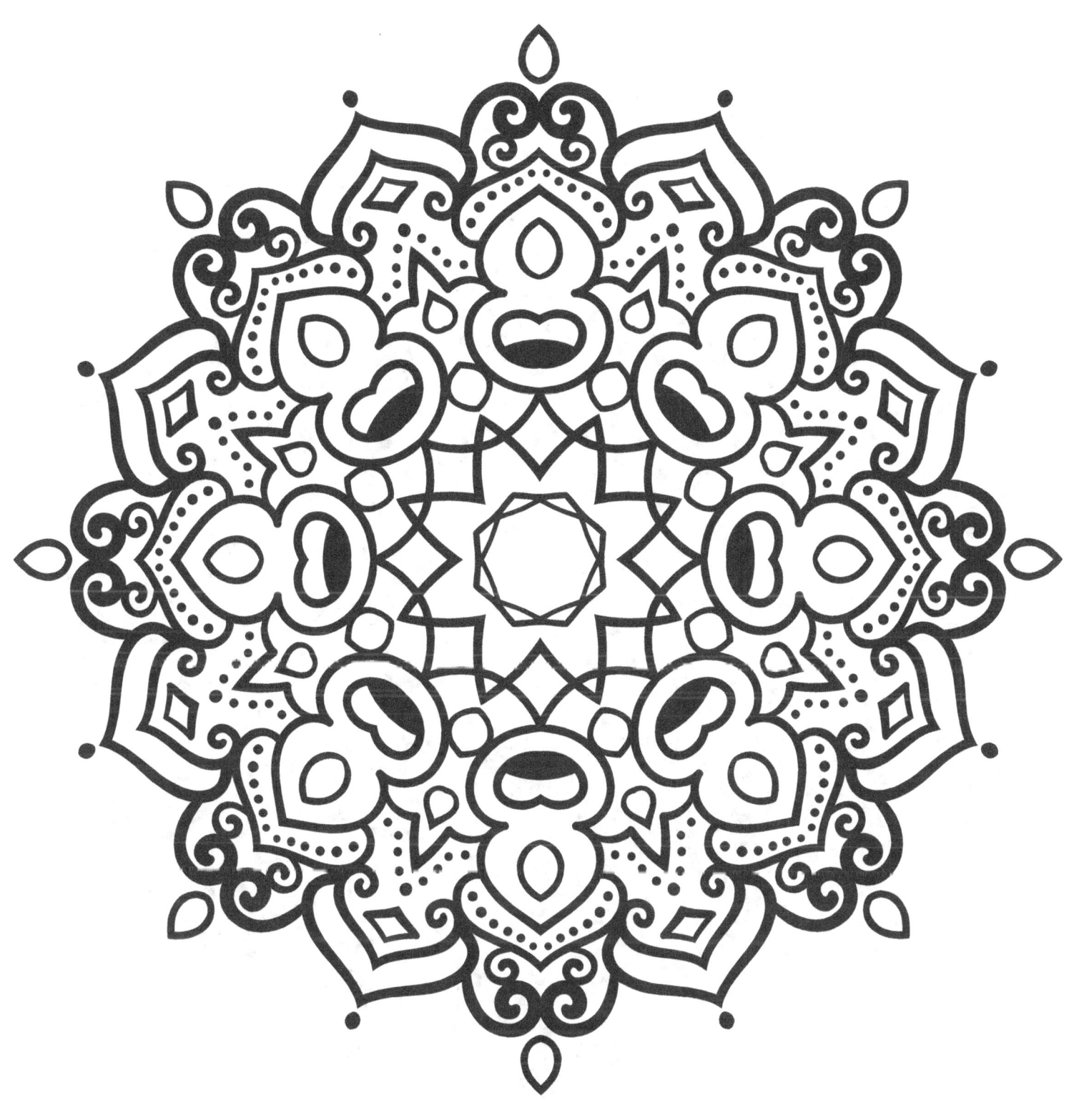

"Anyone who has ever made anything of importance was disciplined."
— Andrew Hendrixson

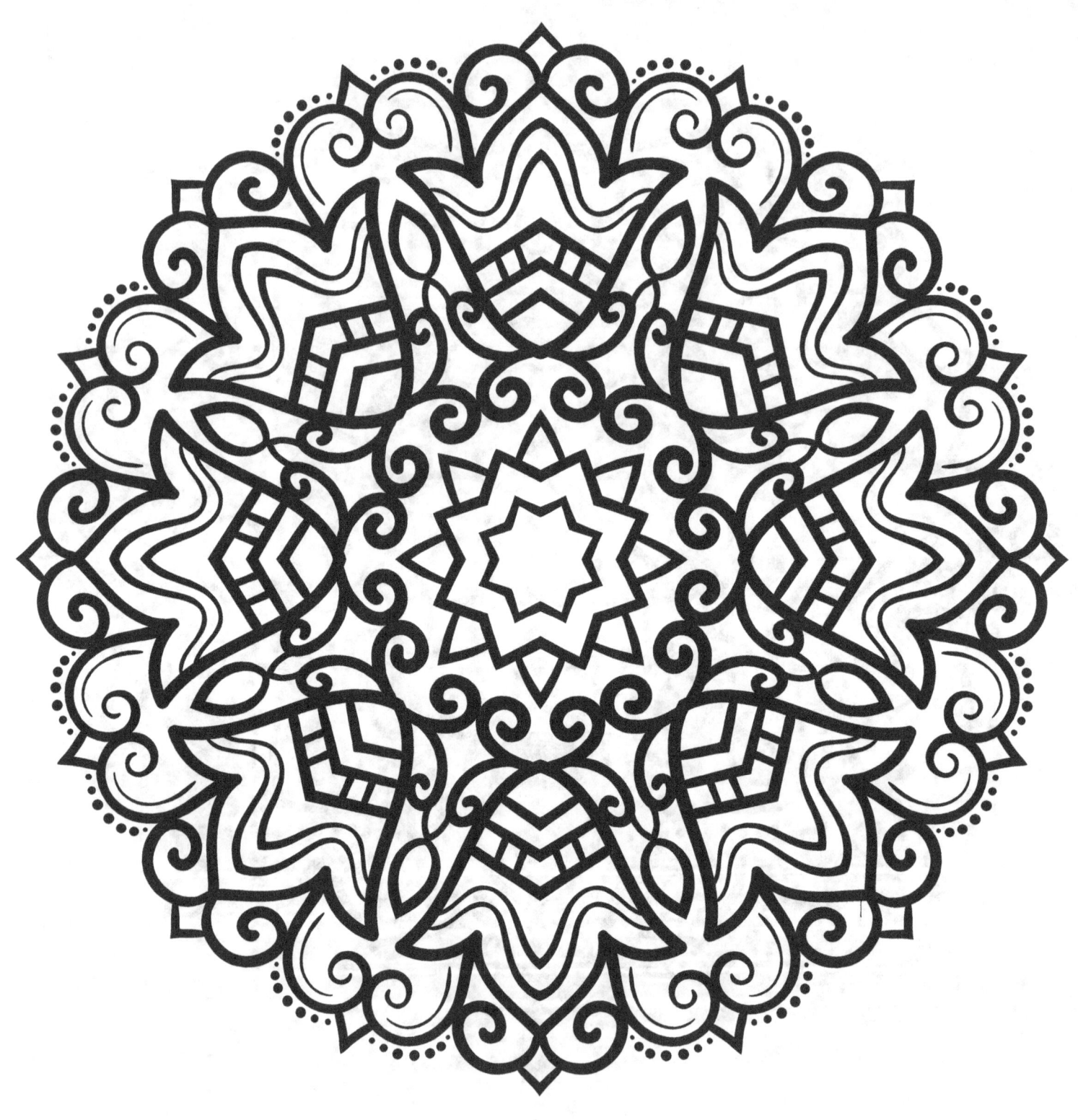

"Don't spend time beating on a wall, hoping to transform it into a door."
— Coco Chanel

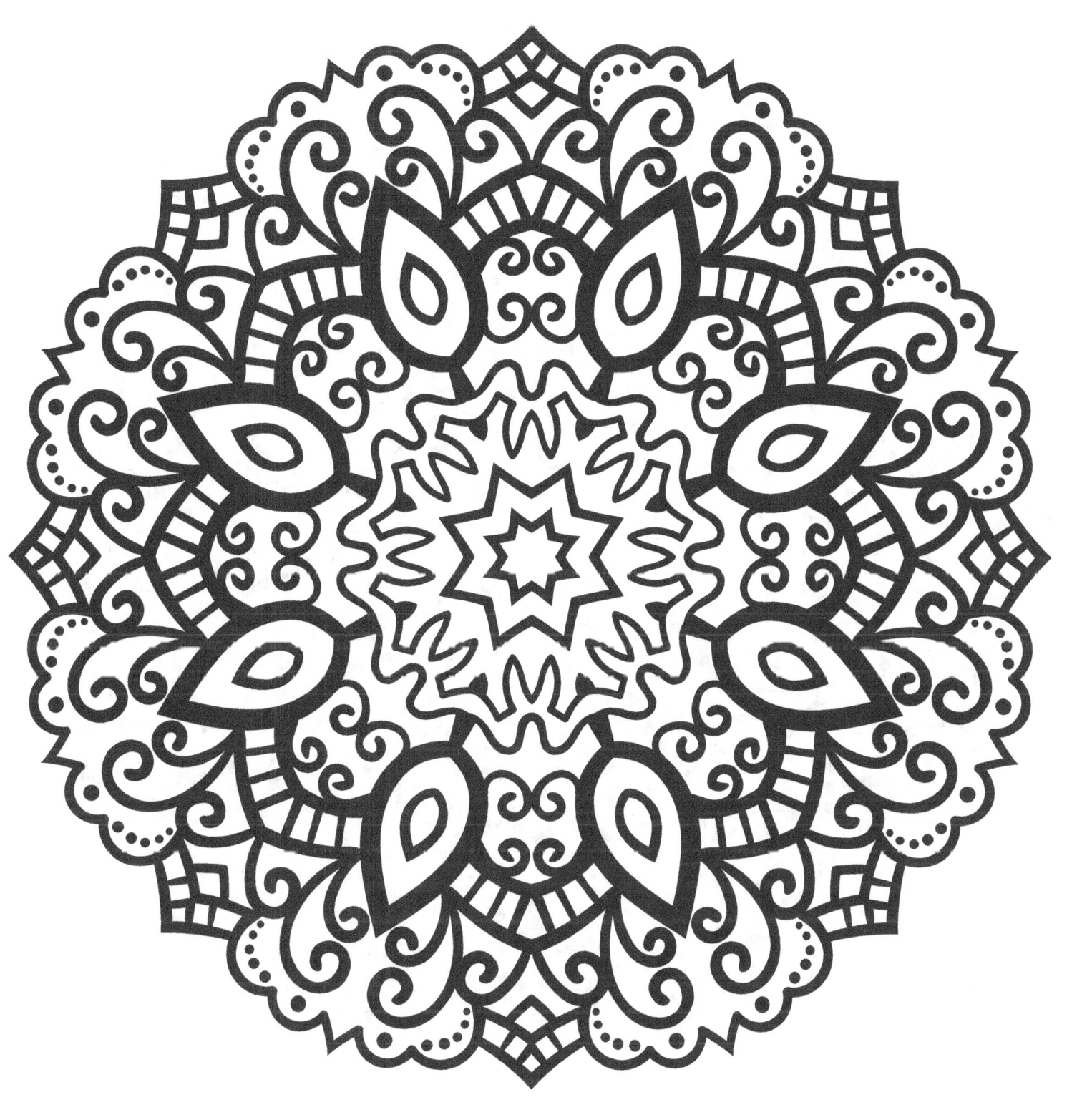

Creativity is intelligence having fun."
— *Albert Einstein*

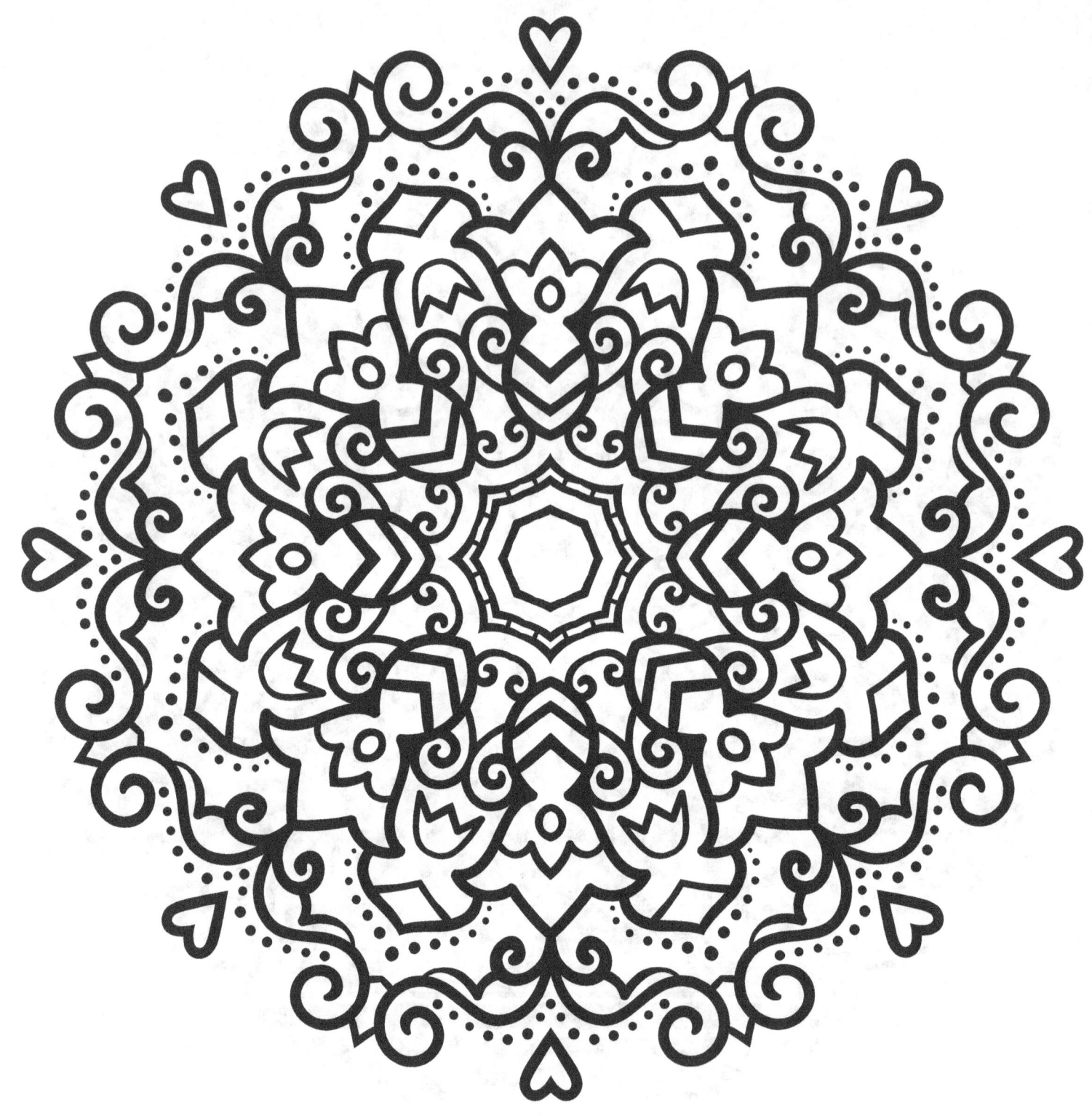

"Optimism is the one quality more associated with success and happiness than any other."
— *Brian Tracy*

Life is not about ALL the wrong moves you made,
Life is about the one right move that made
ALL the difference.
– James Lockhart

Have the passion, take the action &
magic will happen.
— Bar Rafaeli

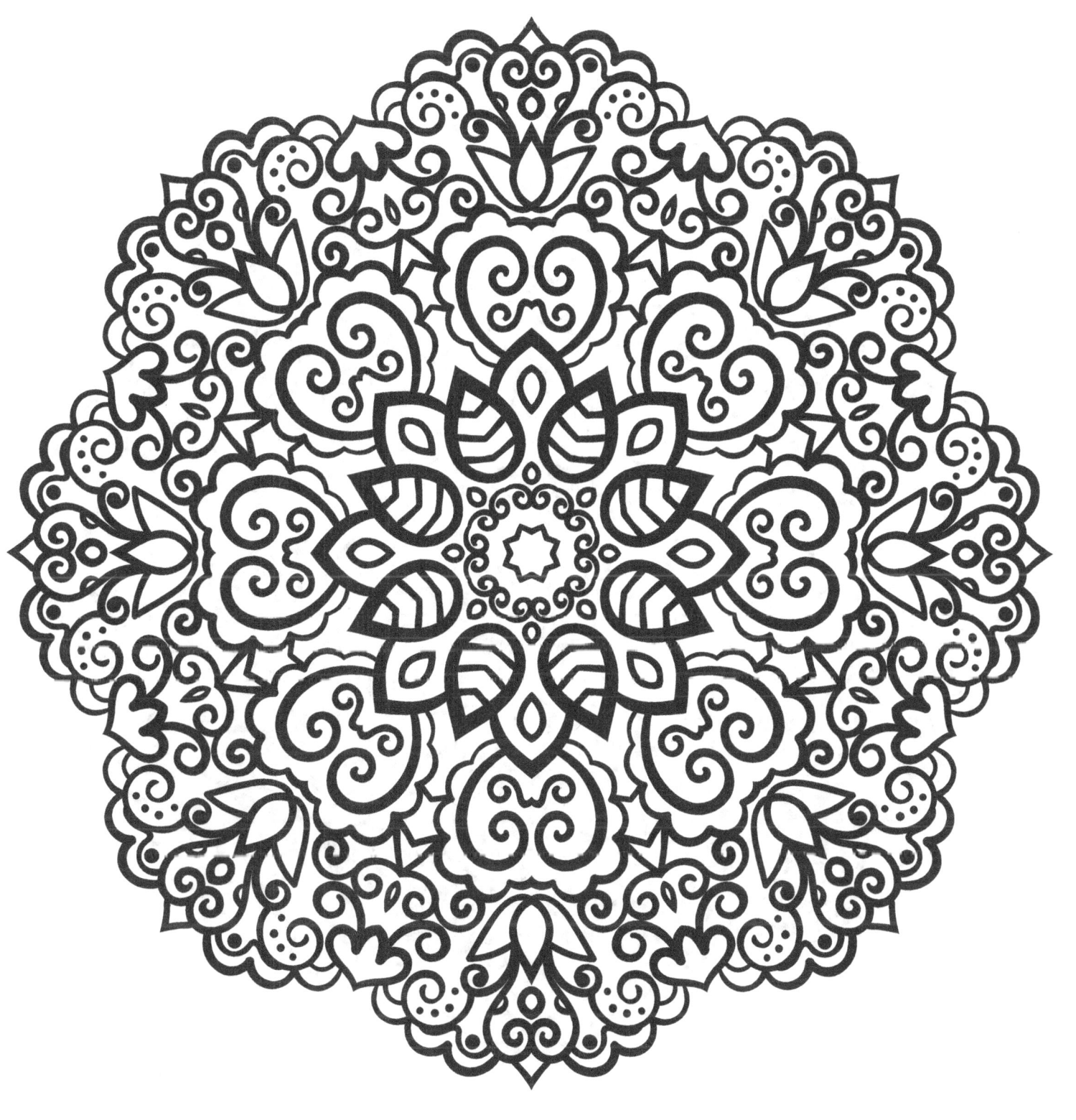

The secret to life is meaningless unless you
discover it yourself.
— W. Somerset Maugham

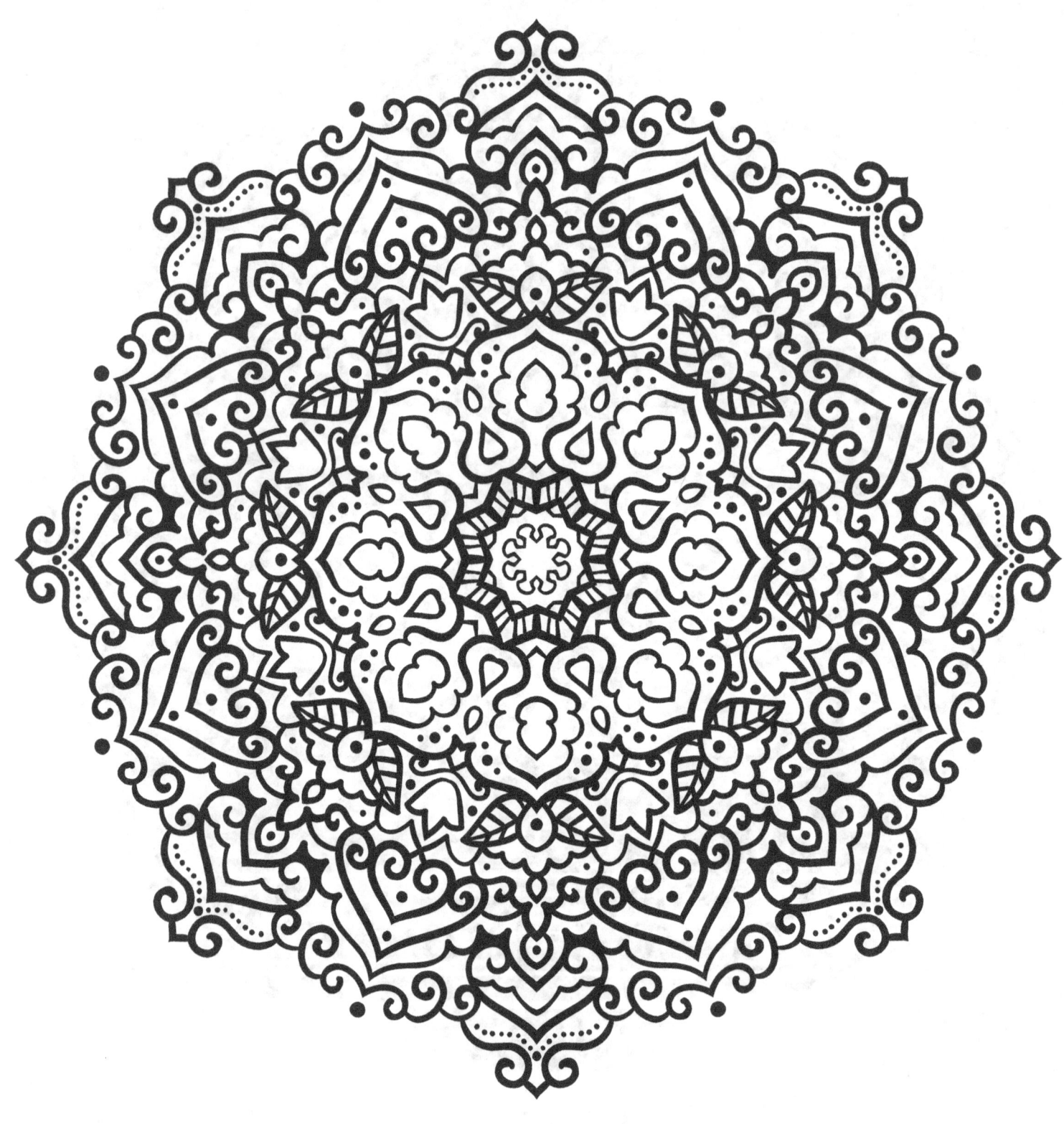

He who has a why to live can bear almost any how.
— Friedrich Nietzsche

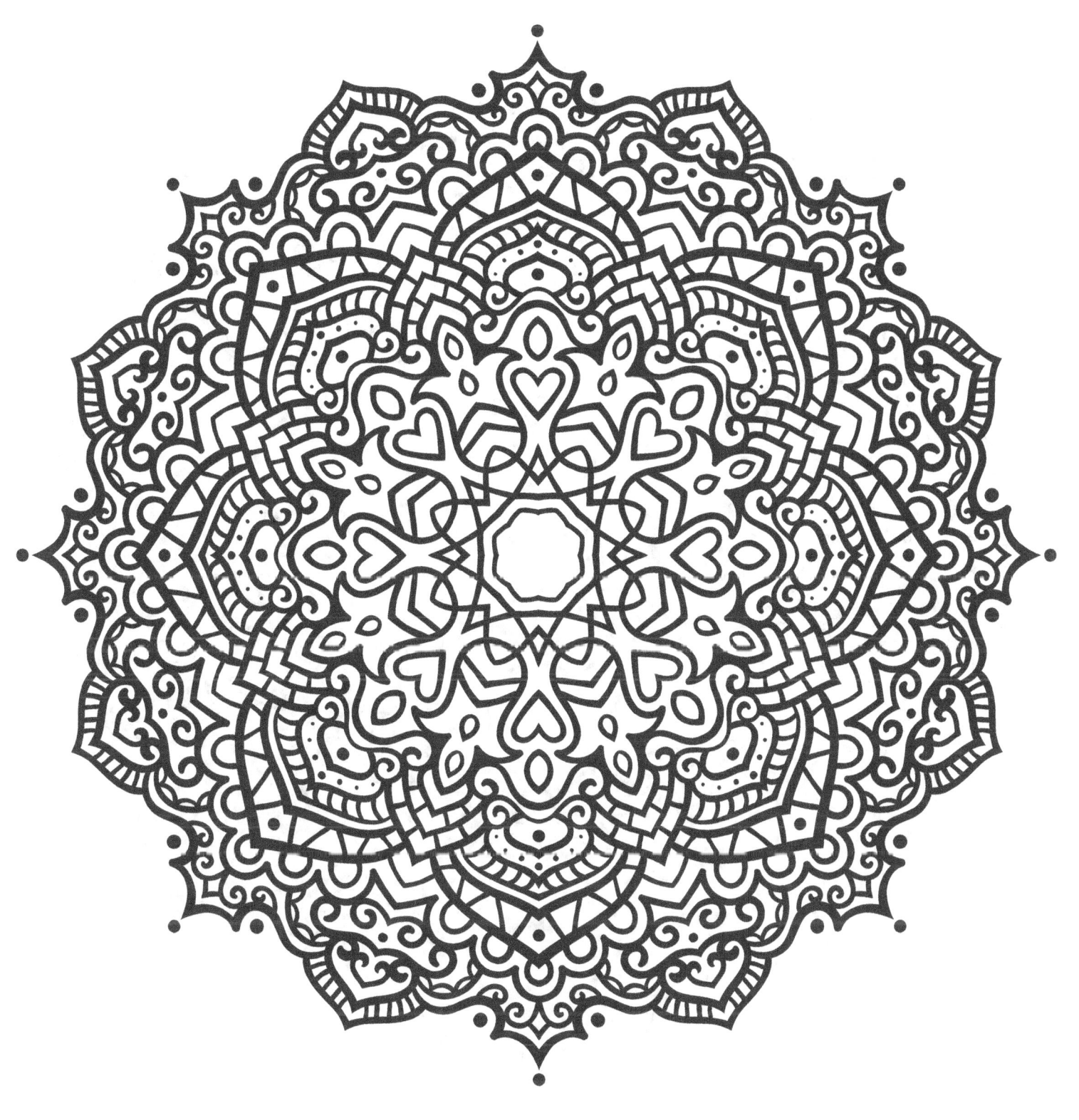

Defeat is not bitter unless you swallow it.
— Joe Clark

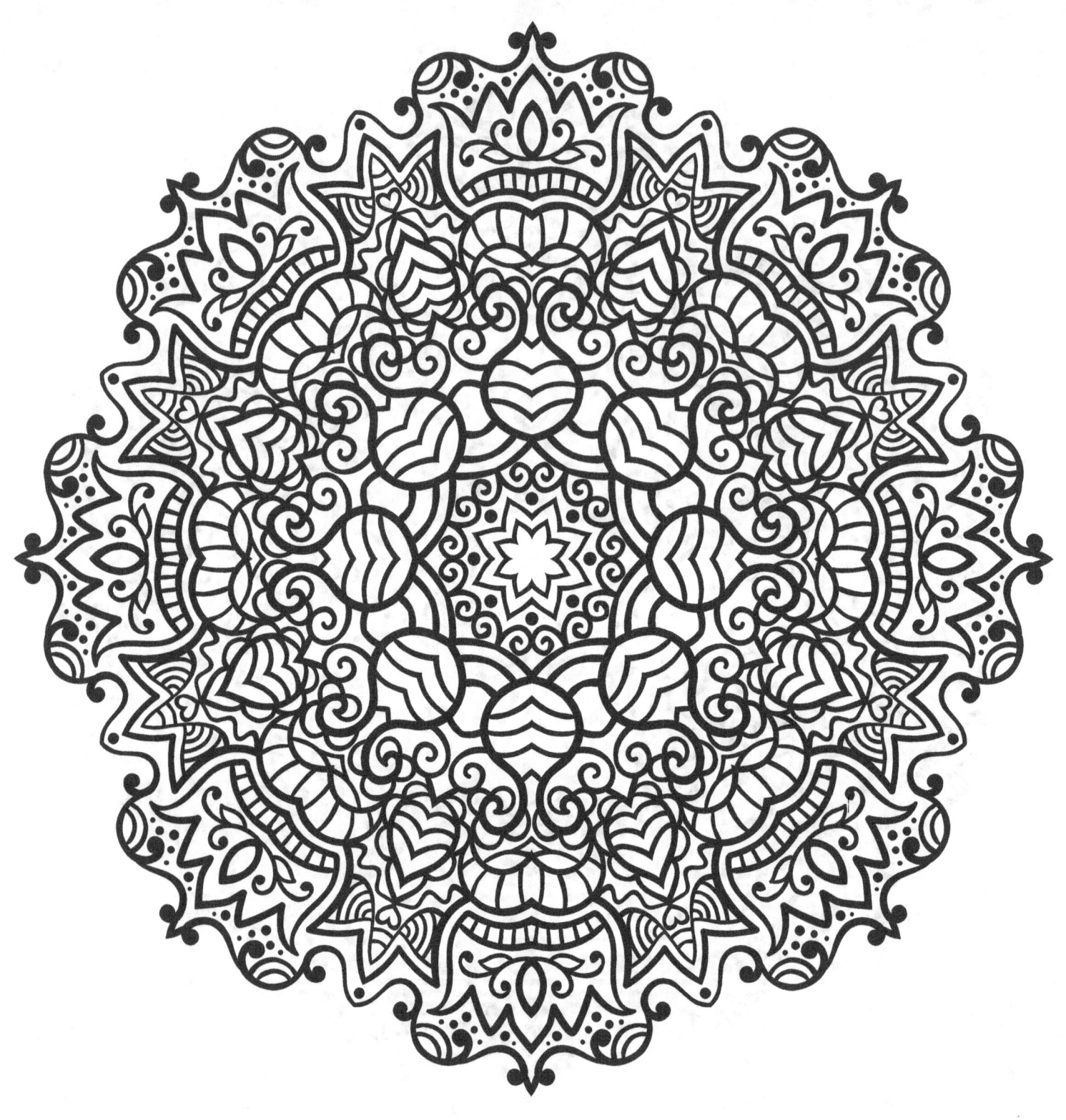

The only people who find what they are looking for in life are the fault finders.
— Foster's Law

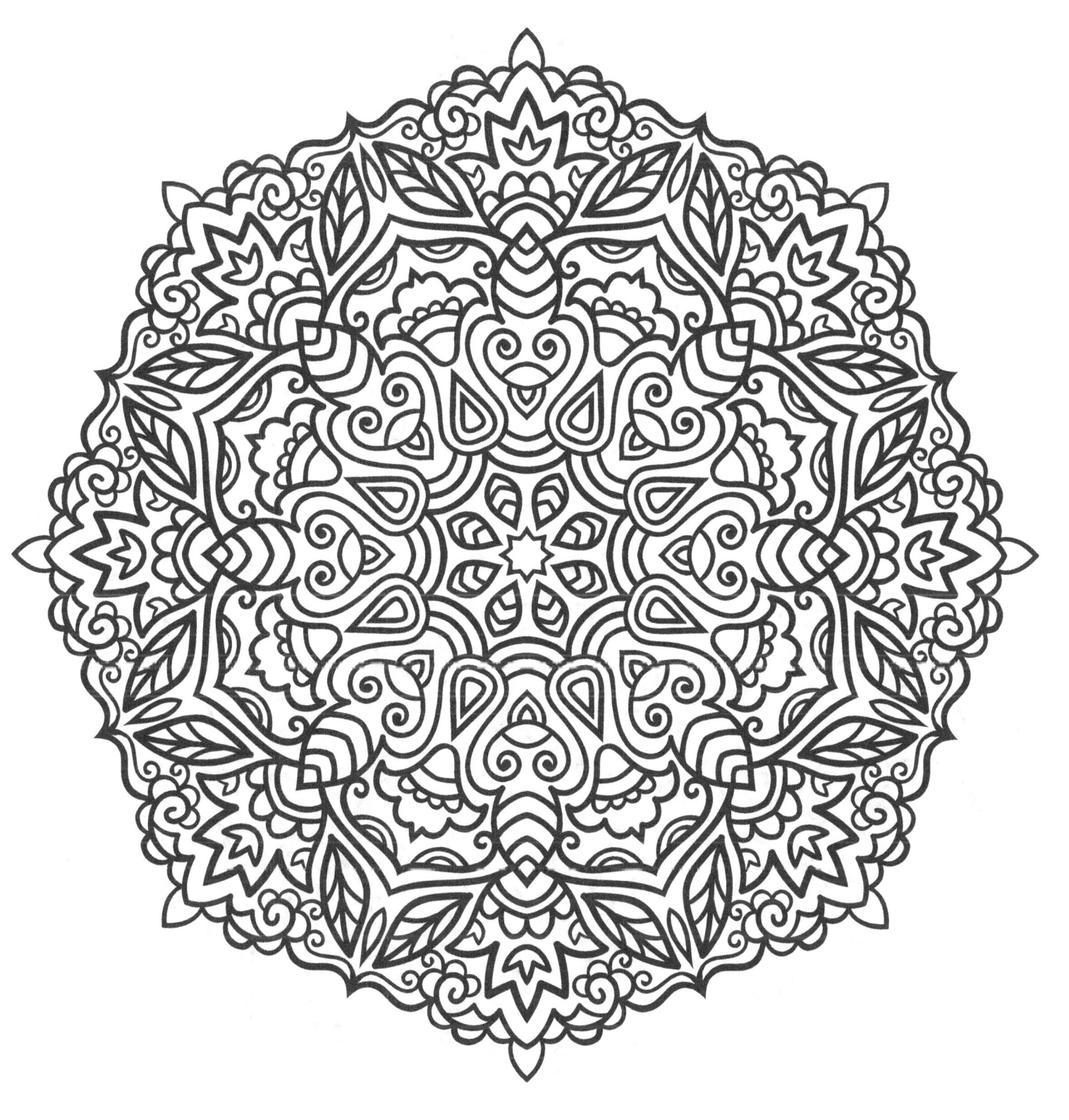

Do first things first, and second things not at all.
– Peter Drucker.

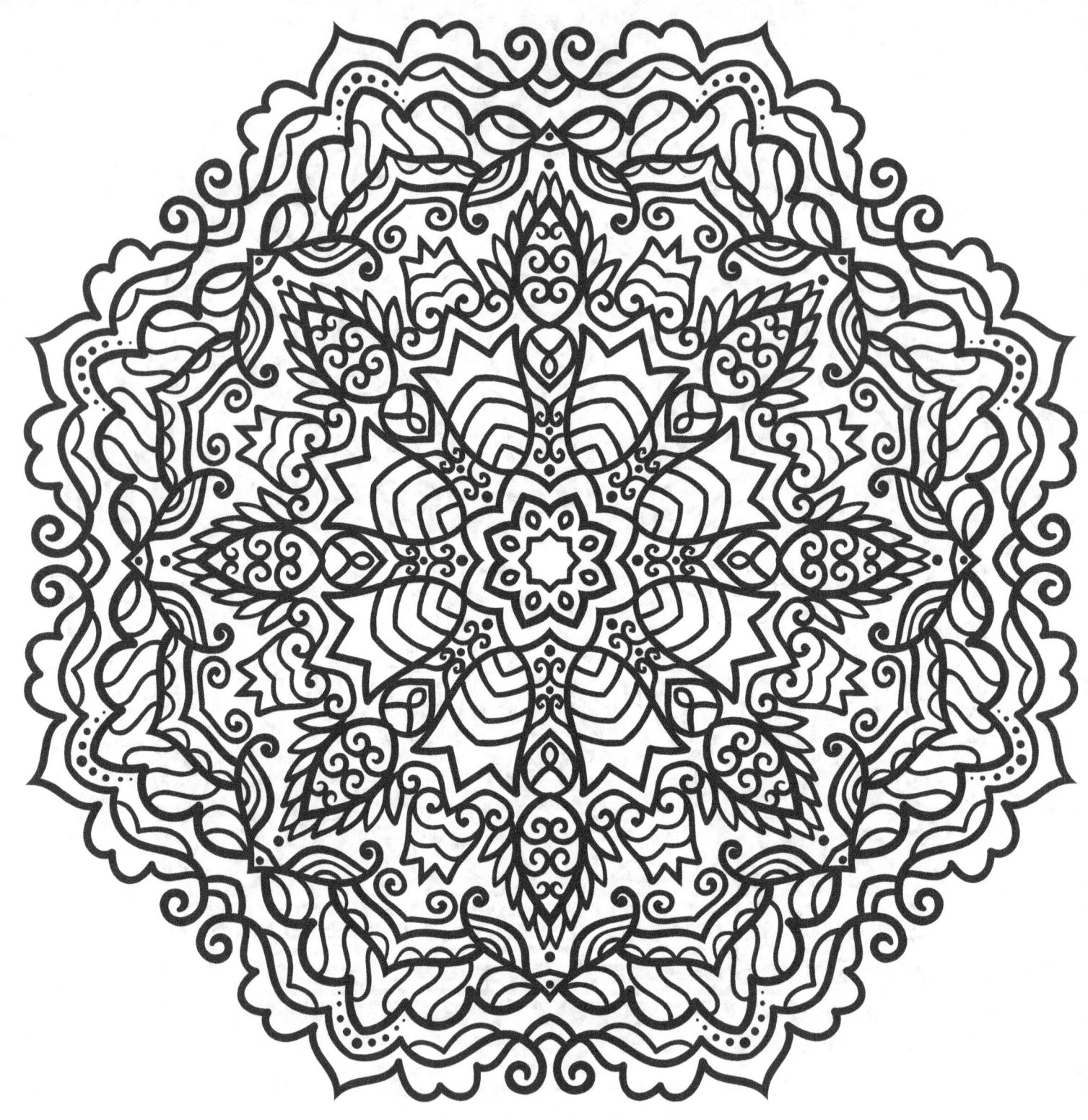

I've learned that no matter what happens, or how bad
it seems today, life does go on,
and it will be better tomorrow.
– Maya Angelou

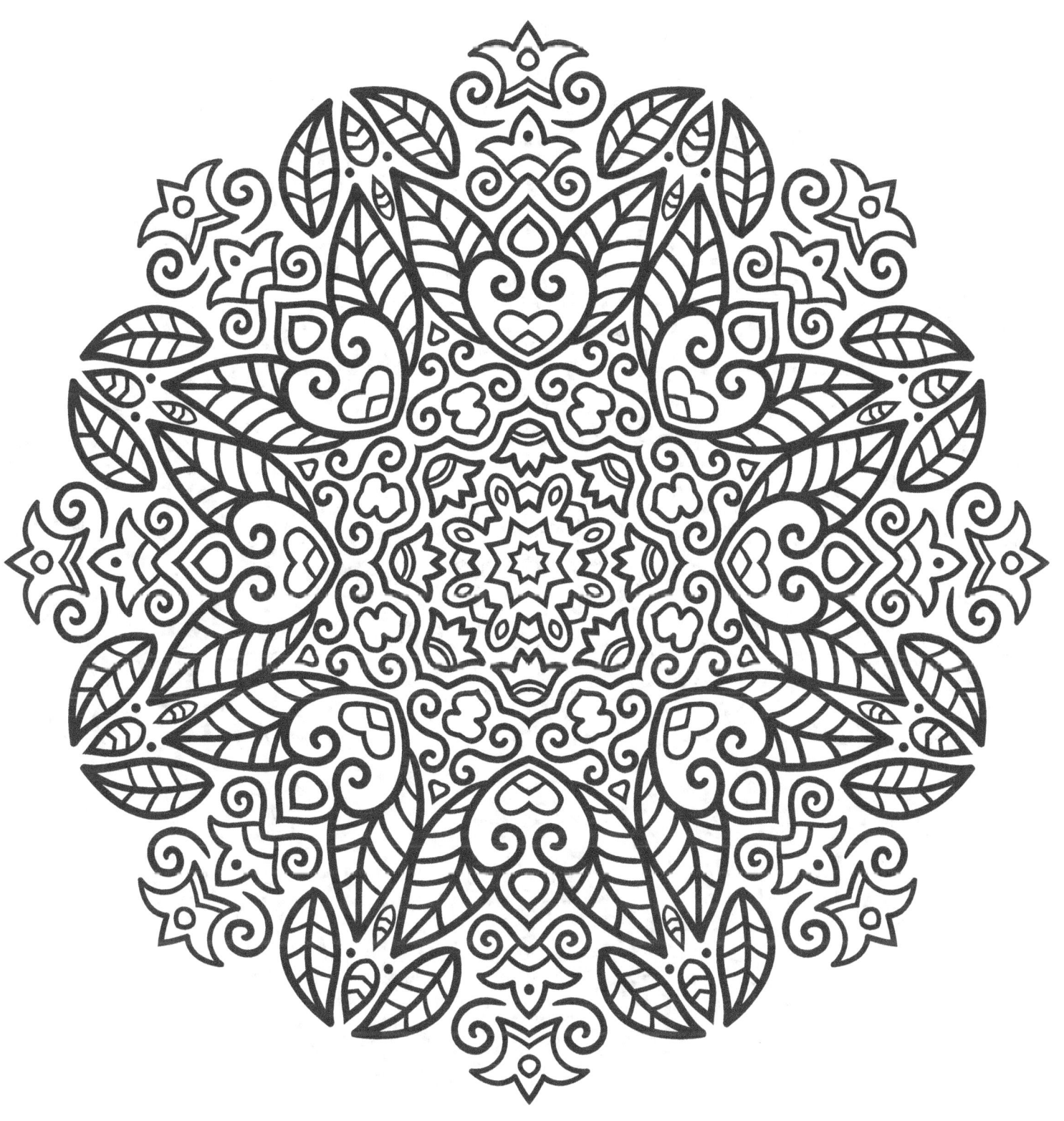

*By working faithfully eight hours a day you may
eventually get to be boss and work twelve hours a day
– Robert Frost*

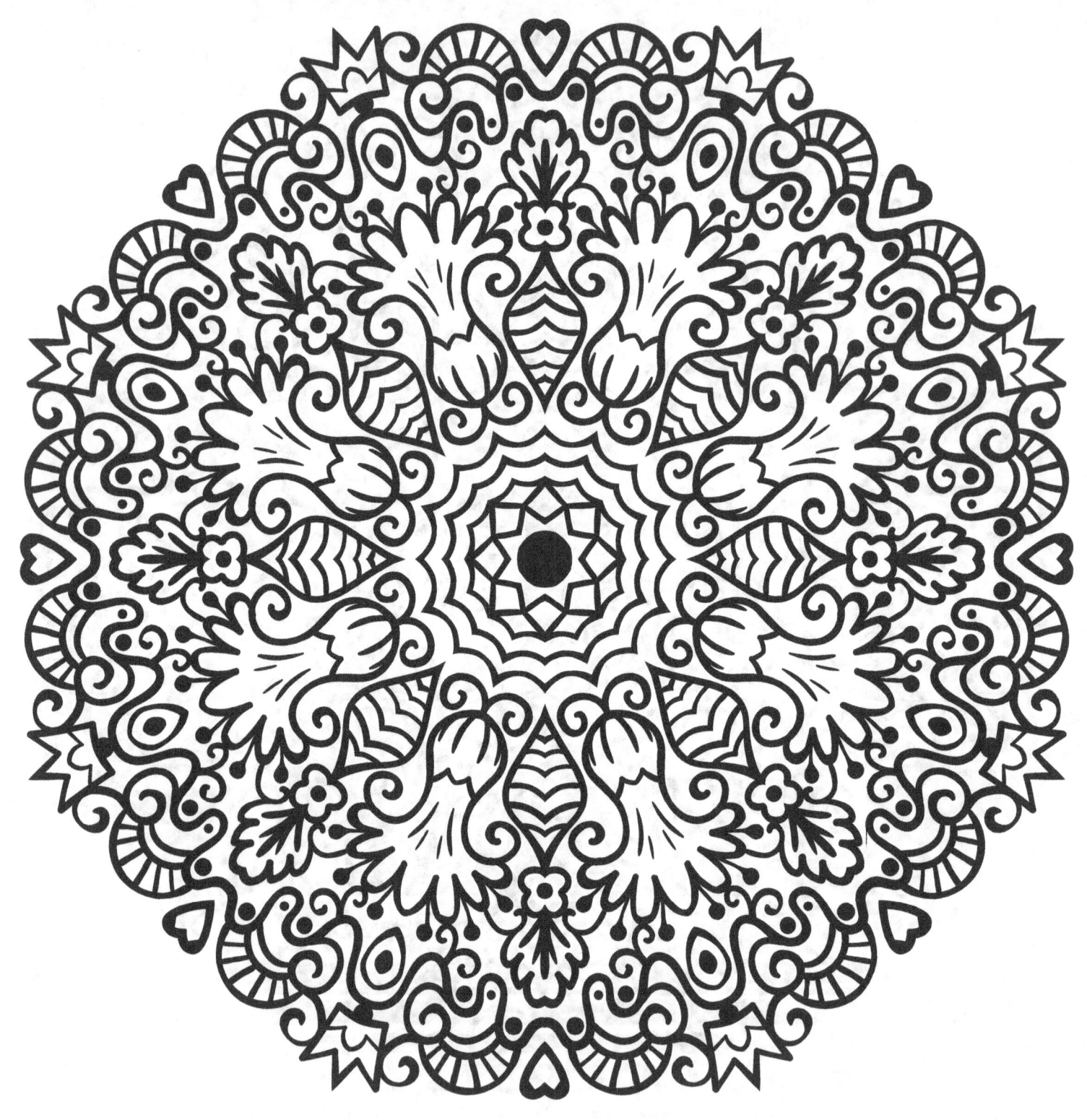

To avoid criticism do nothing,
say nothing, be nothing.
– Elbert Hubbard

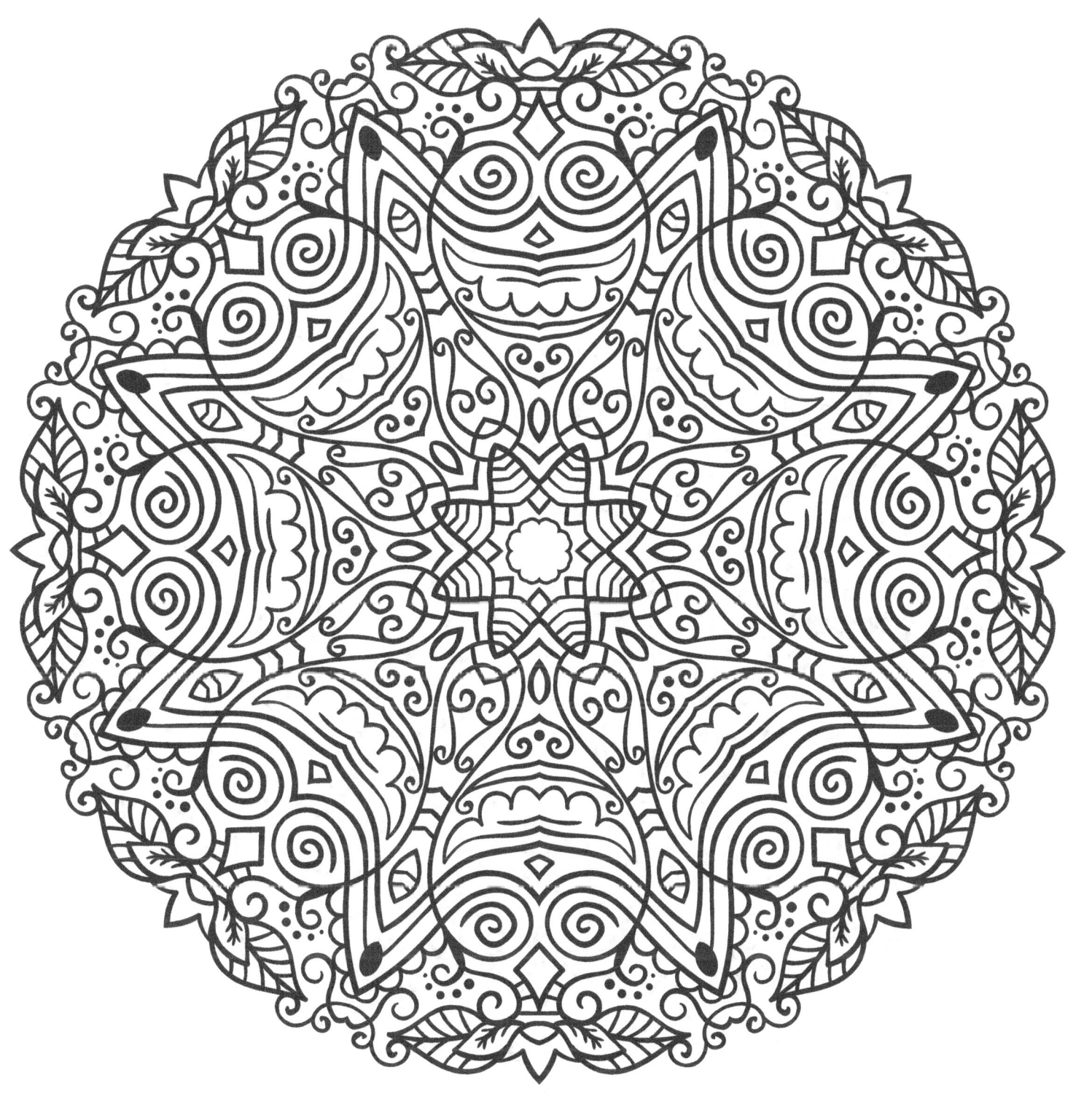

What you do speaks so loudly that
I cannot hear what you say"
— Ralph Waldo Emerson"

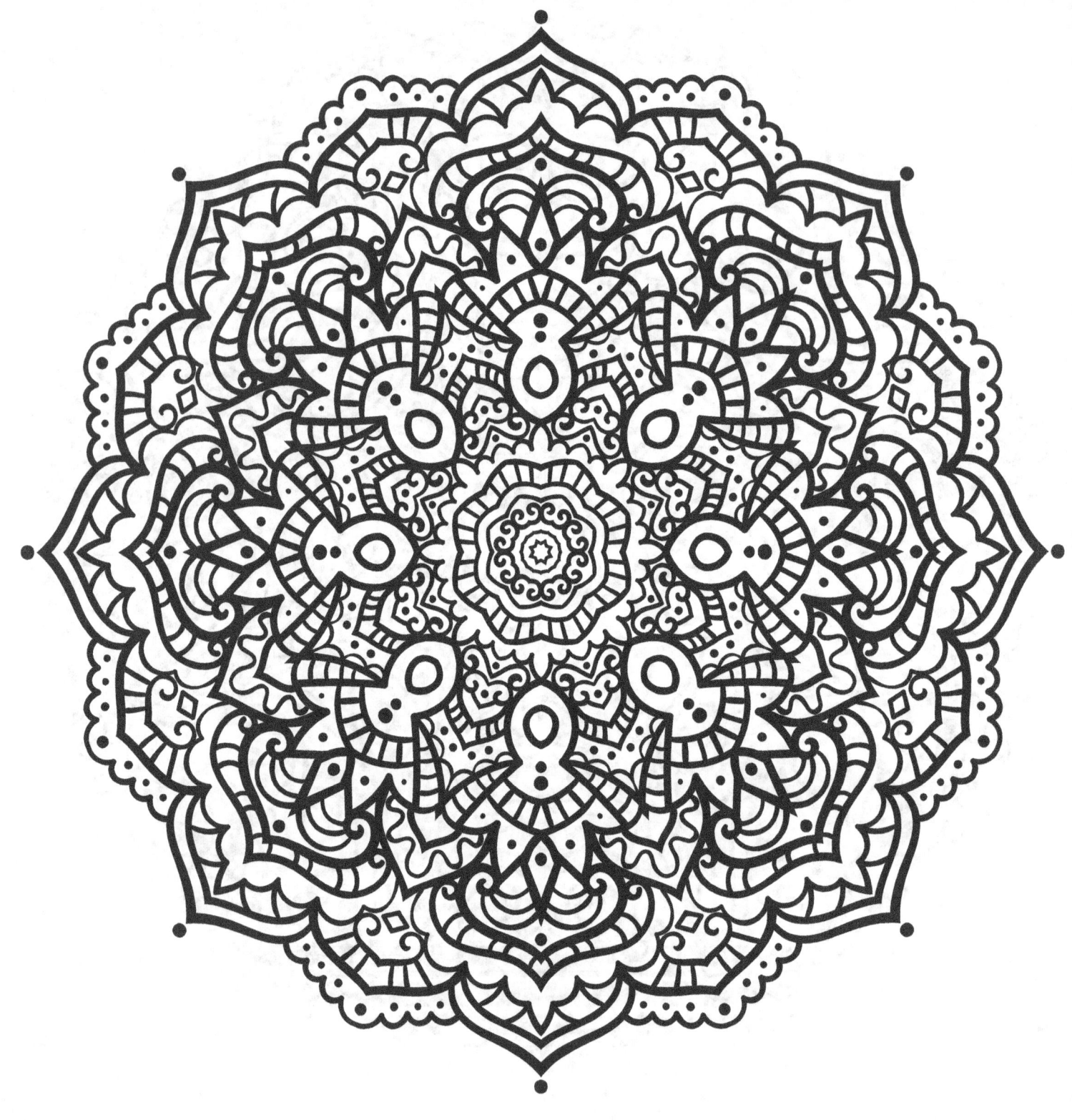

"You are what you think about all day long."
— *Dr. Robert Schuller*

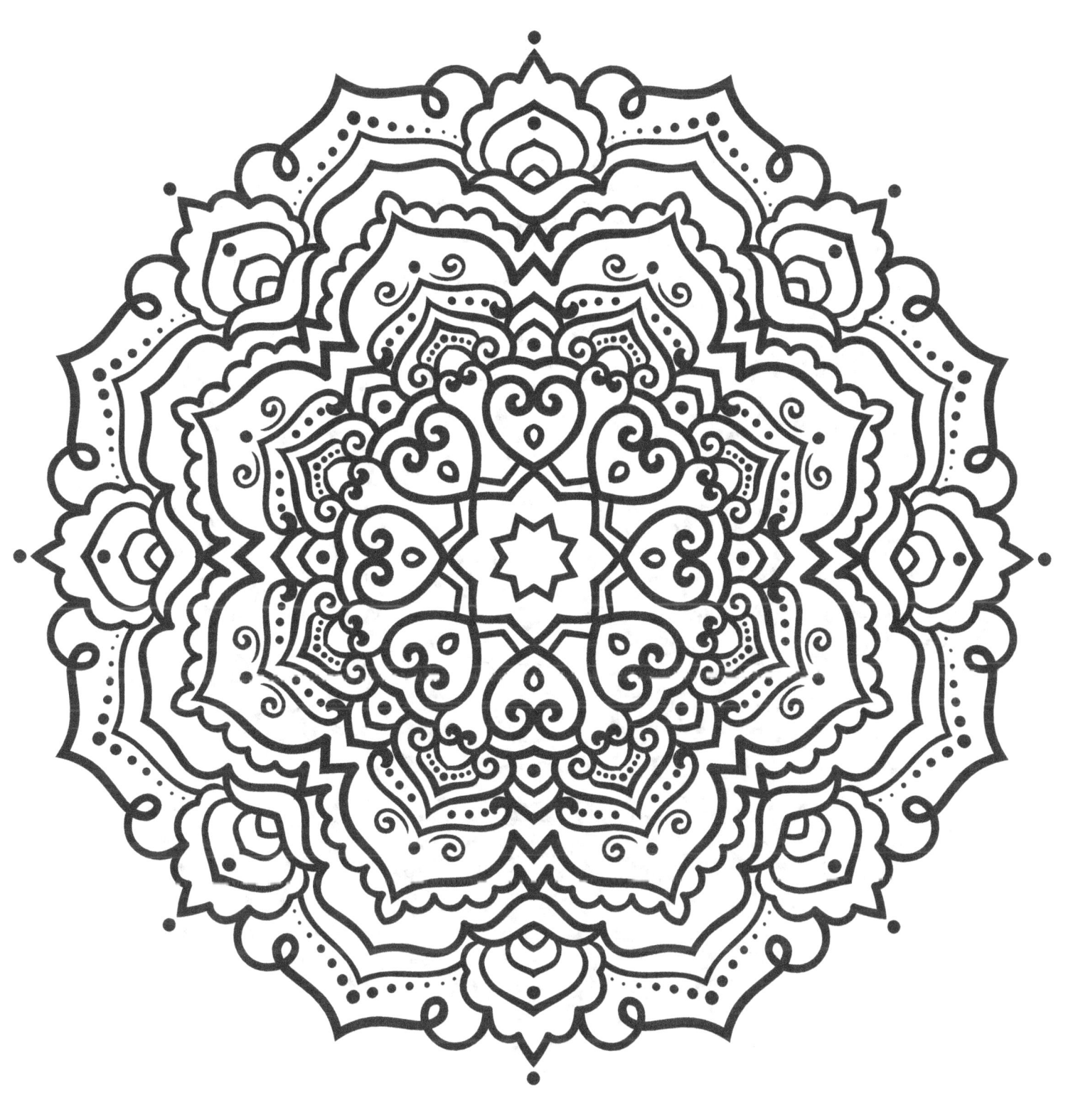

In matters of style, swim with the current; i
n matters of principle, stand like a rock.
-Thomas Jefferson

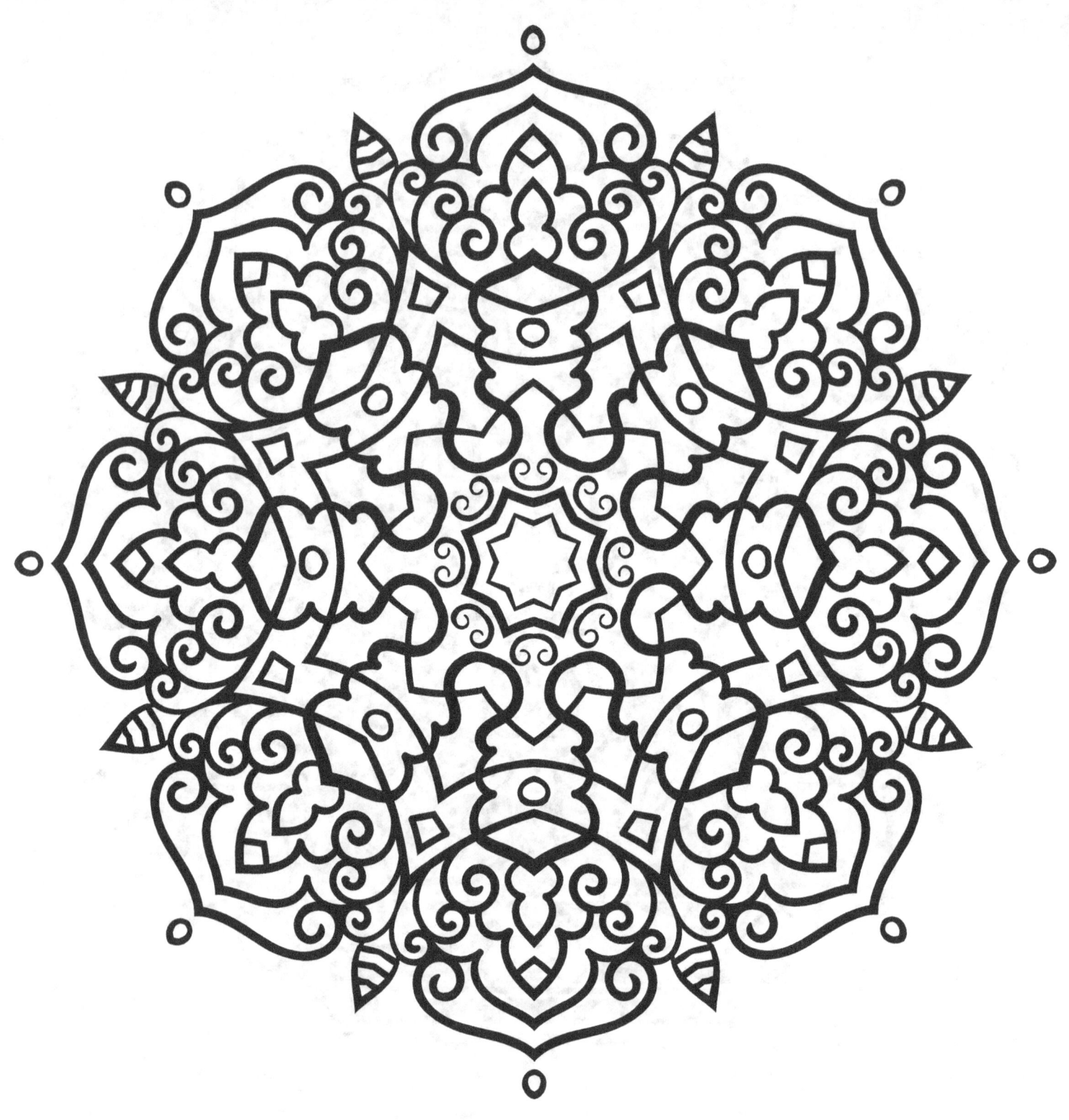

I think and think for months and years. Ninety-nine times, the conclusion is false.
The hundredth time I am right.
-Albert Einstein

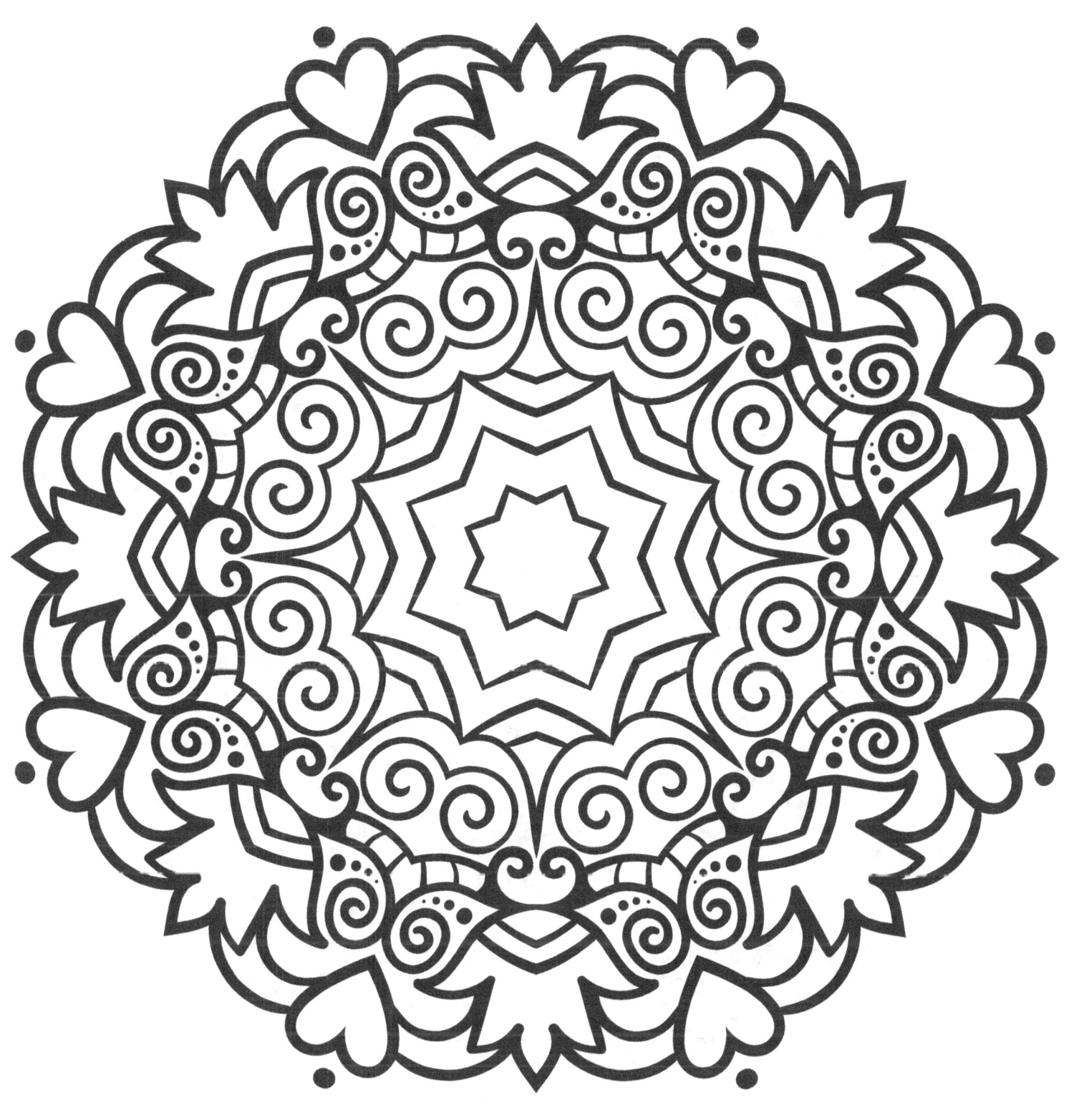

Winners lose much more often than losers.
So if you keep losing but you're still trying,
keep it up! You're right on track.
– Matthew Keith Groves

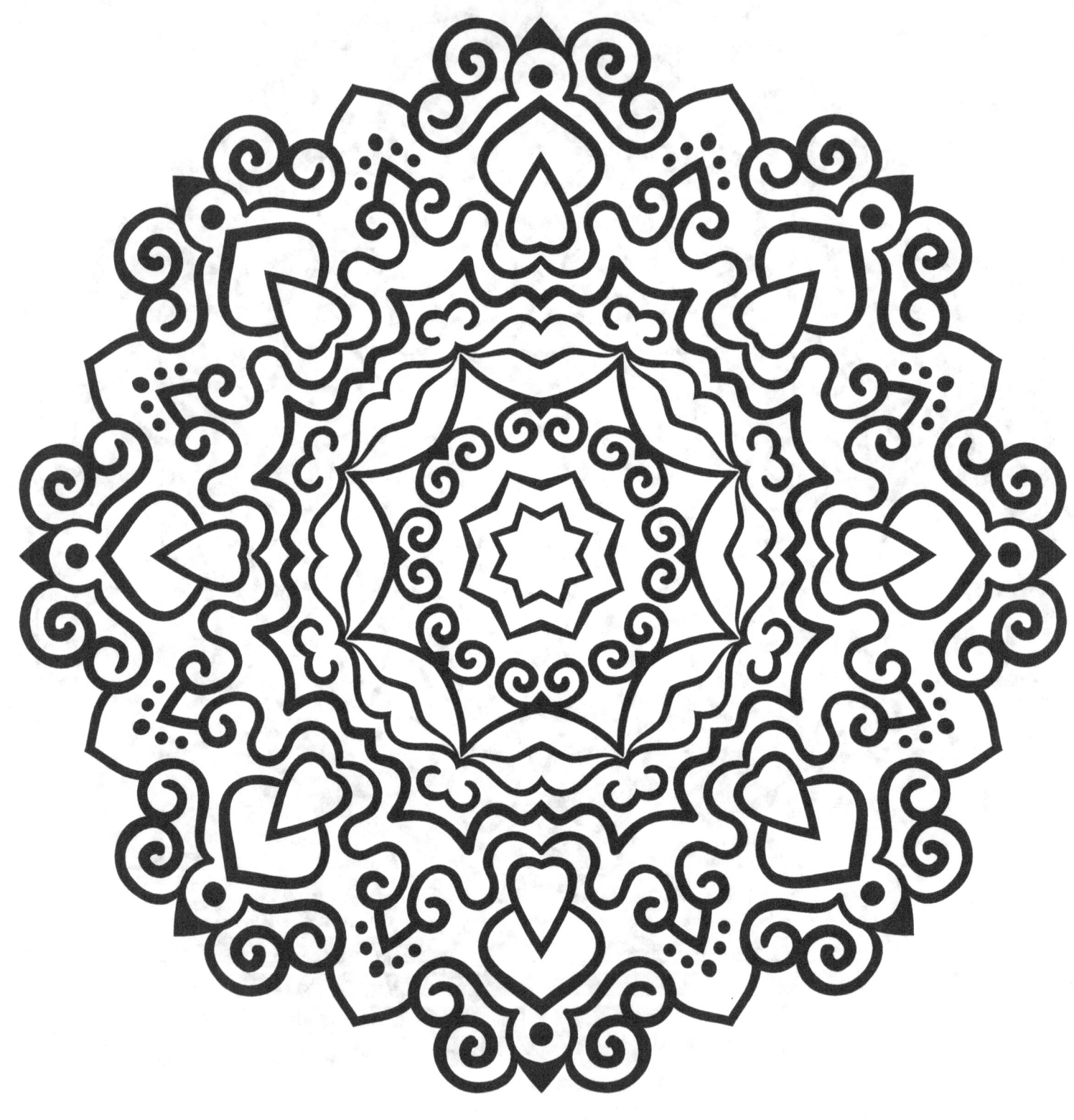

*An idea can turn to dust or magic, depending on
the talent that rubs against it.*
– Bill Bernbach

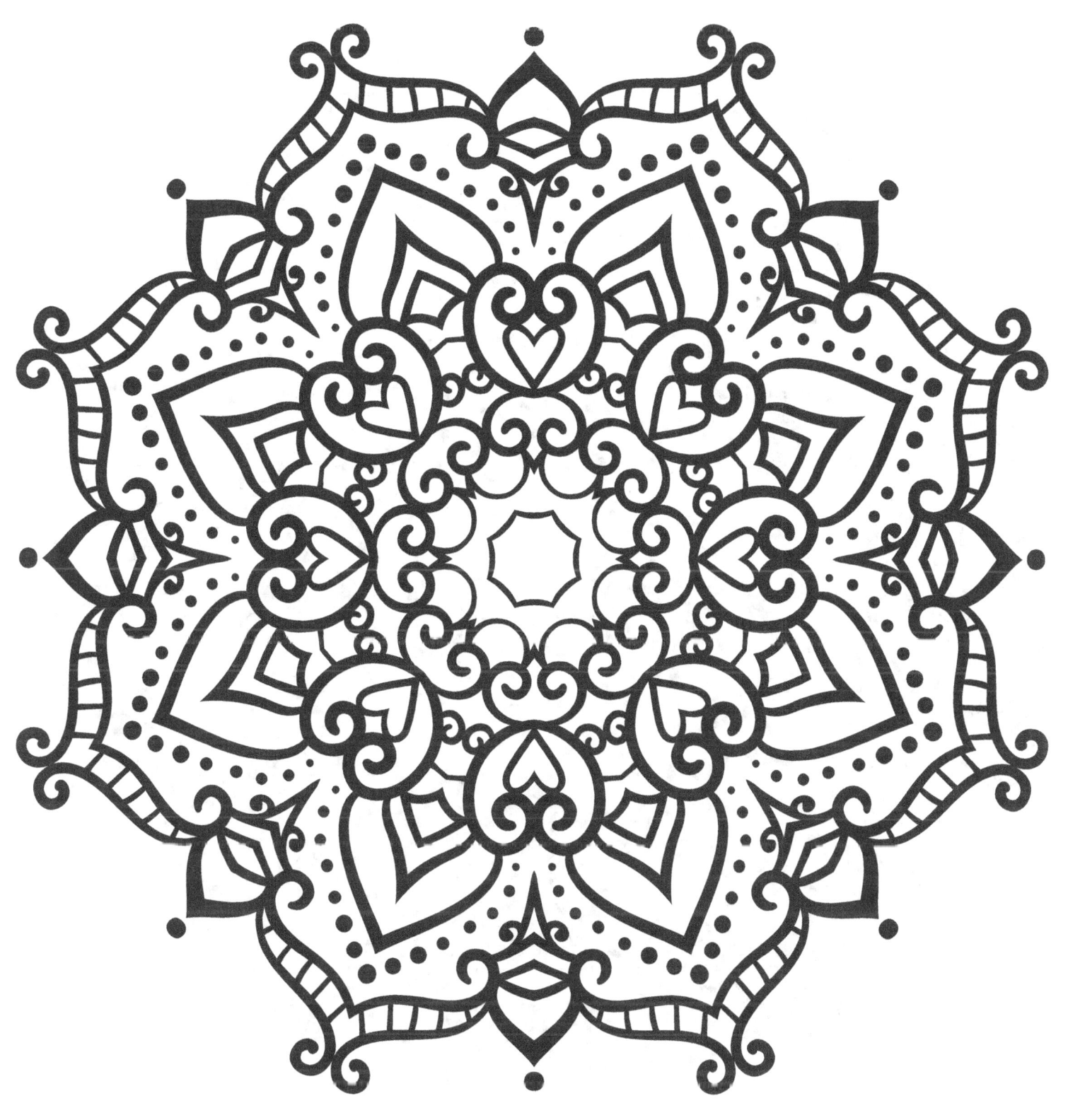

Success is a state of mind. If you want success, start thinking of yourself as a success. – Dr. Joyce Brothers

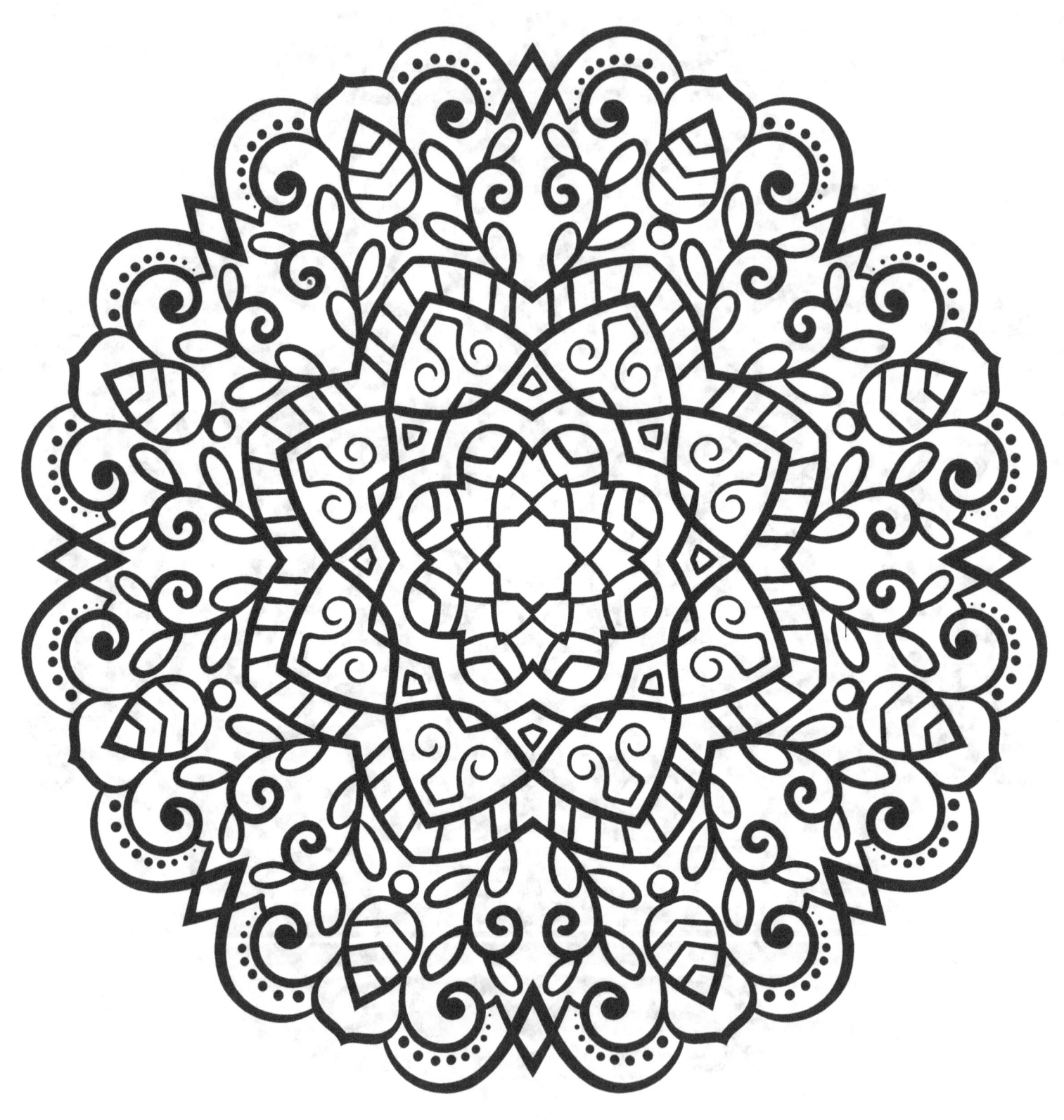

Ever tried. Ever failed. No matter.
Try Again. Fail again. Fail better.
– Samuel Beckett

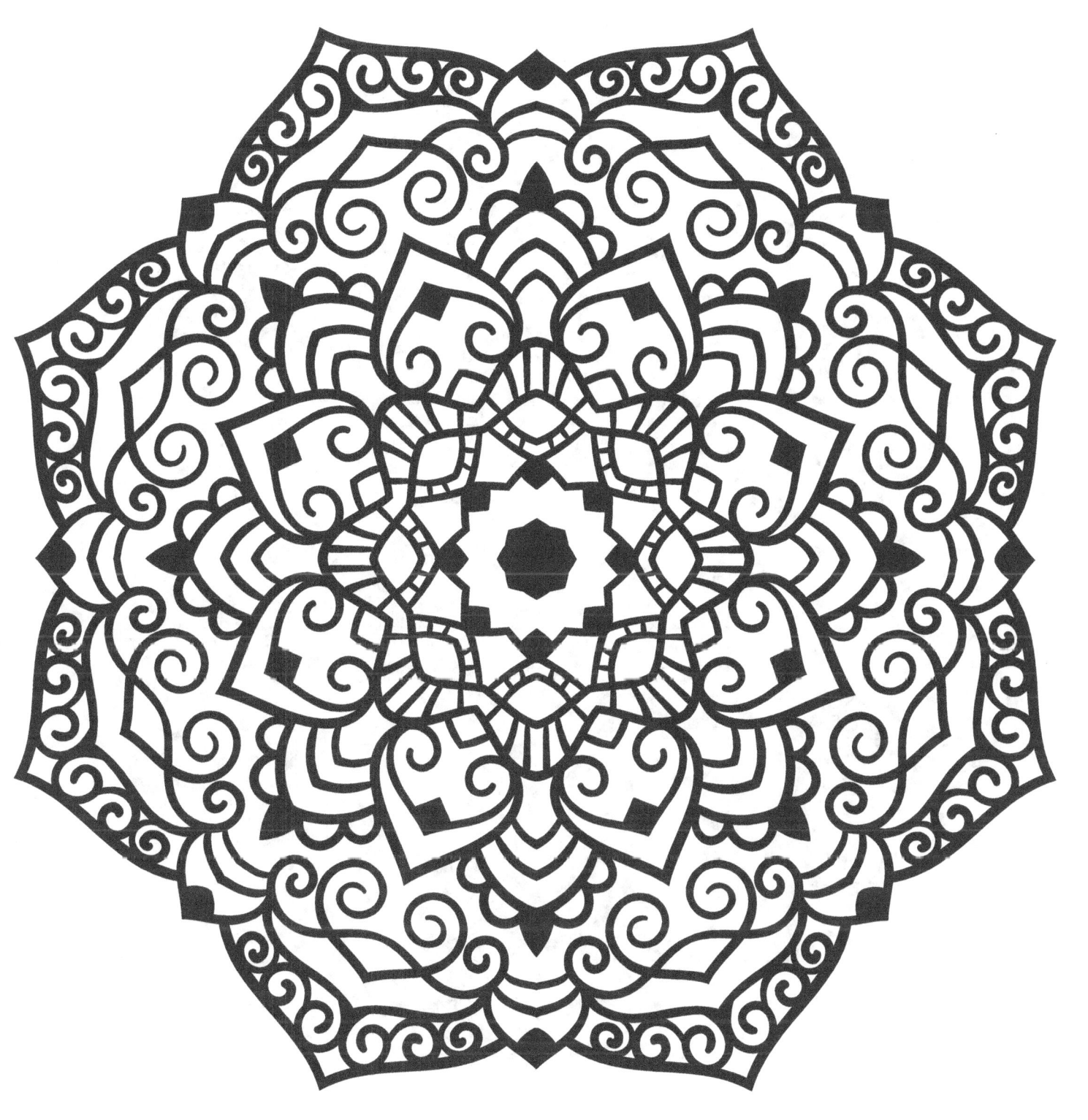

Life is "trying things to see if they work"
-Ray Bradbury

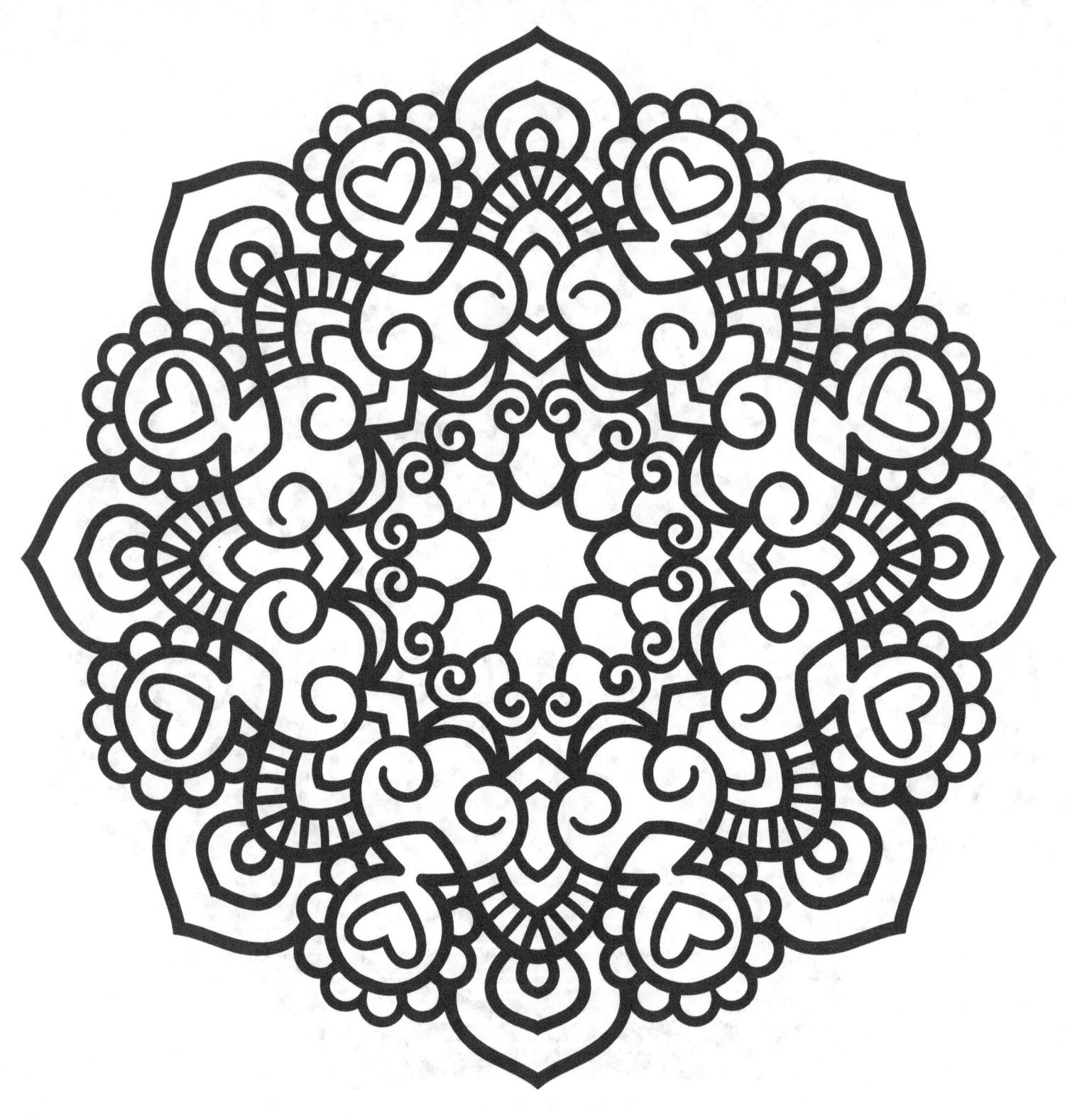

Life is 10% what happens to us and
90% how we react to it.
-Dennis P. Kimbro

We are all inventors, each sailing out on a voyage of
discovery, guided each by a private chart,
of which there is no duplicate.
The world is all gates, all opportunities.
-Ralph Waldo Emerson

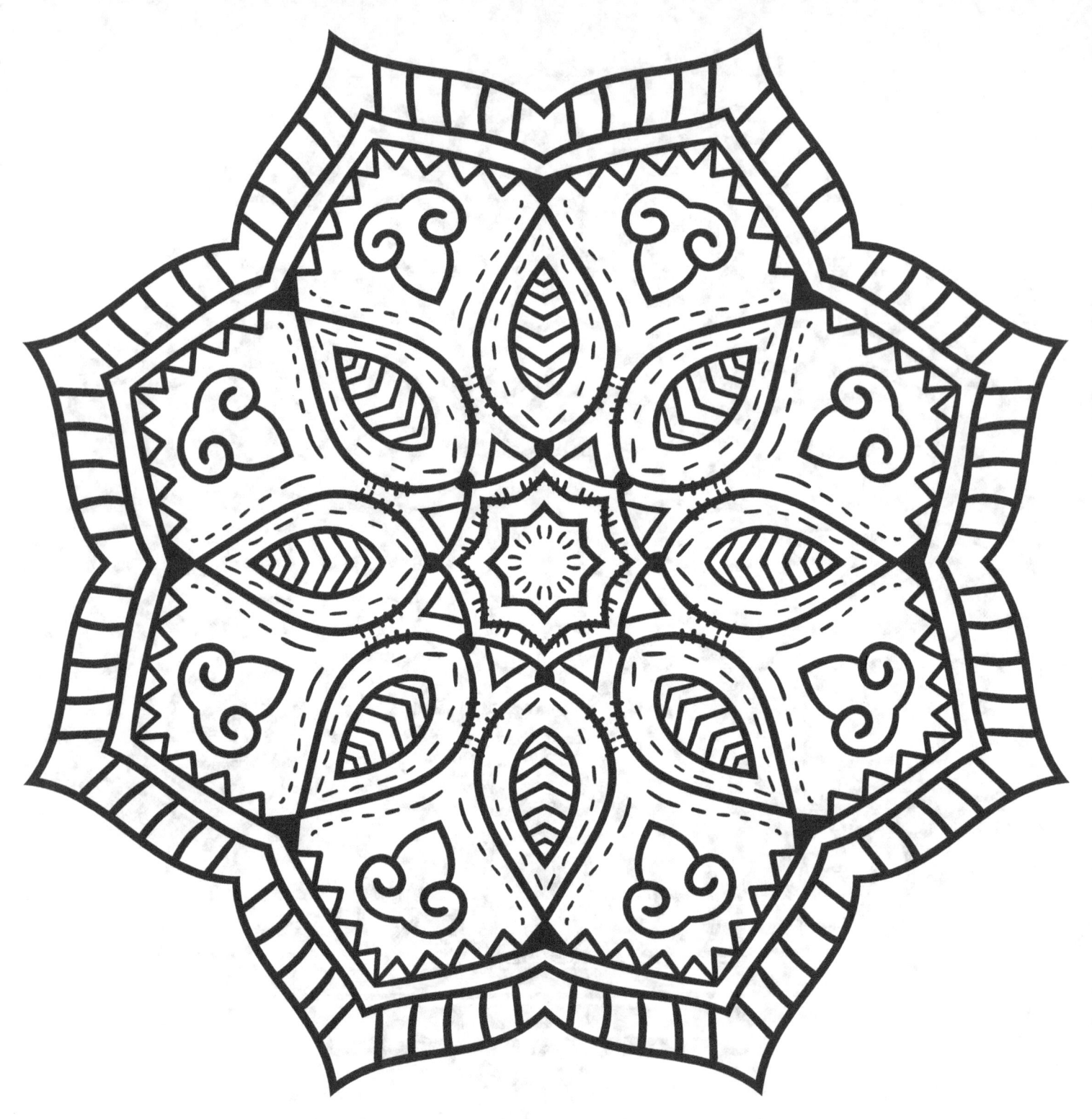

Knowing is not enough; we must apply.
Willing is not enough; we must do.
-Johann Wolfgang von Goethe

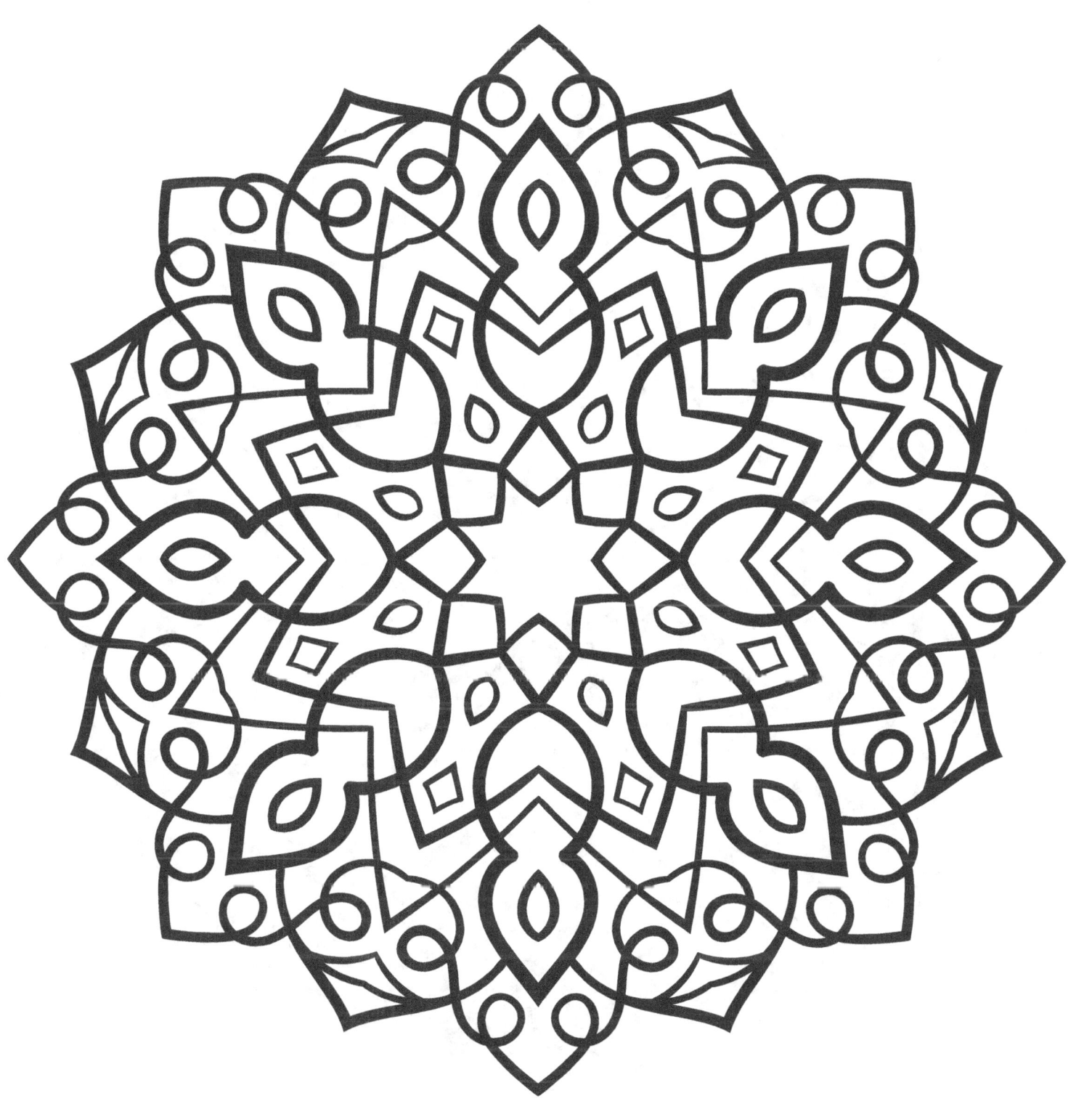

Vision doesn't usually come as a lightening bolt.
Rather it comes as a slow crystallization of life
challenges that we one day recognize as a beautiful
diamond with great value to ourselves and others.
– Dr. Michael Norwood

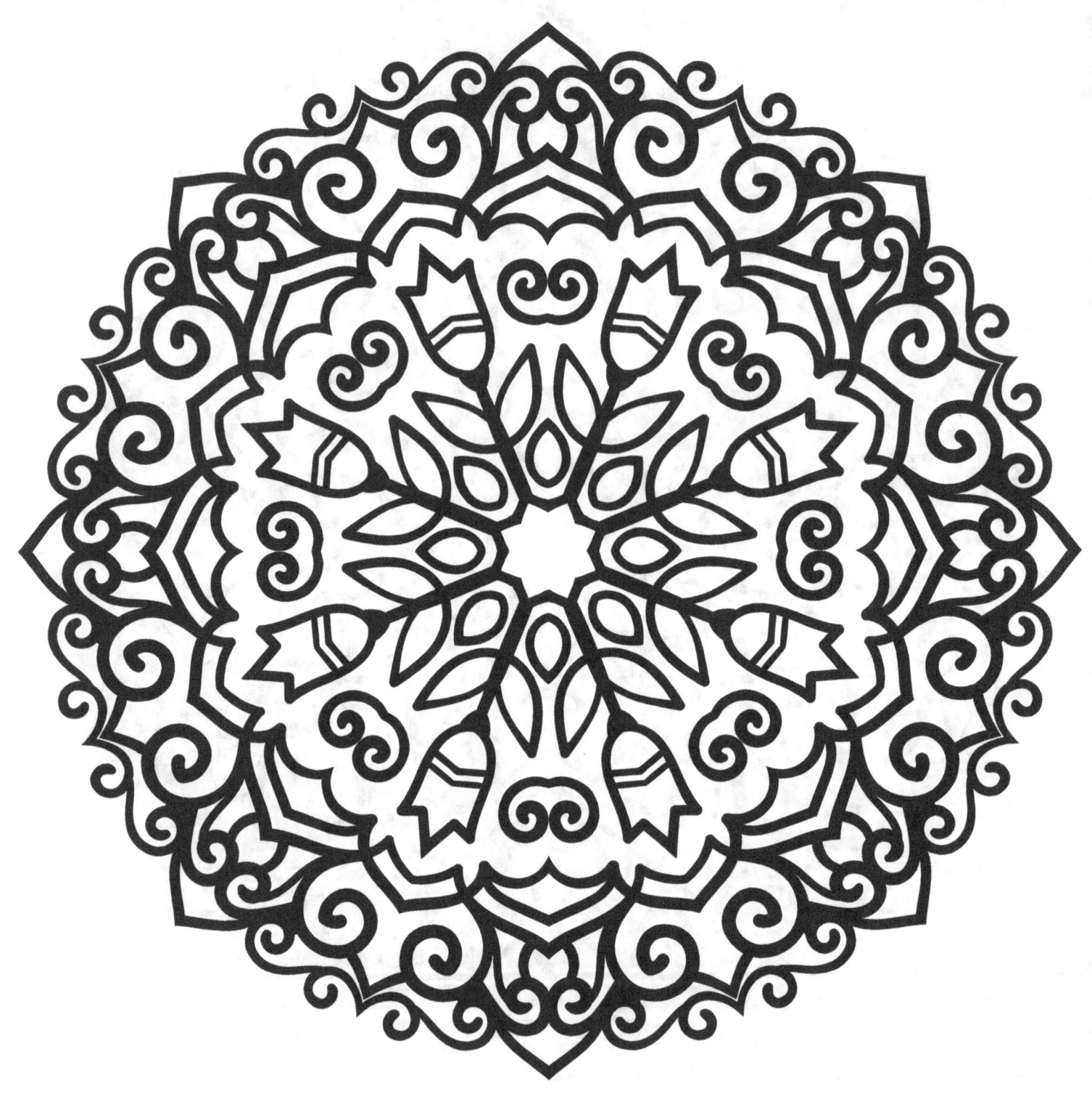

Flops are a part of life's menu and
I've never been a girl to miss out on any
of the courses.
– Rosalind Russell

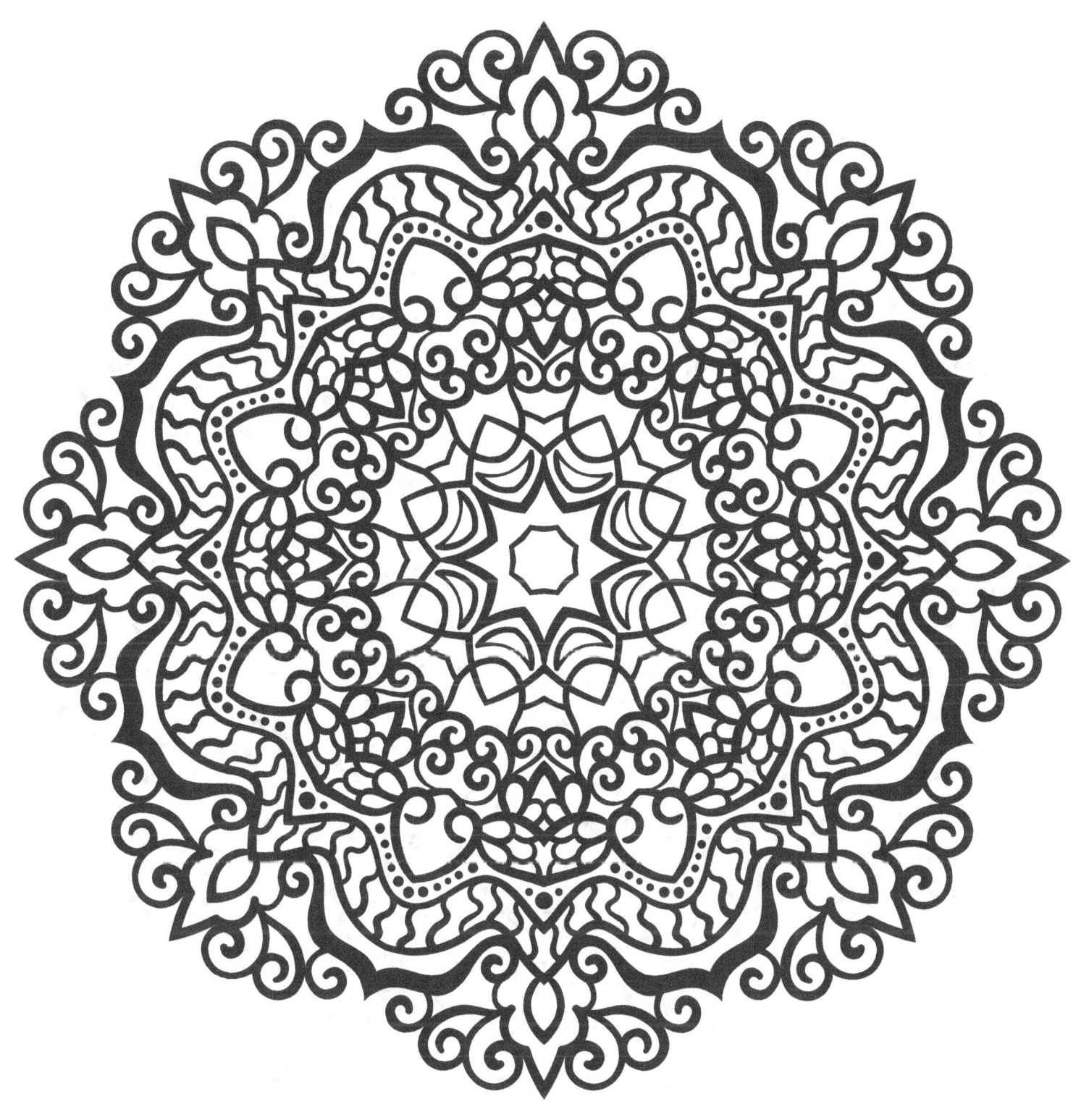

Sooner or later, those who win
are those who think they can.
– Richard Bach

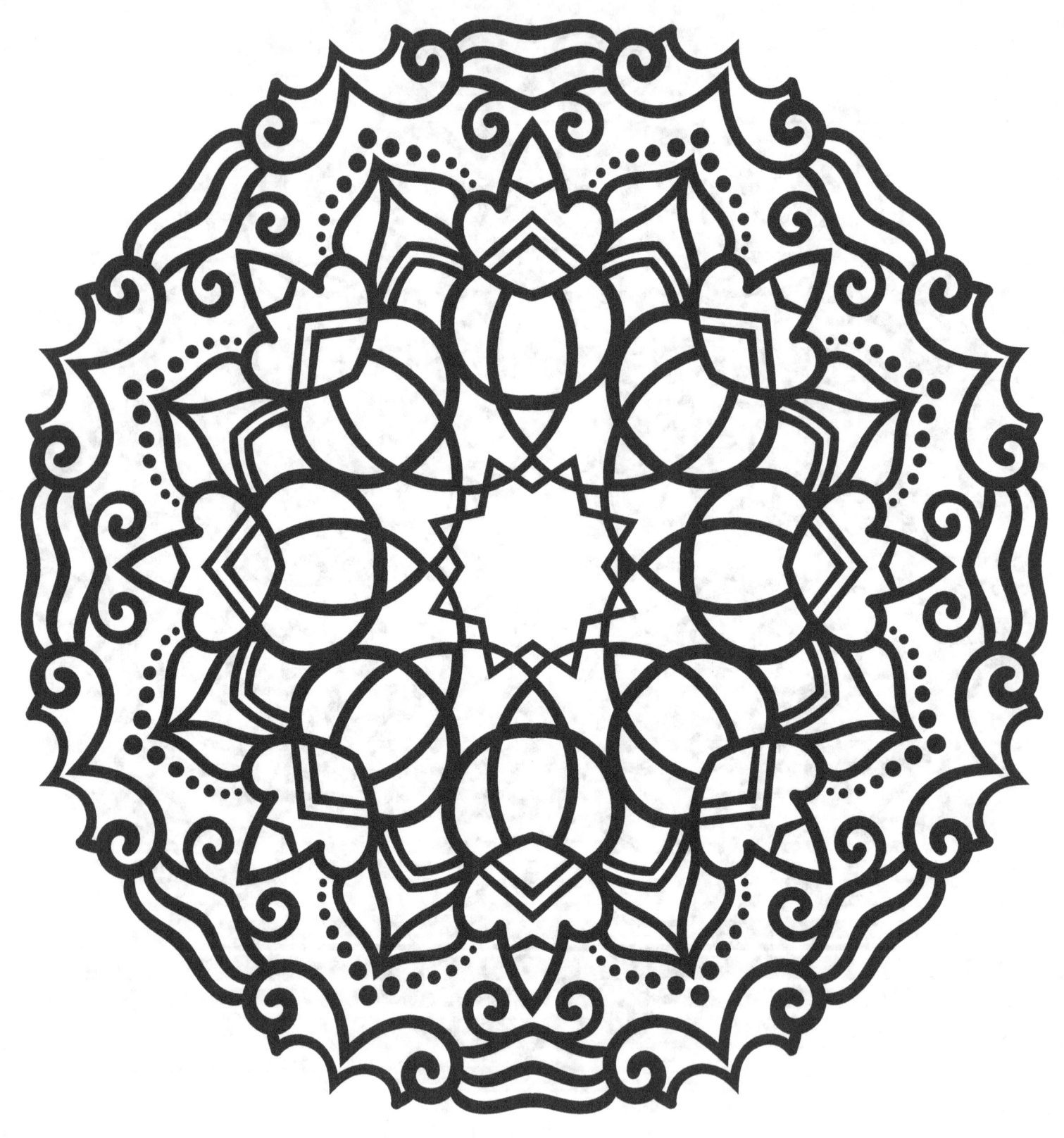

Where the willingness is great,
the difficulties cannot be great.
-Machiavelli.

Strength does not come from physical capacity.
It comes from an indomitable will.
-Mahatma Gandhi

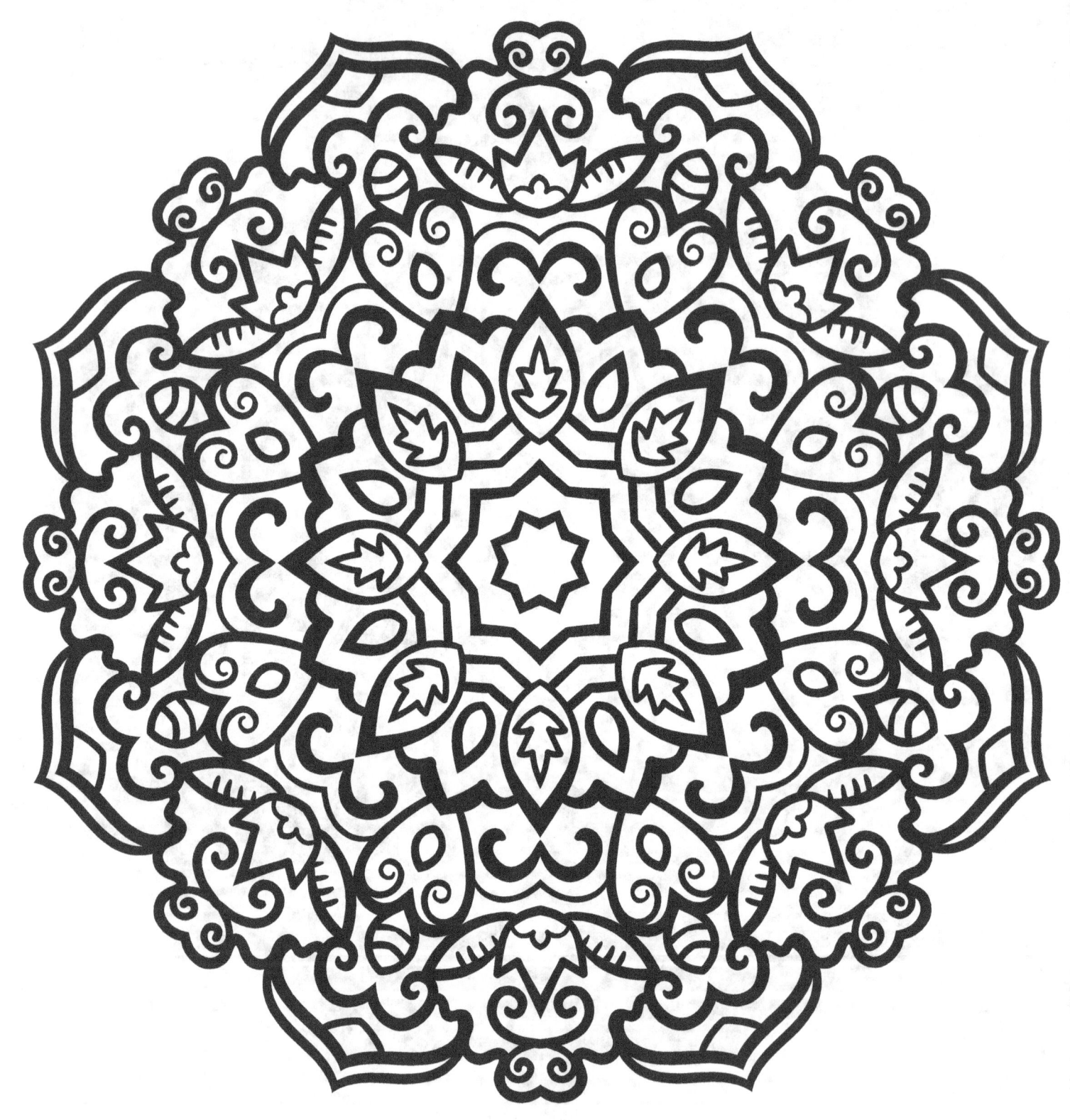

Cause Change & Lead
Accept Change & Survive
Resist Change & Die
– Ray Norda, Chairman, Novellist

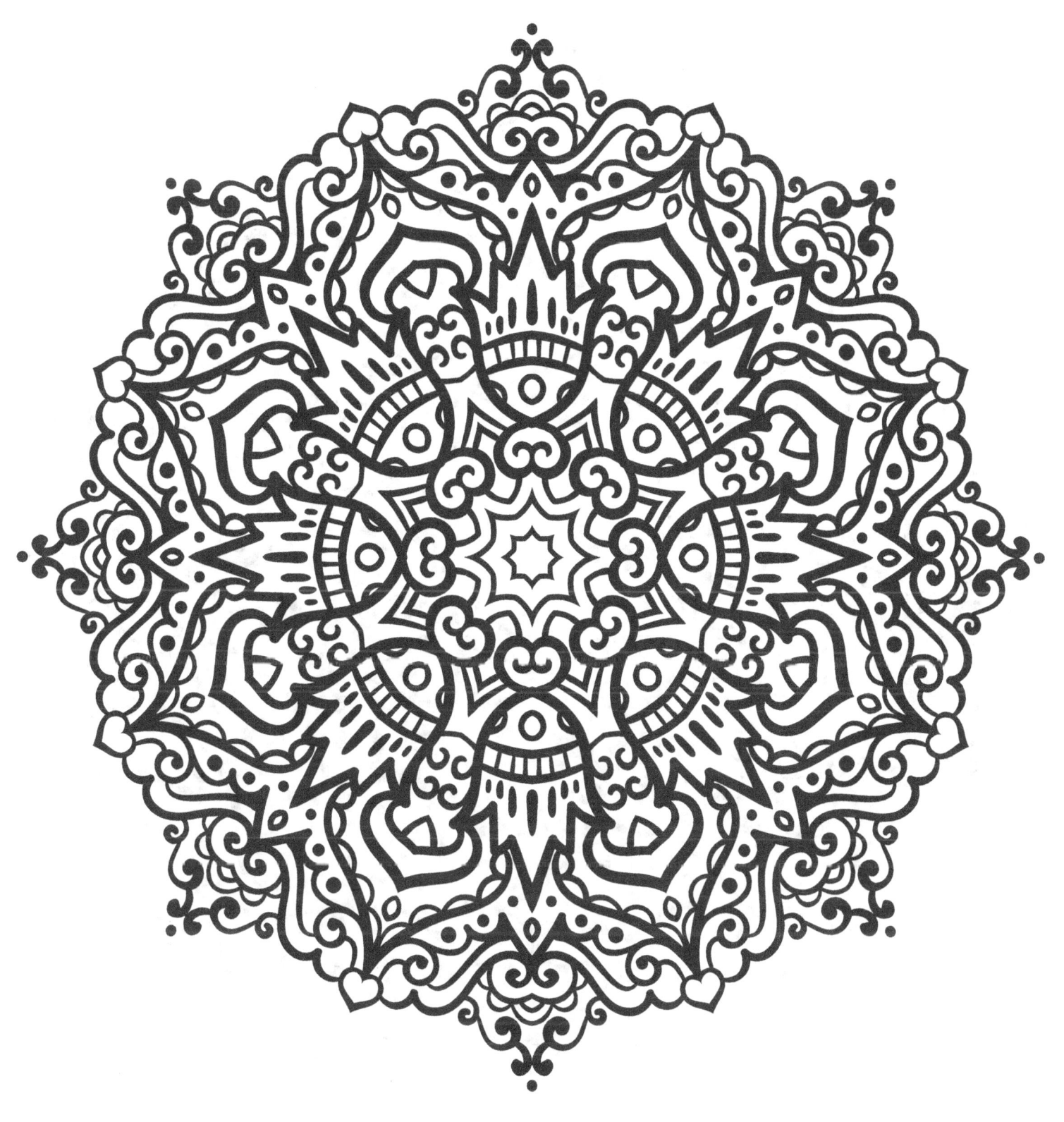

Whenever you find the whole world is against you just turn around and lead the world.
— Anonymous

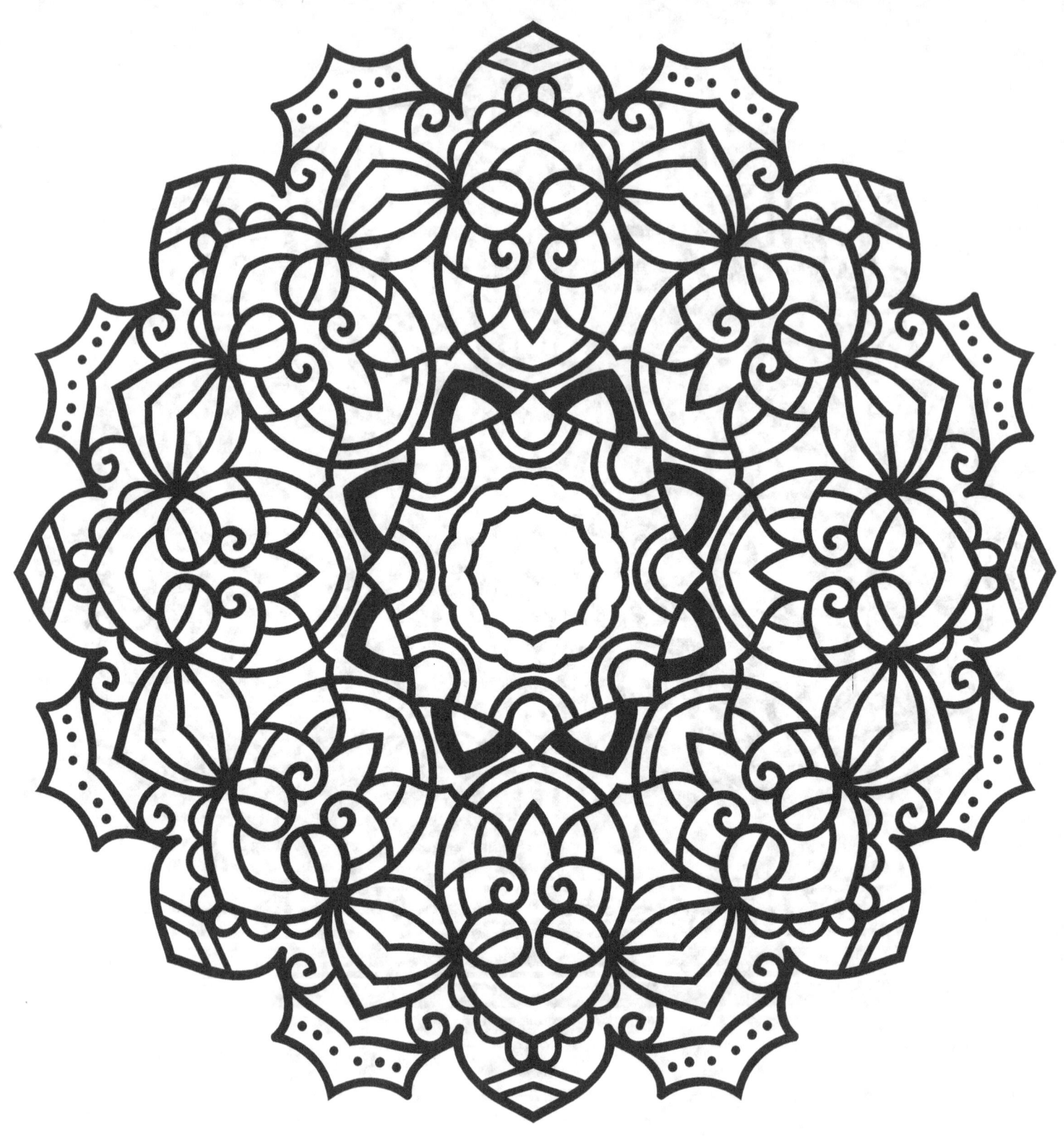

People become really quite remarkable
when they start thinking that they can do things.
When they believe in themselves
they have the first secret of success.
— Norman Vincent Peale

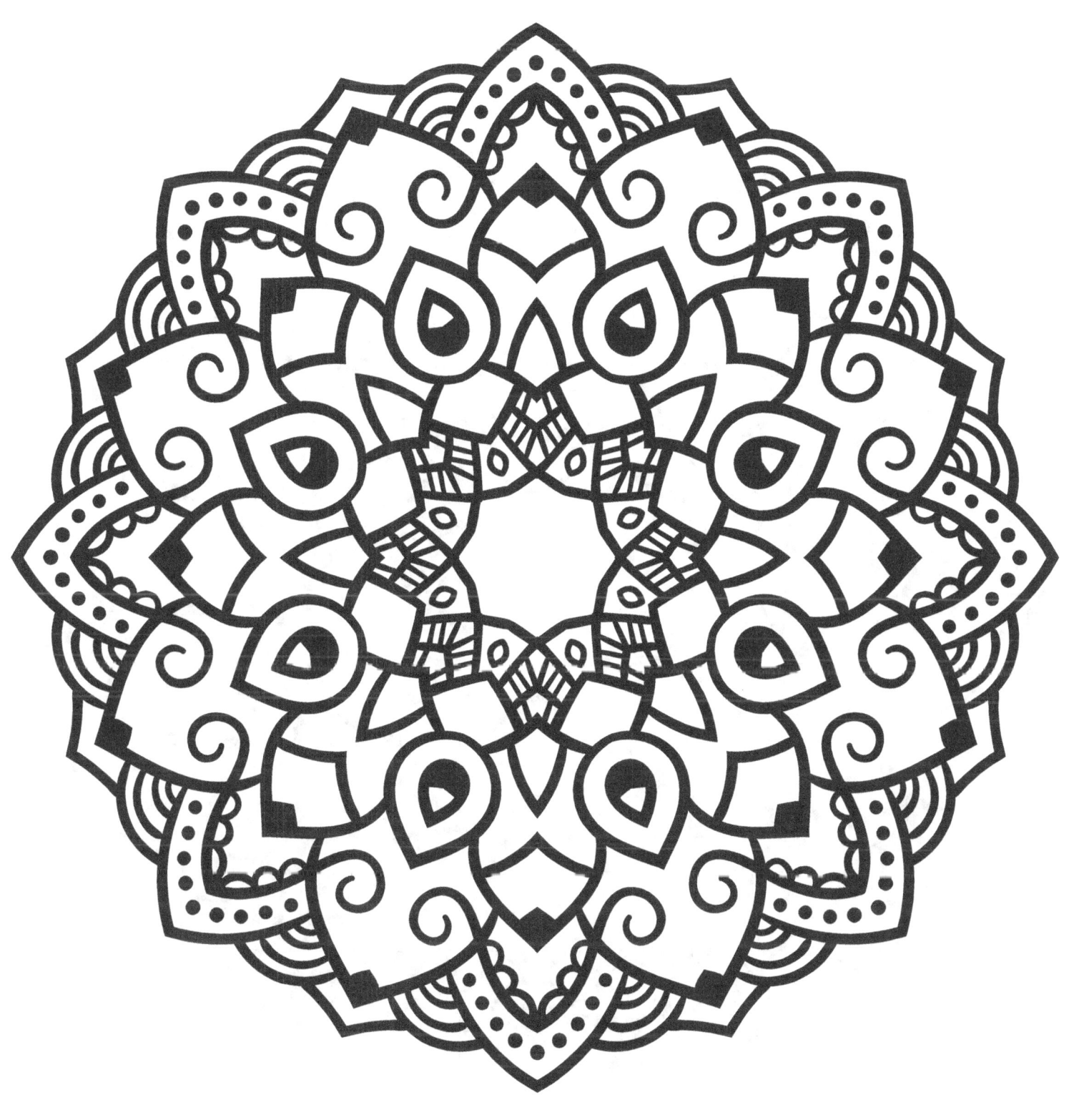

Being defeated is only a temporary condition;
giving up is what makes it permanent.
– Marilyn vos Savant,
Author and Advice Columnist

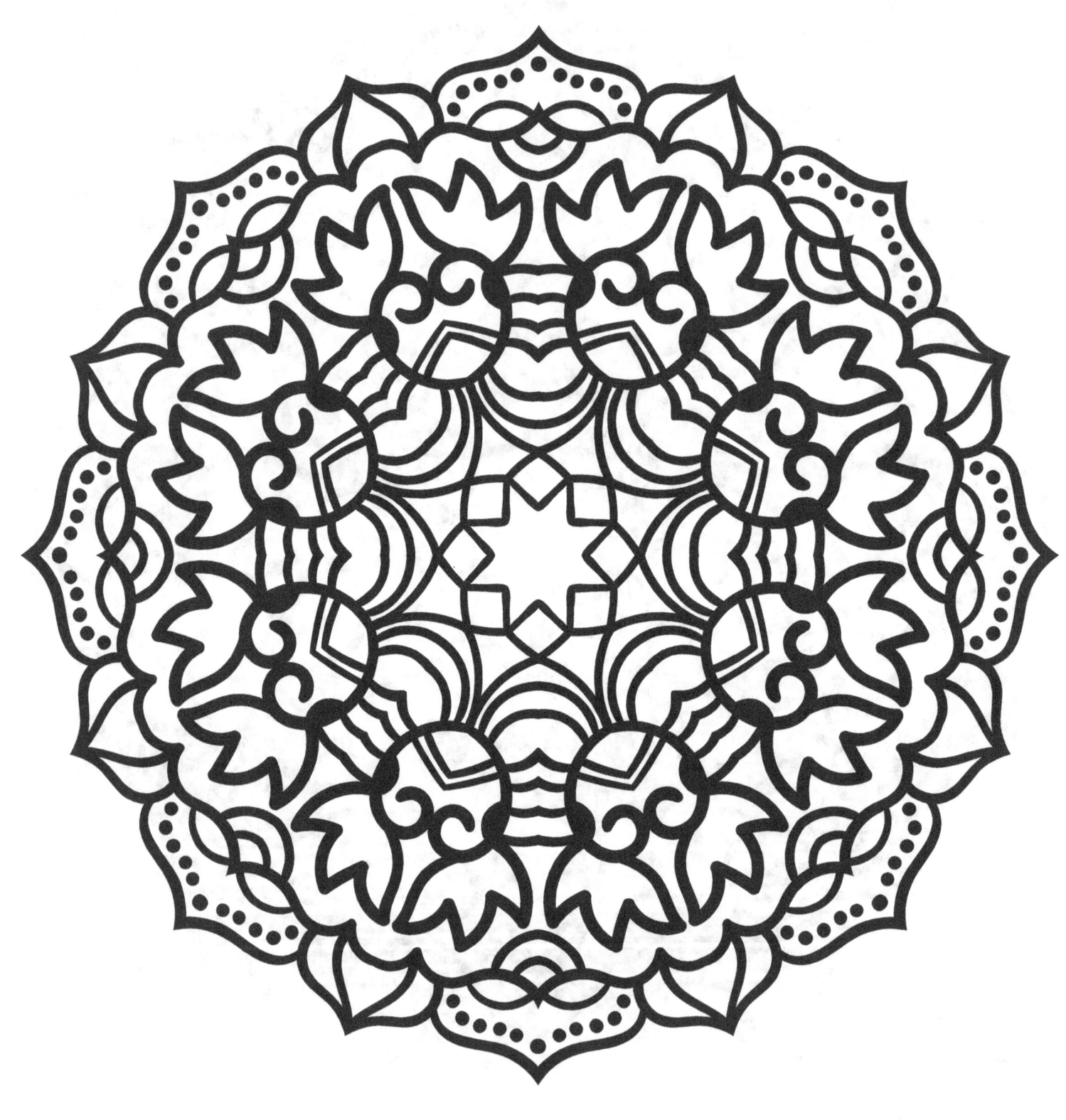

The best way to predict the future is to create it.
– Unknown

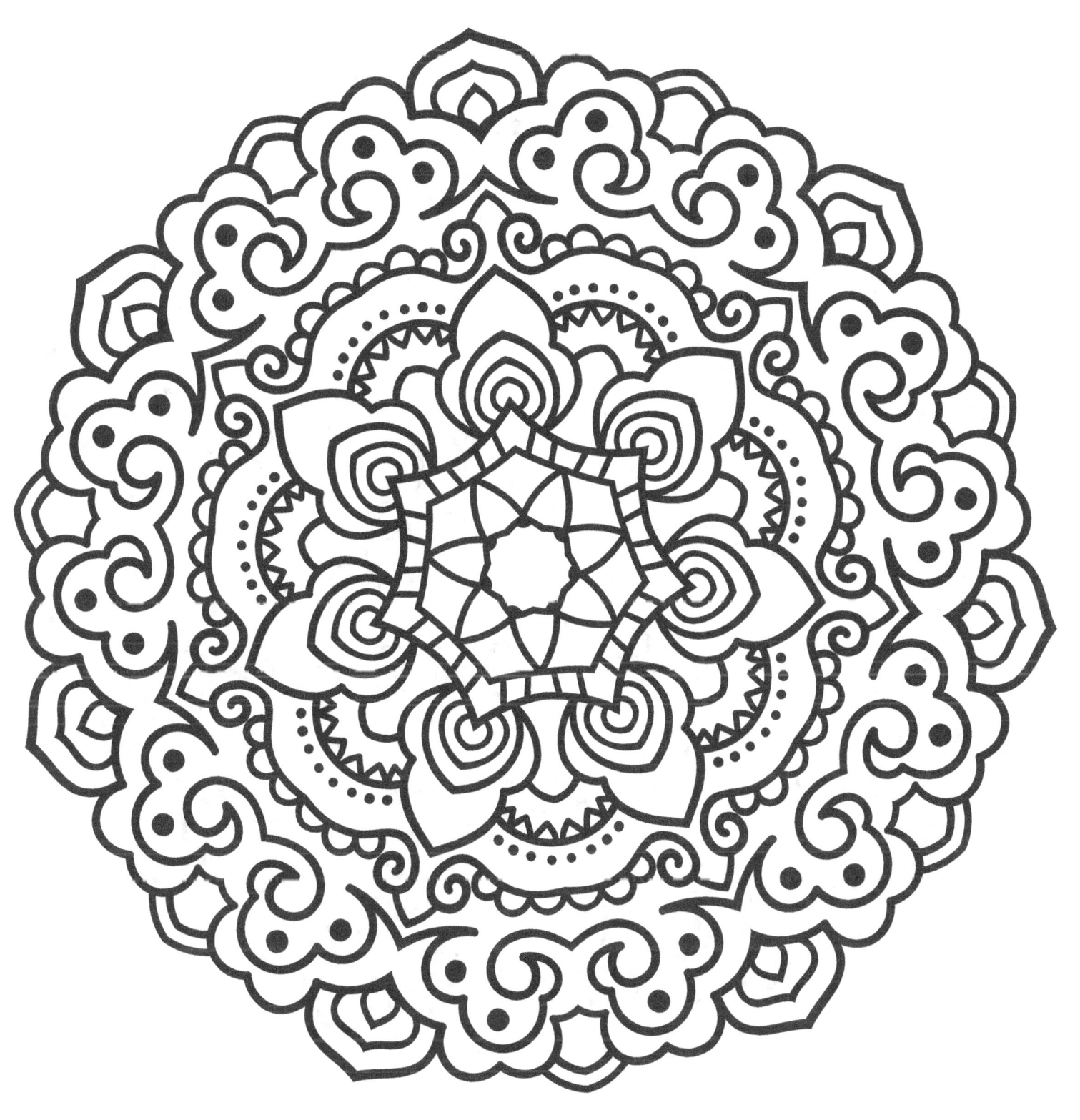

*The difference between ordinary
and extraordinary is that little extra.
— Unknown*

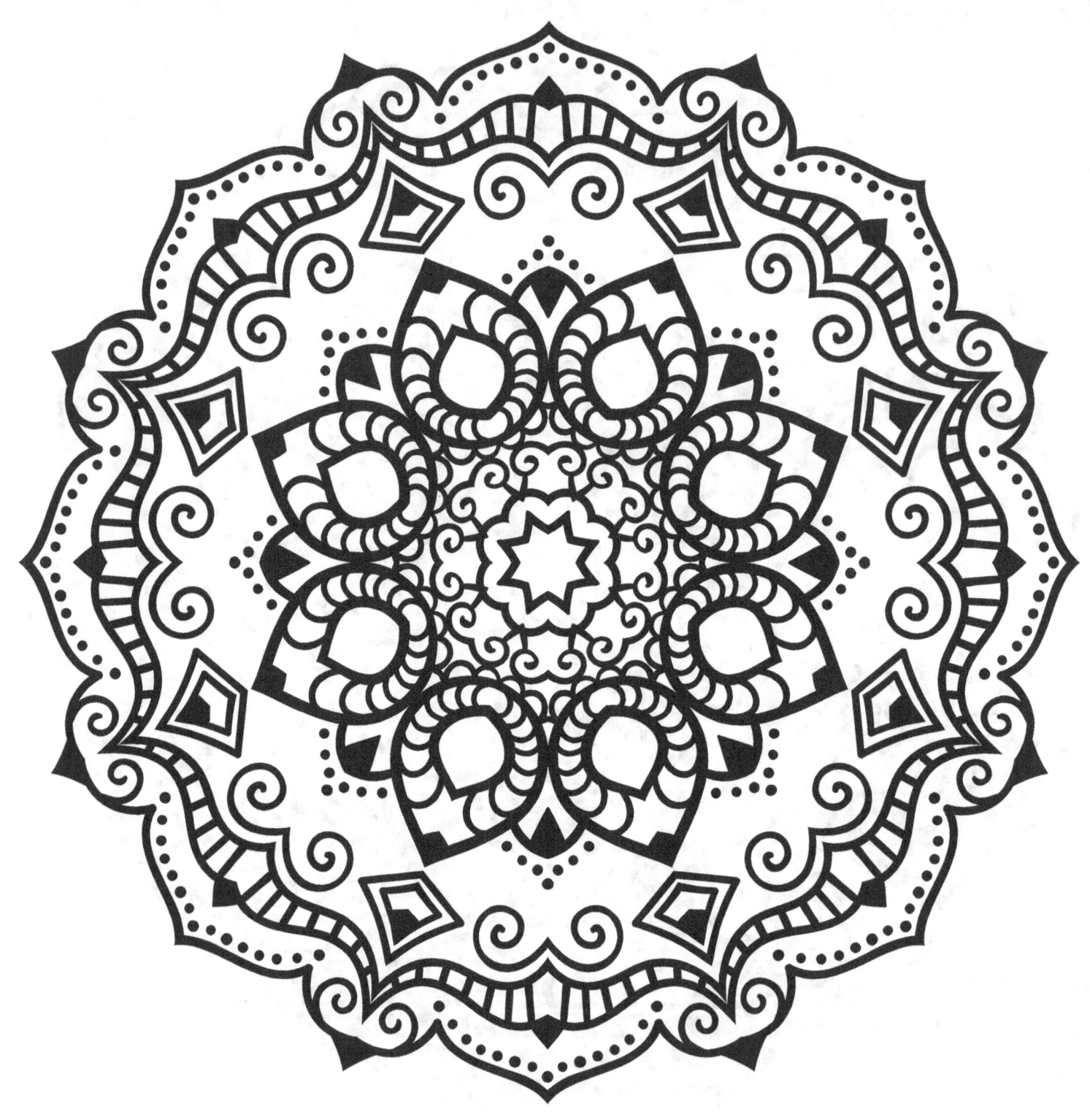

Anyone can do something when they WANT to do it.
Really successful people do things when they
don't want to do it.
– Dr. Phil

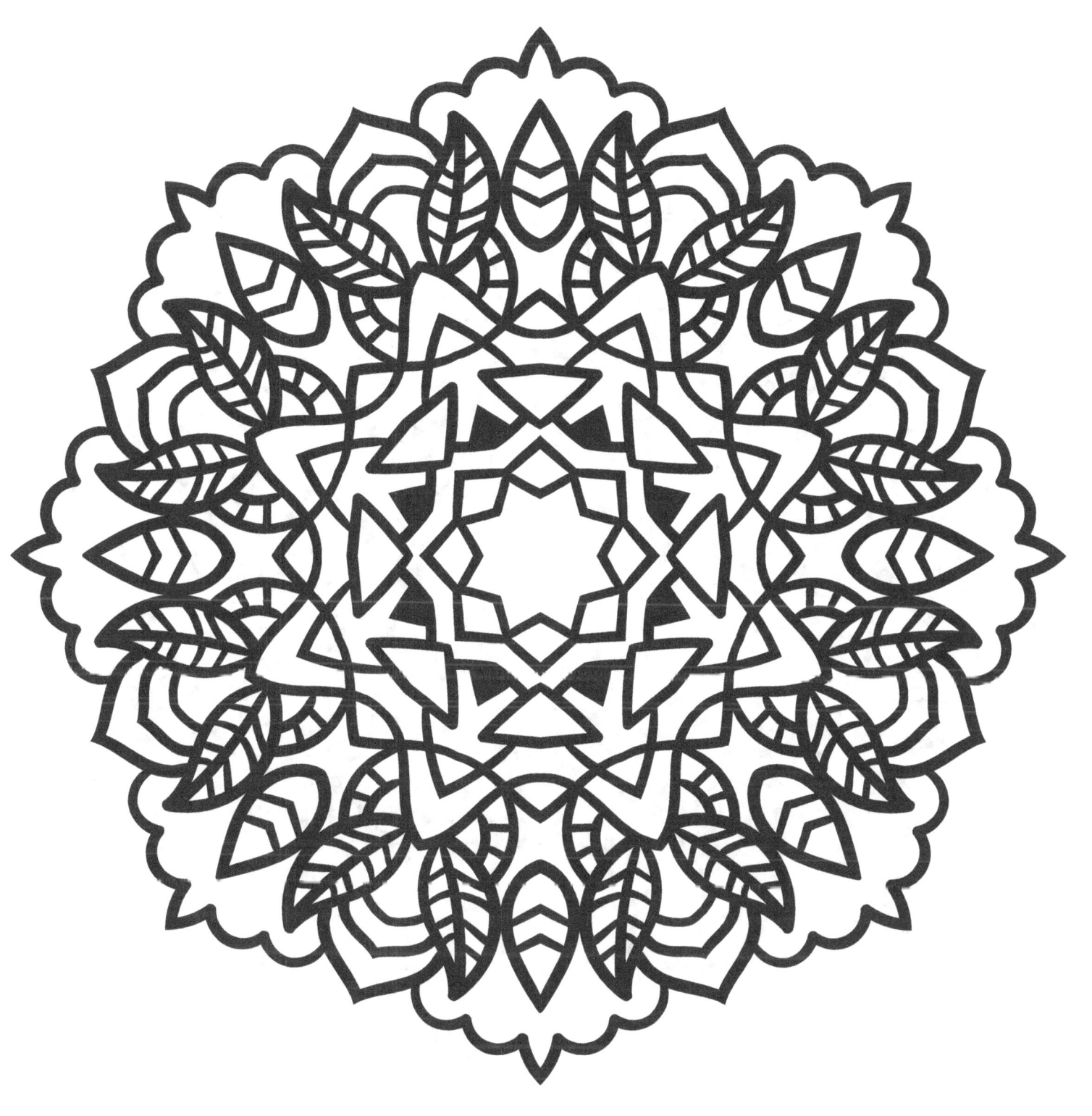

There are two primary choices in life: to accept conditions as they exist, or accept the responsibility for changing them.
- Denis Waitley

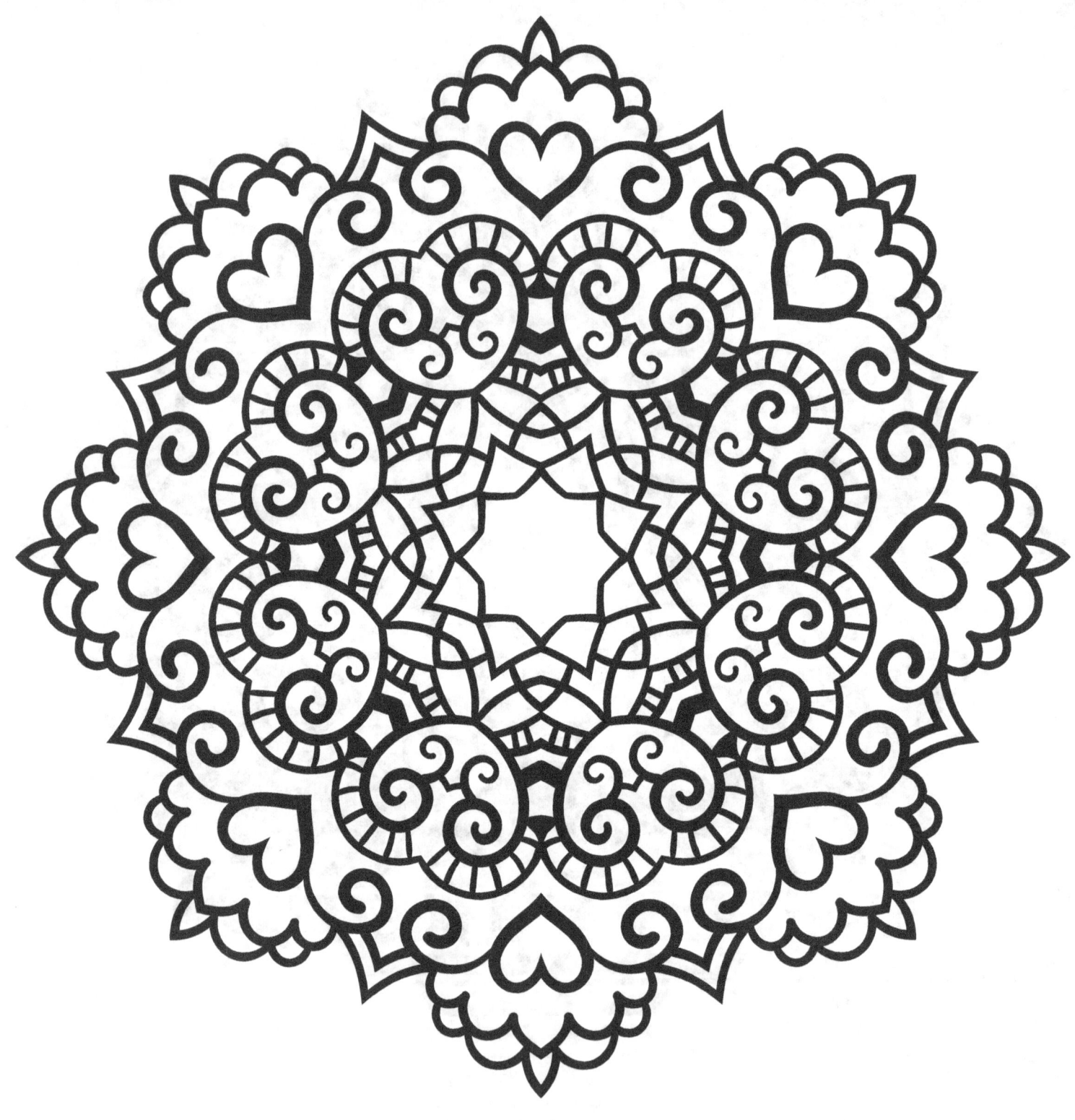

Success seems to be connected with action.
Successful people keep moving.
They make mistakes but don't quit.
— Conrad Hilton

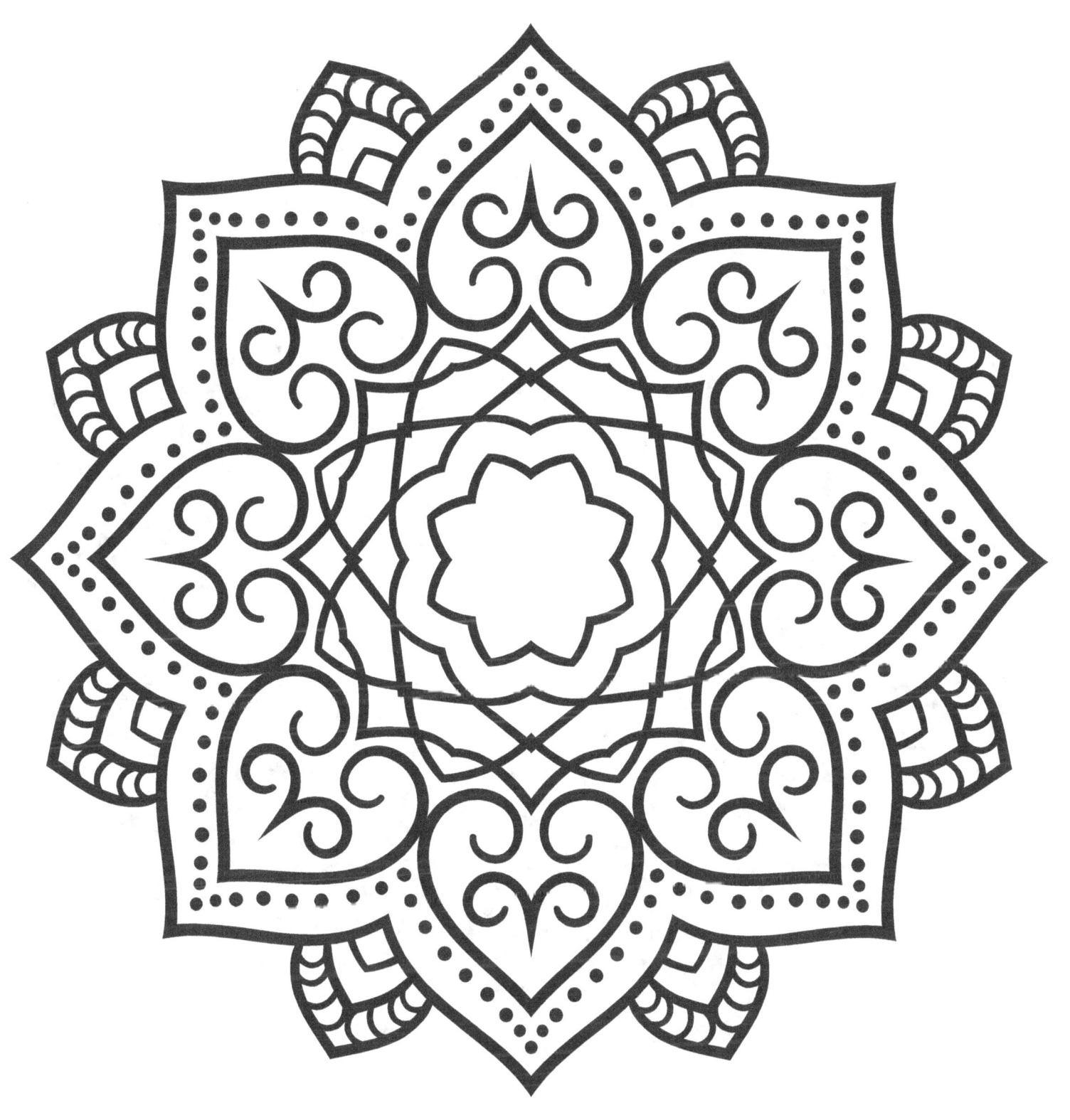

*There are only two rules for being successful.
One, figure out exactly what you want to do,
and two, do it.*
– Mario Cuomo

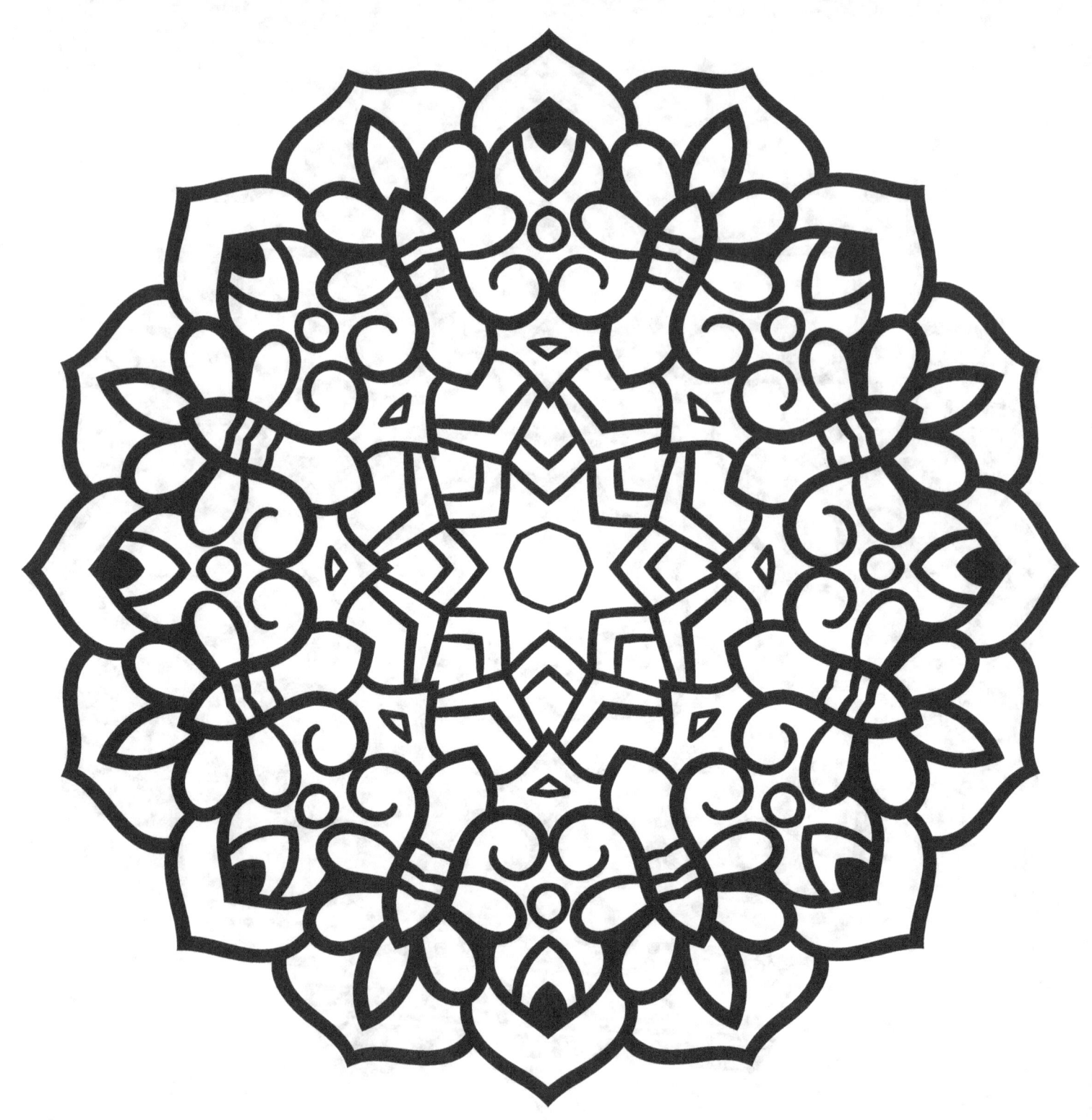

Motivation is a fire from within.
If someone else tries to light that fire under you,
chances are it will burn very briefly.
– Stephen R. Covey

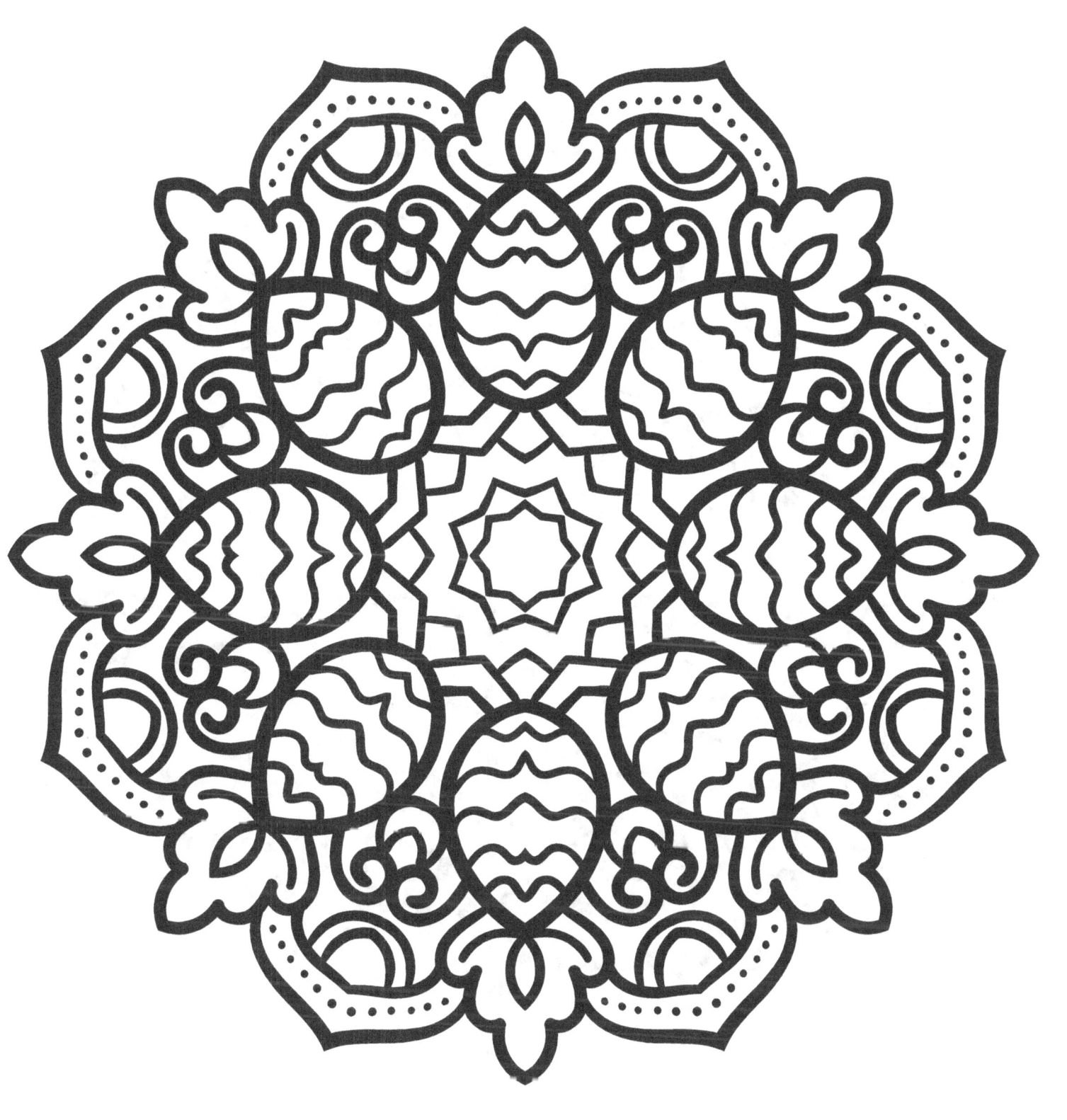

I can't understand why people are frightened by new ideas. I'm frightened by old ones.
— John Cage

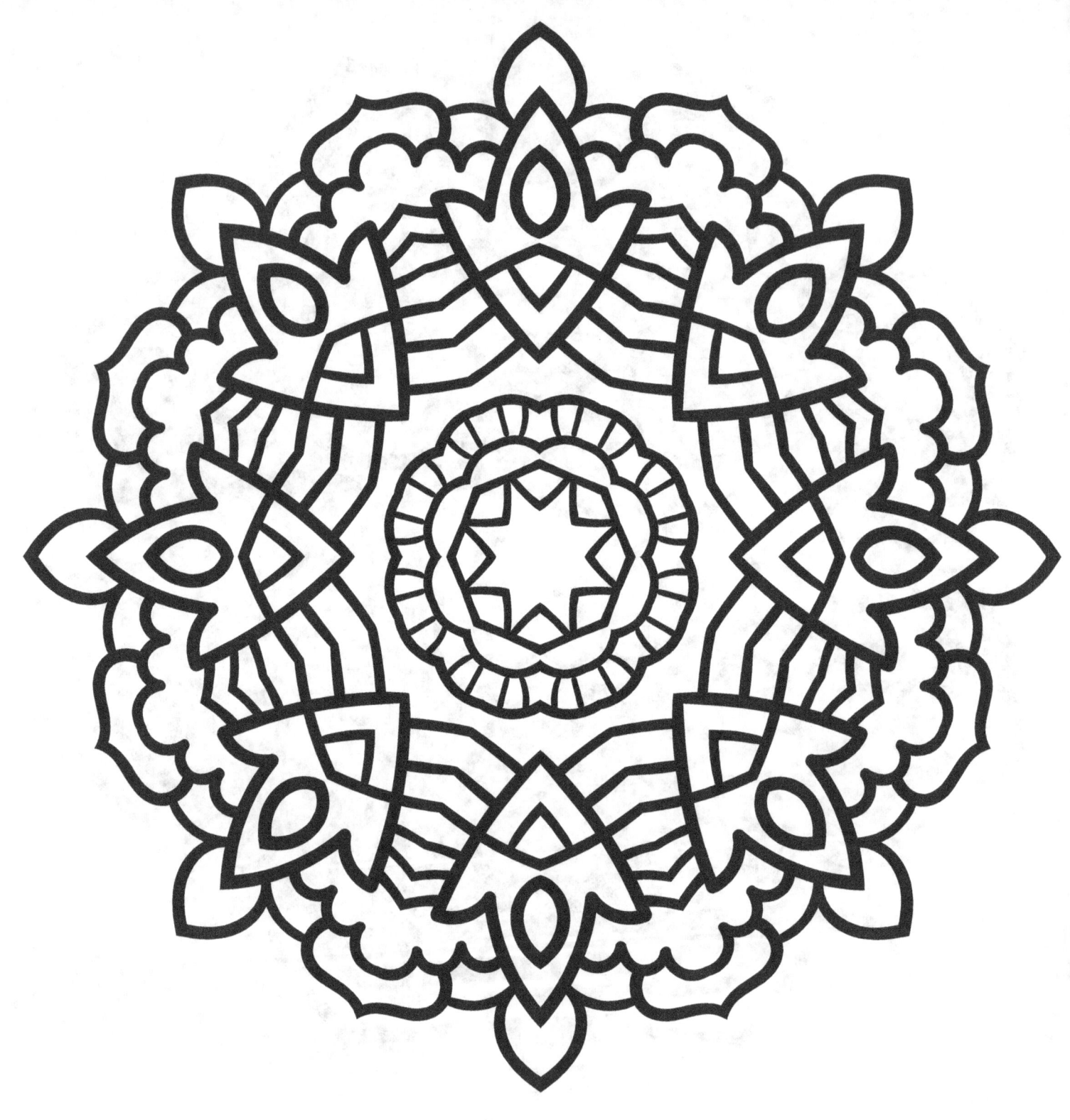

Fall down seven times, get up eight.
-Â Japanese Proverb

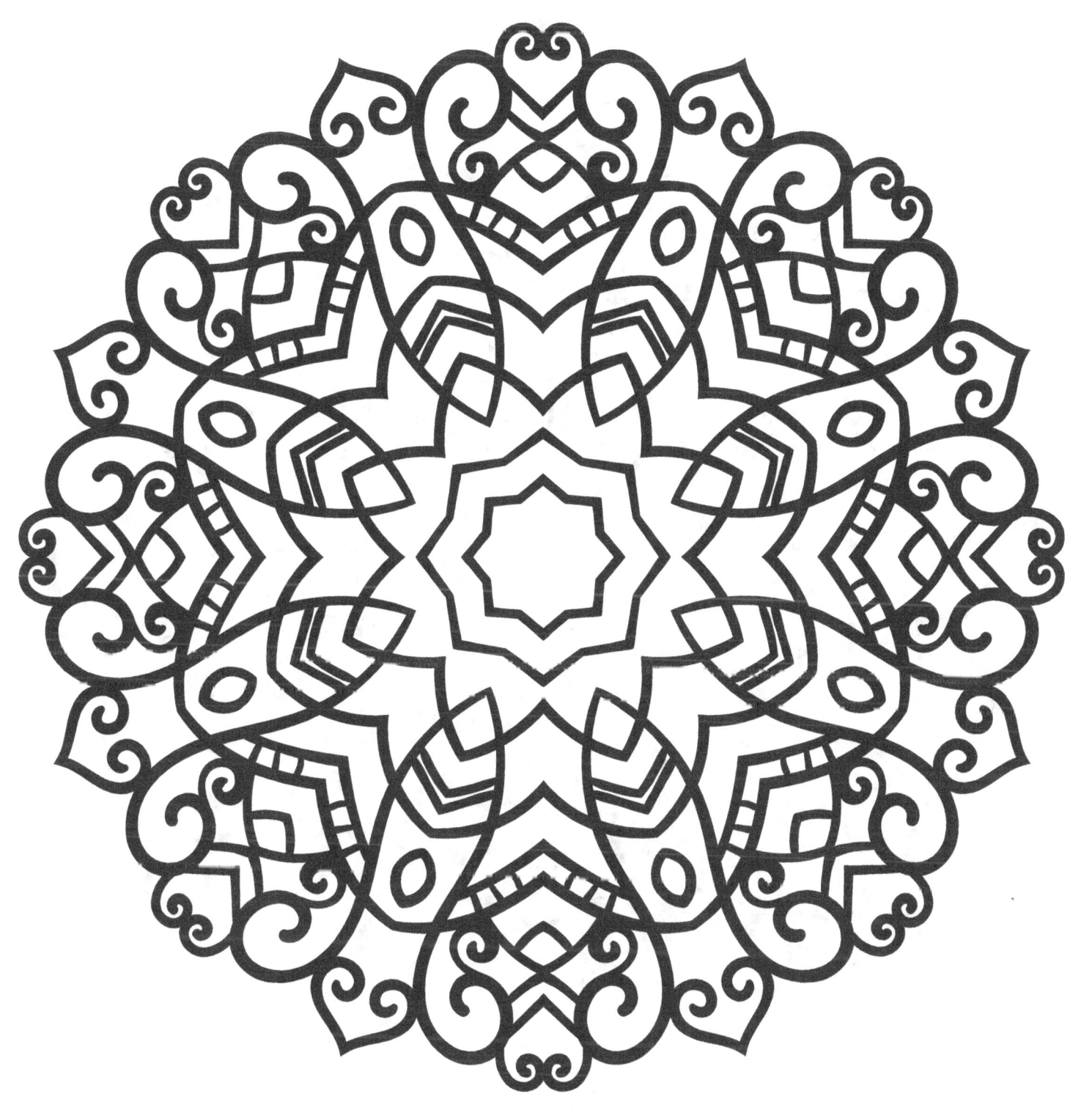

Attitudes are contagious.
Make yours worth catching.
– Unknown

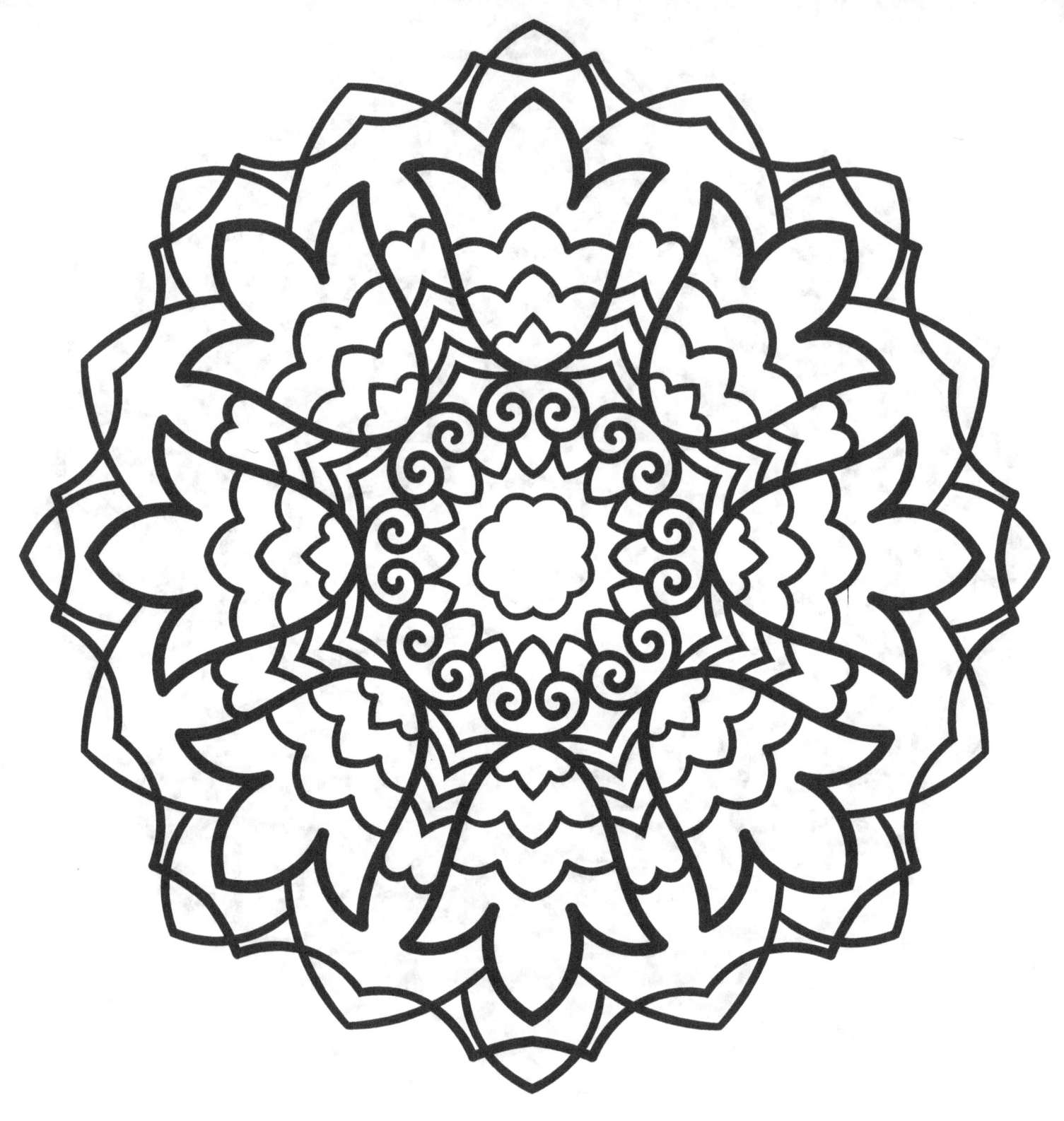

Take the first step in faith. You don't have to see the whole staircase, just take the first step."
– Dr. Martin Luther King Jr.

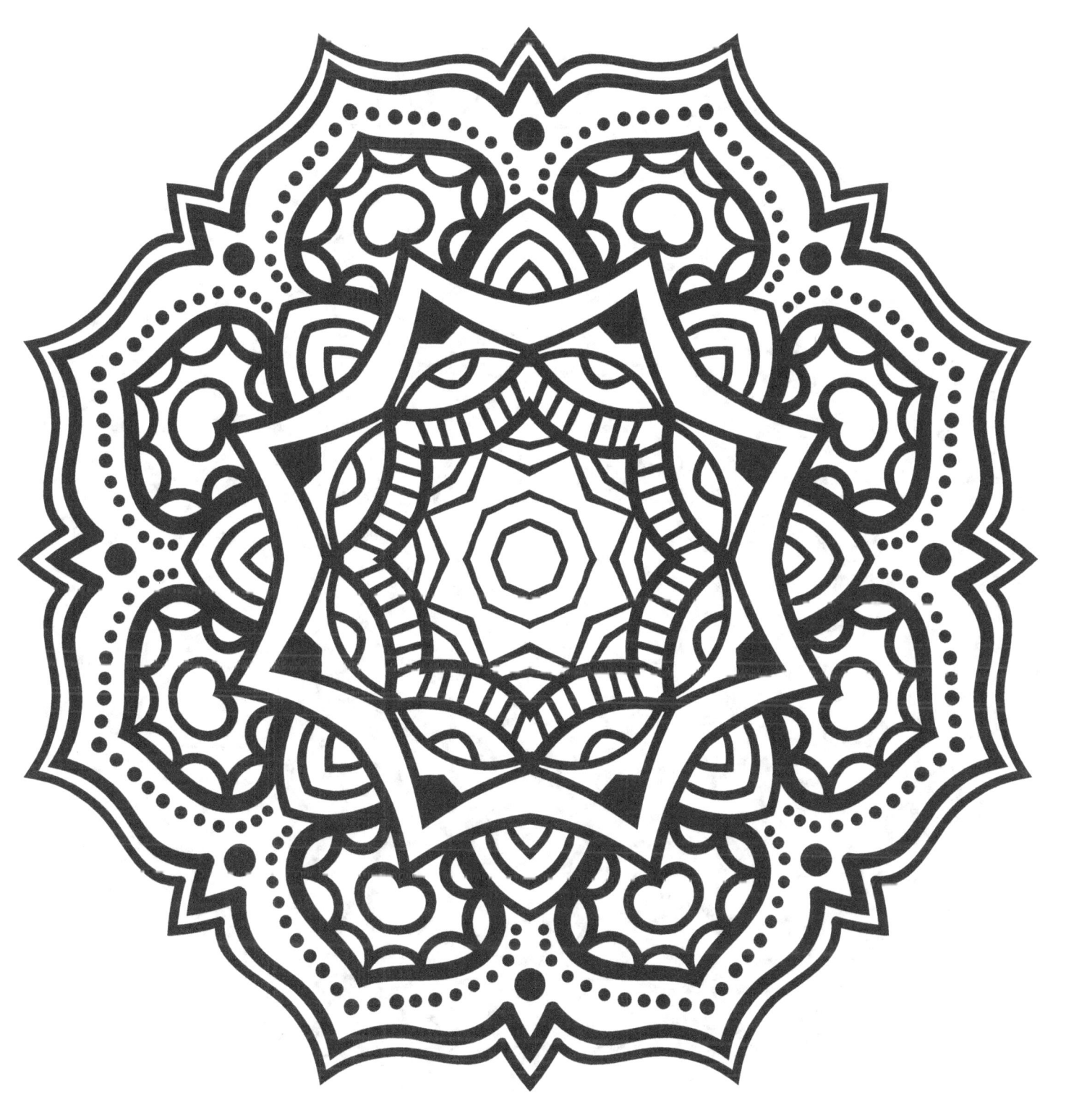

*Many great ideas go unexecuted,
and many great executioners are without ideas.
One without the other is worthless.
– Tim Blixseth*

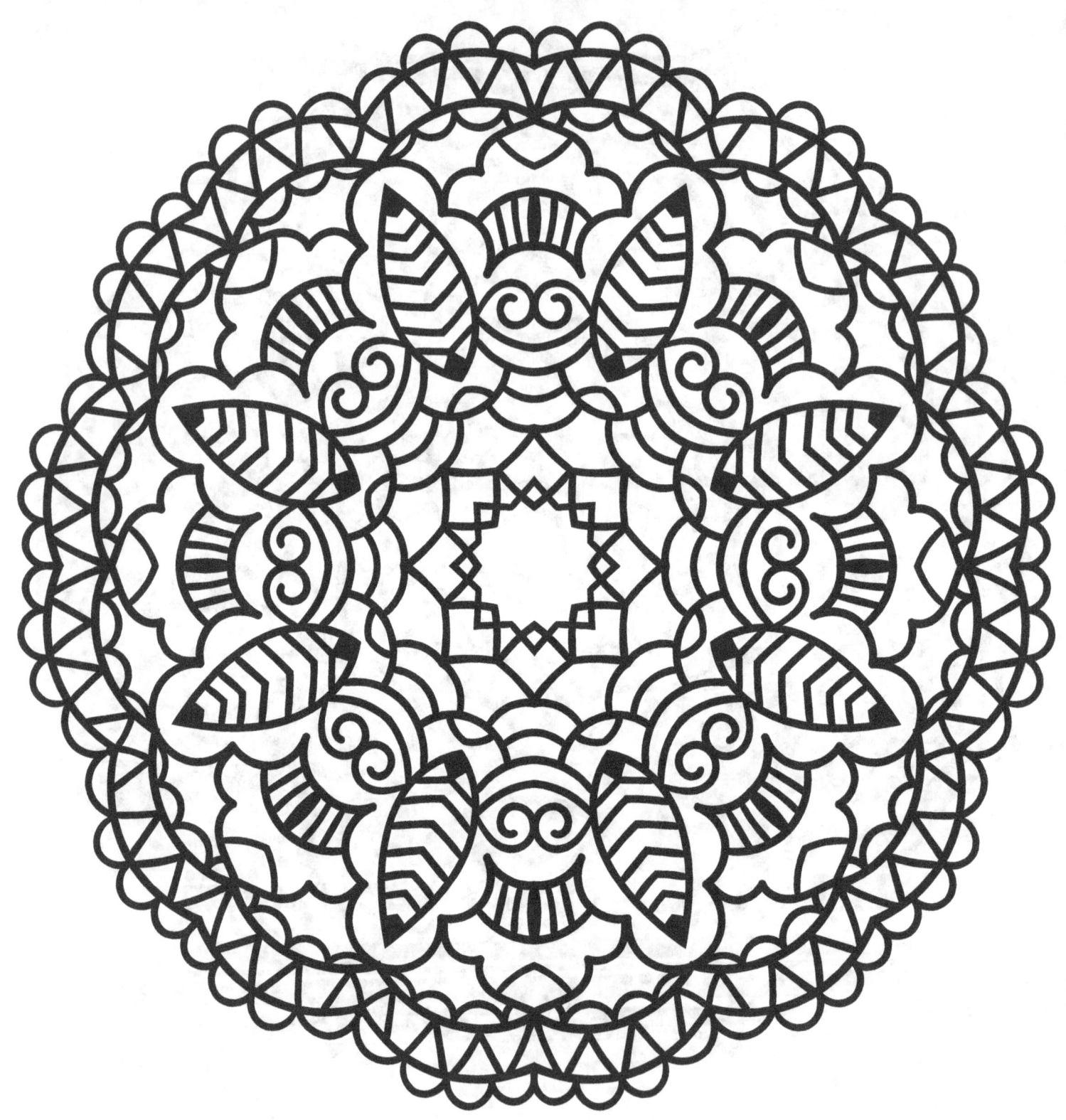

The world is more malleable than you think and it's waiting for you to hammer it into shape.
— Bono

The surest way not to fail is to determine to succeed.
— Richard B. Sheridan

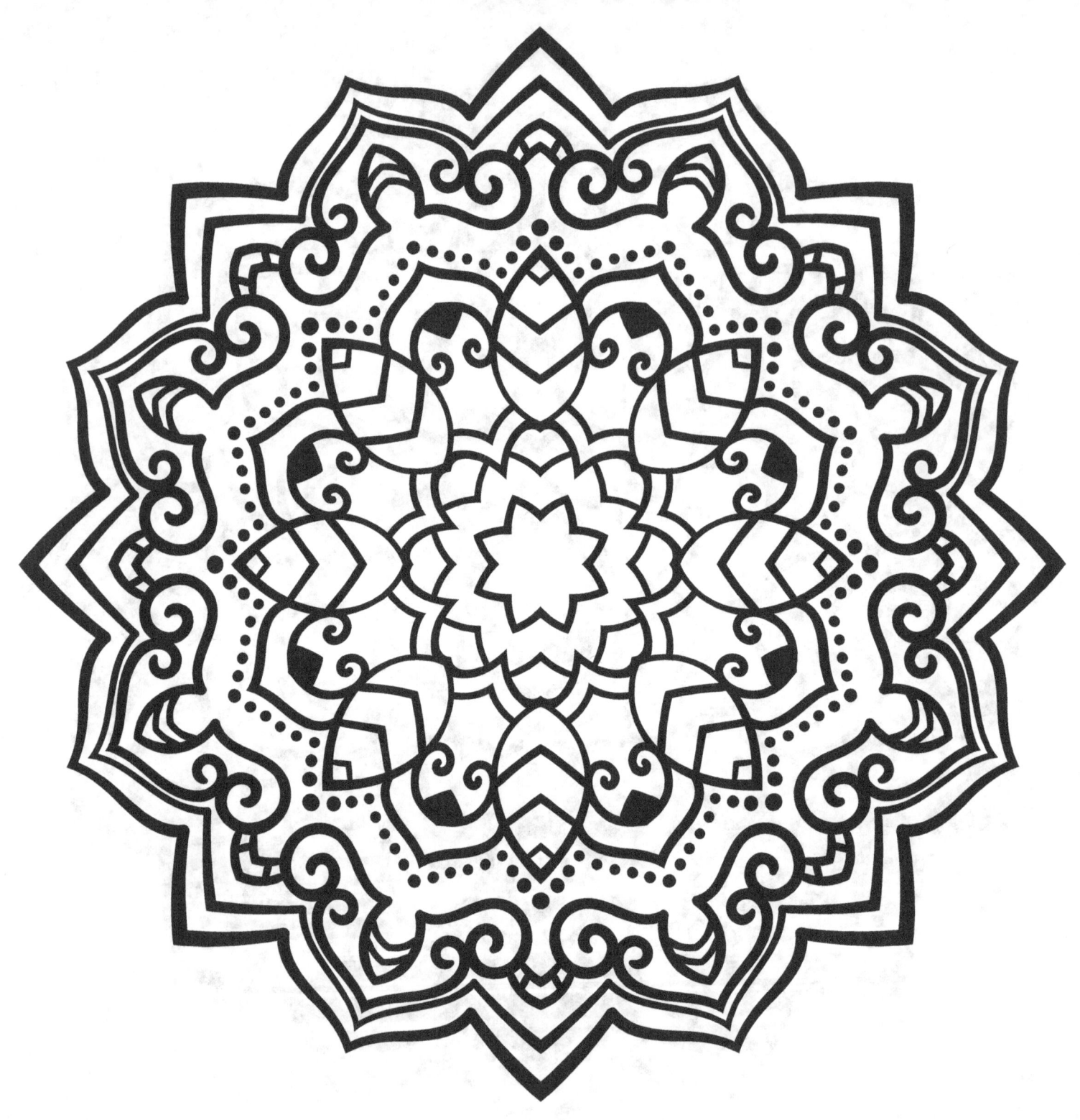

Keep away from people who try to belittle your ambitions. Small people always do that, but the really great make you feel that you, too, can become great.
– Mark Twain

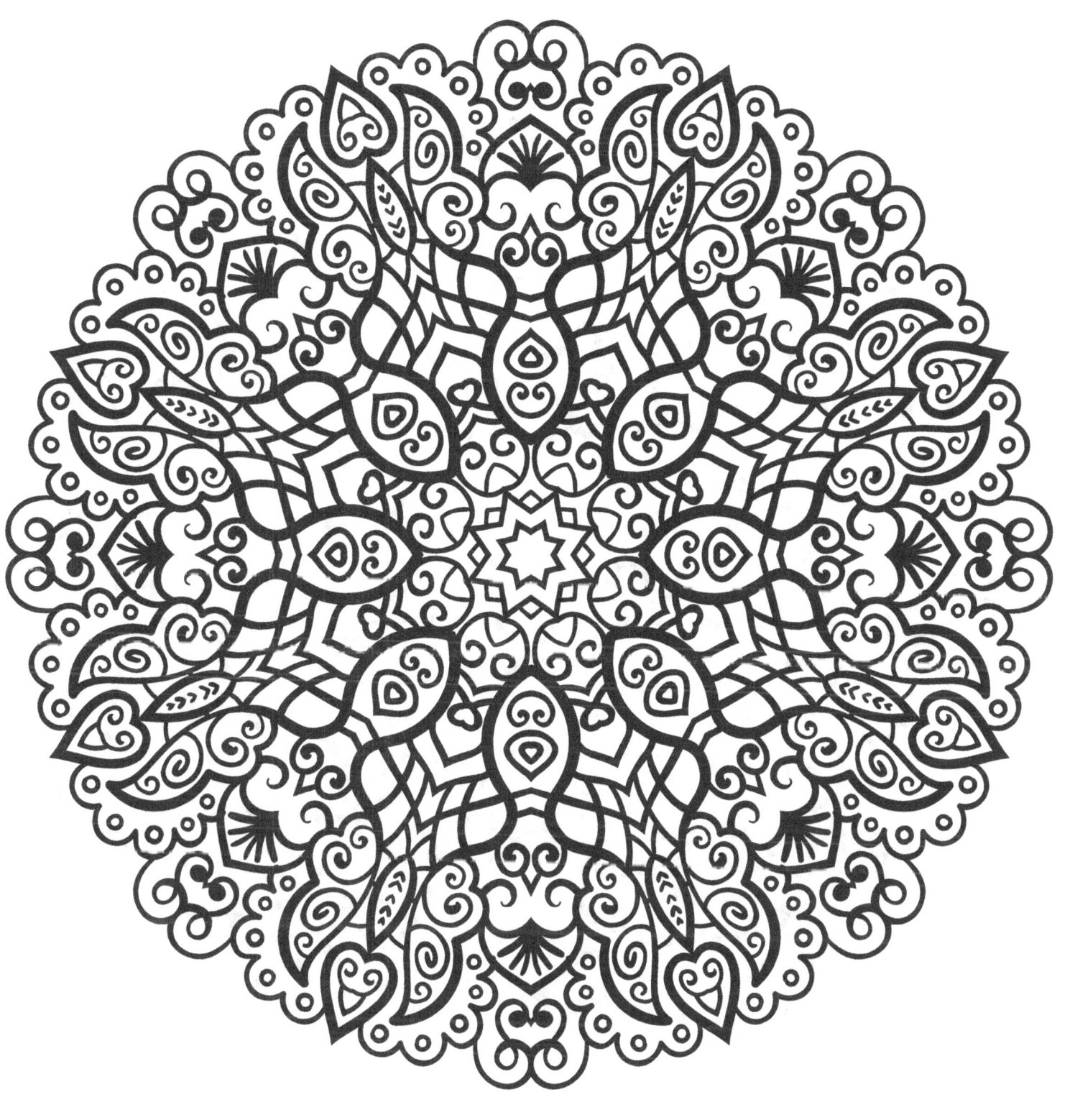

What lies behind us and what lies before us are tiny matters compared to what lies within us.
— Ralph Waldo Emerson

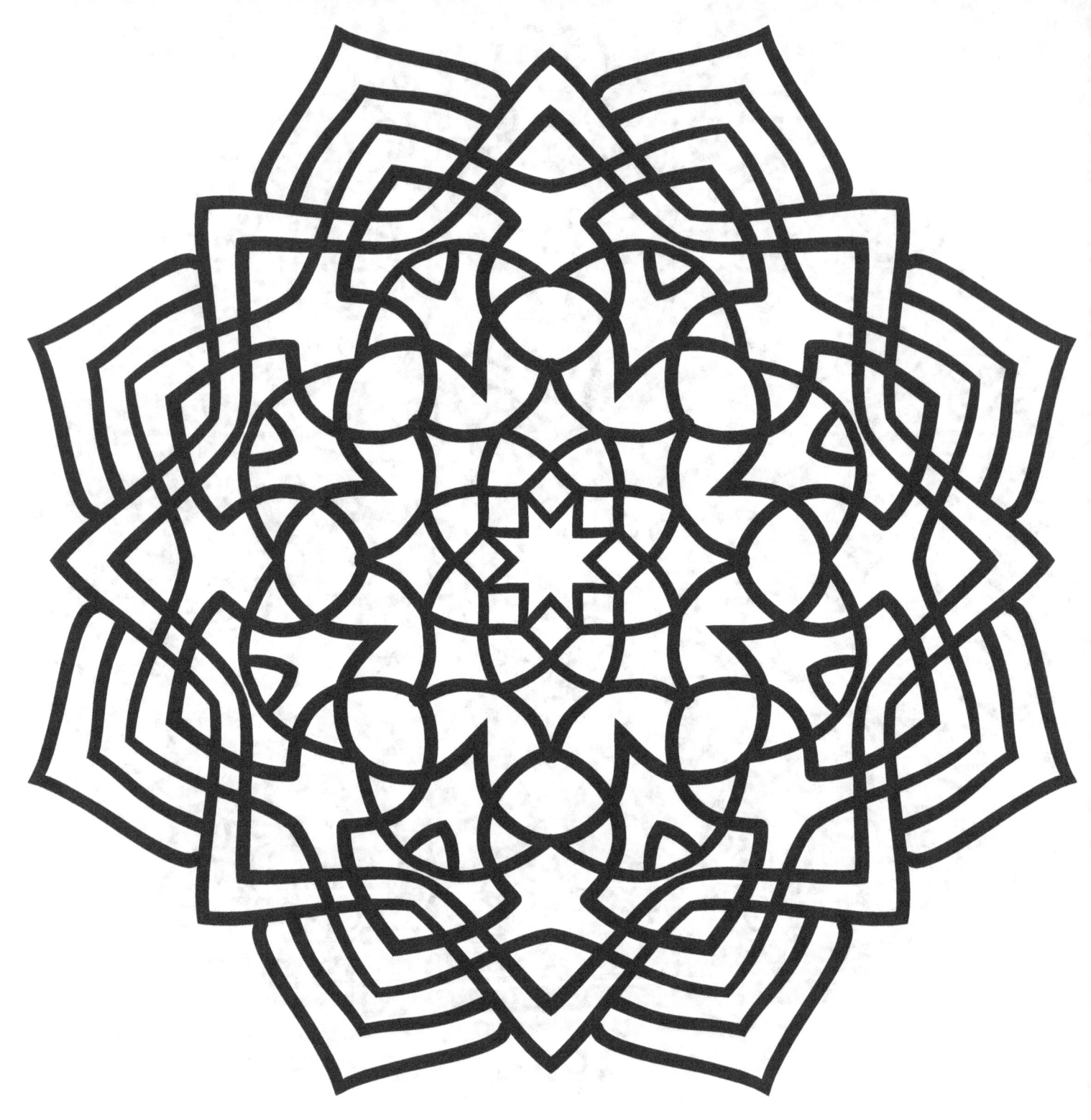

Age is an issue of mind over matter.
If you don't mind, it doesn't matter.
— Mark Twain

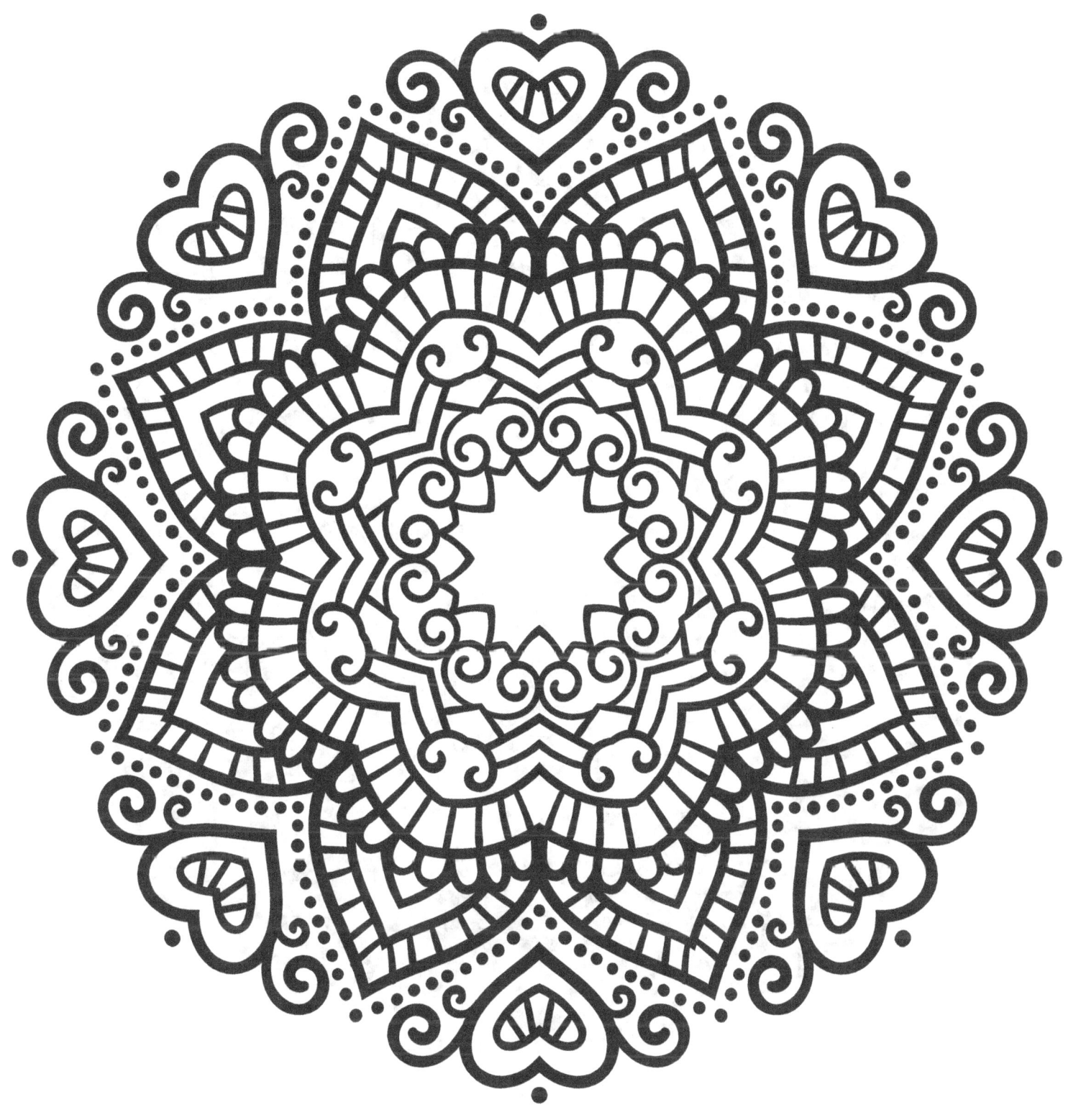

Whenever you find yourself on the side of the majority, it's time to pause and reflect.
— Mark Twain

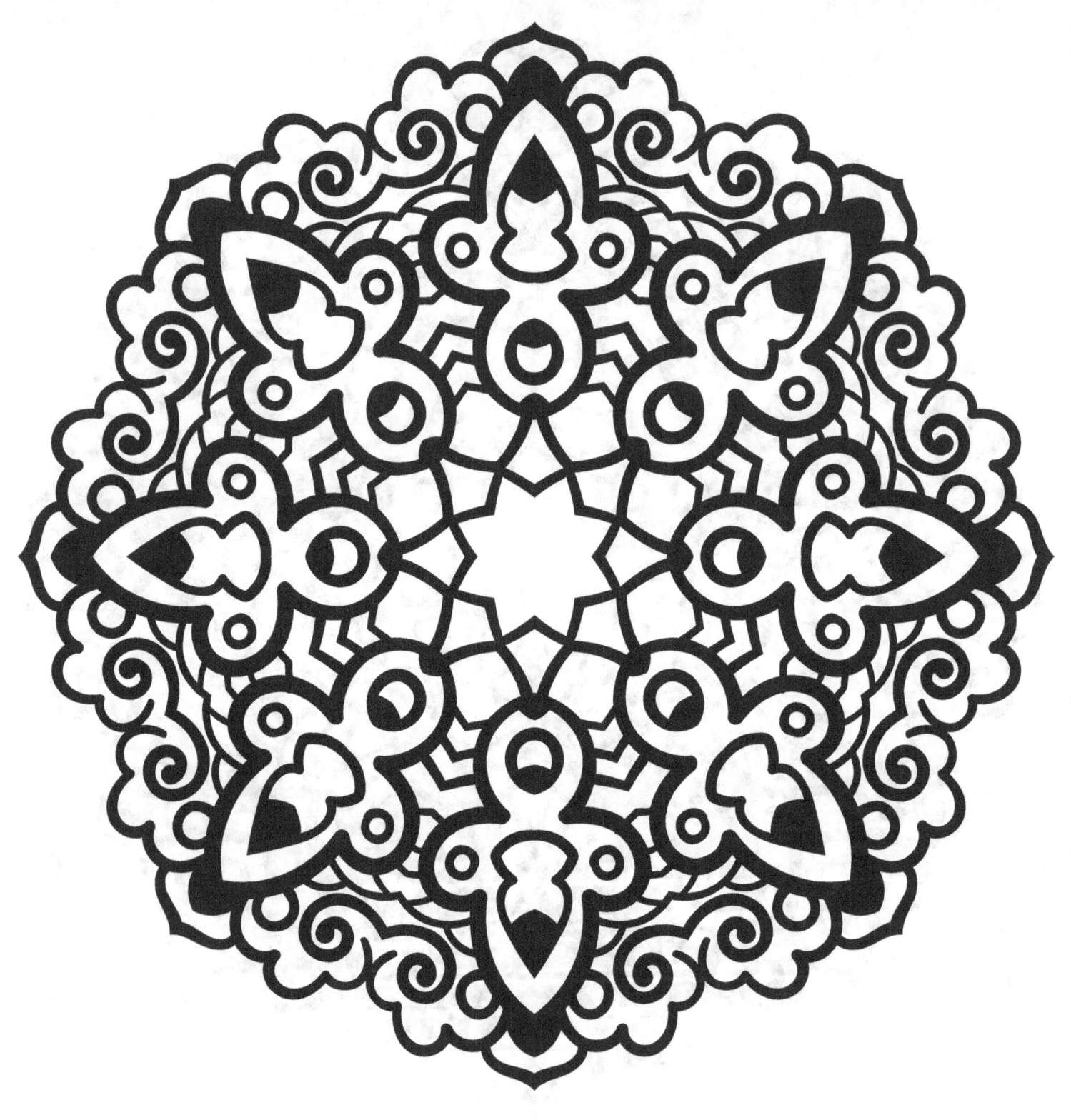

We judge of man's wisdom by his hope.
— Ralph Waldo Emerson

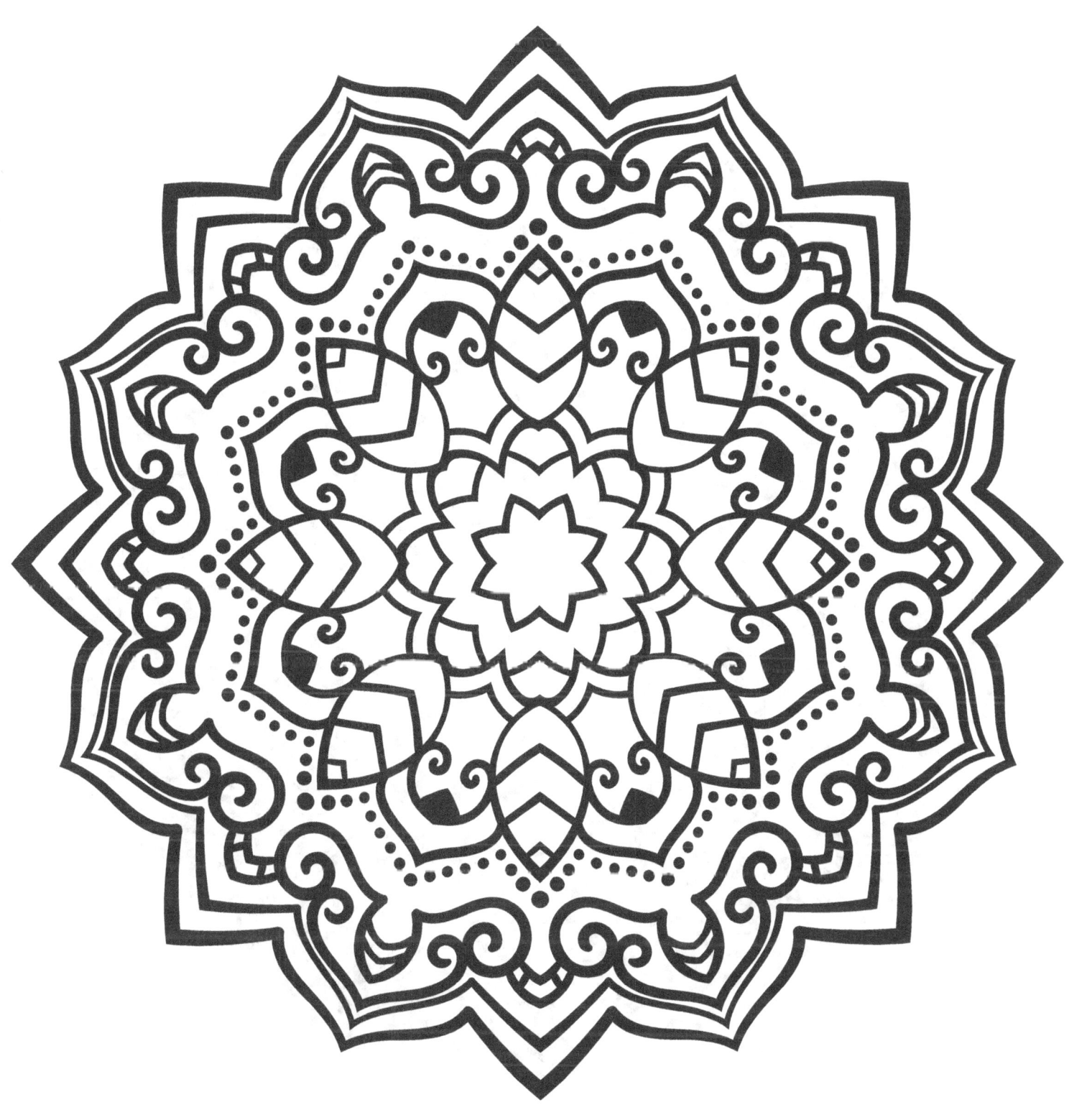

Keep away from people who try to belittle your ambitions. Small people always do that, but the really great make you feel that you, too, can become great.
— Mark Twain

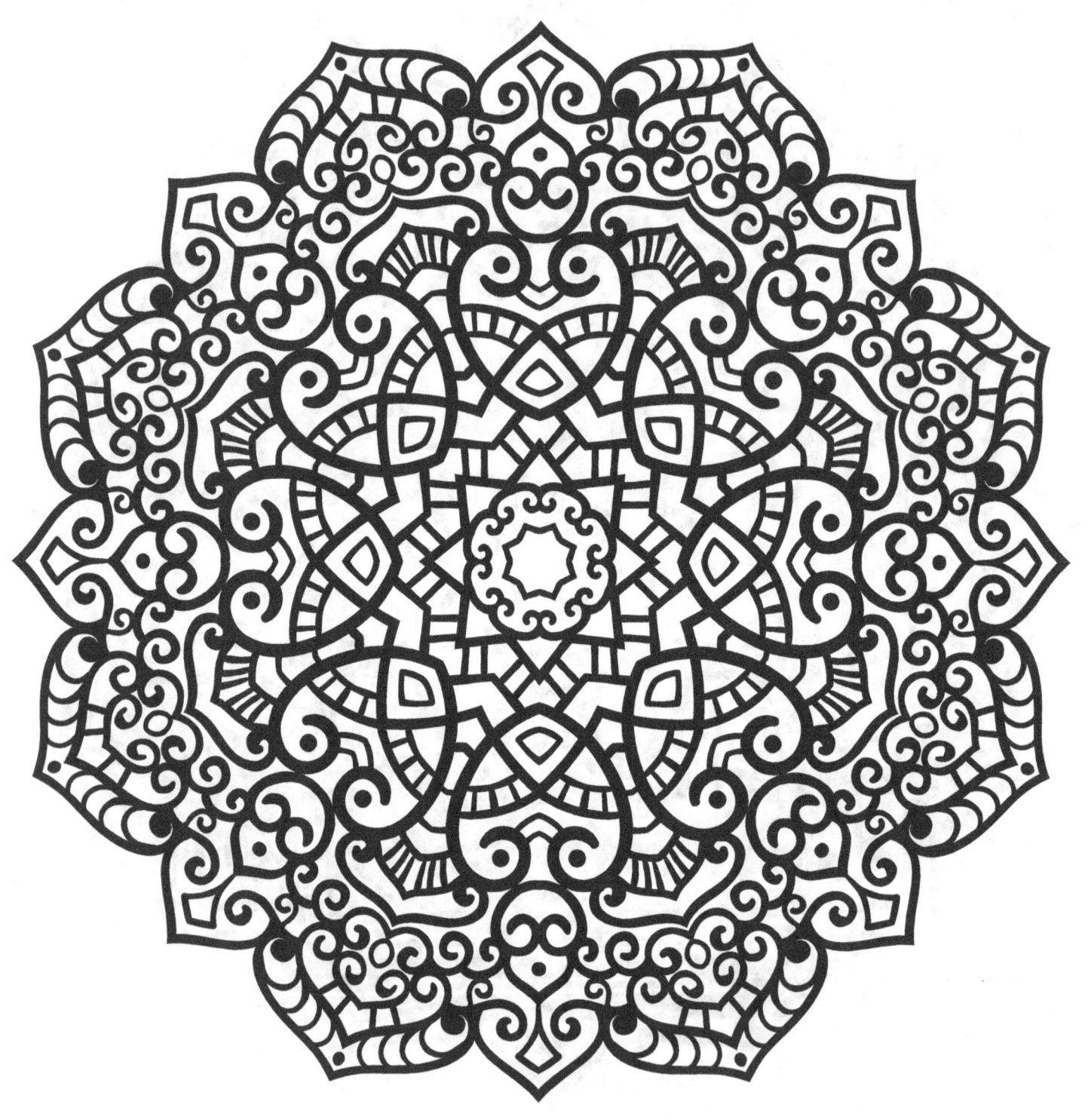

*Remember that happiness is a way
of travel, not a destination.
– Roy Goodman*

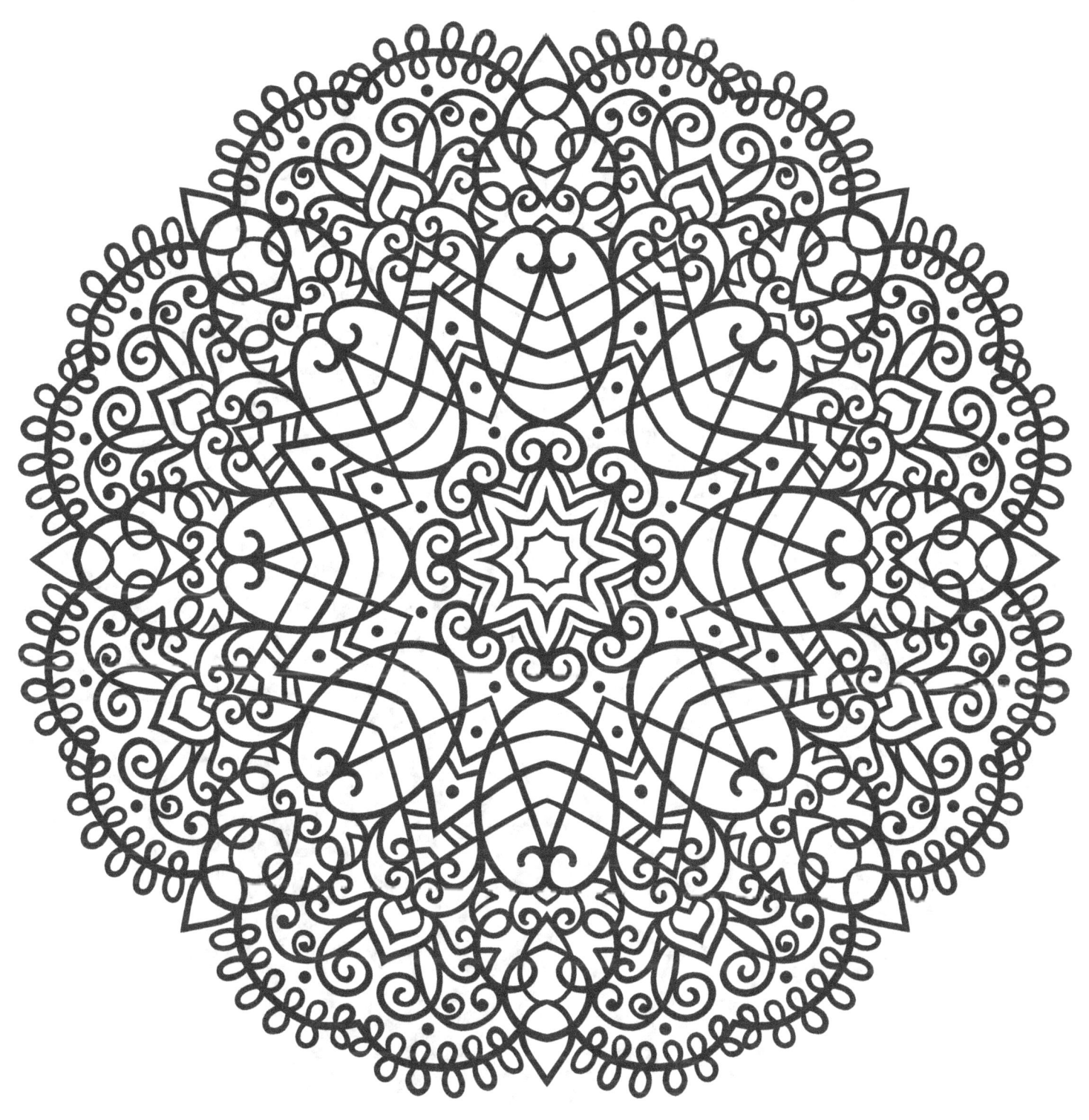

Setting an example is not the main means of influencing others; it is the only means.
– Albert Einstein

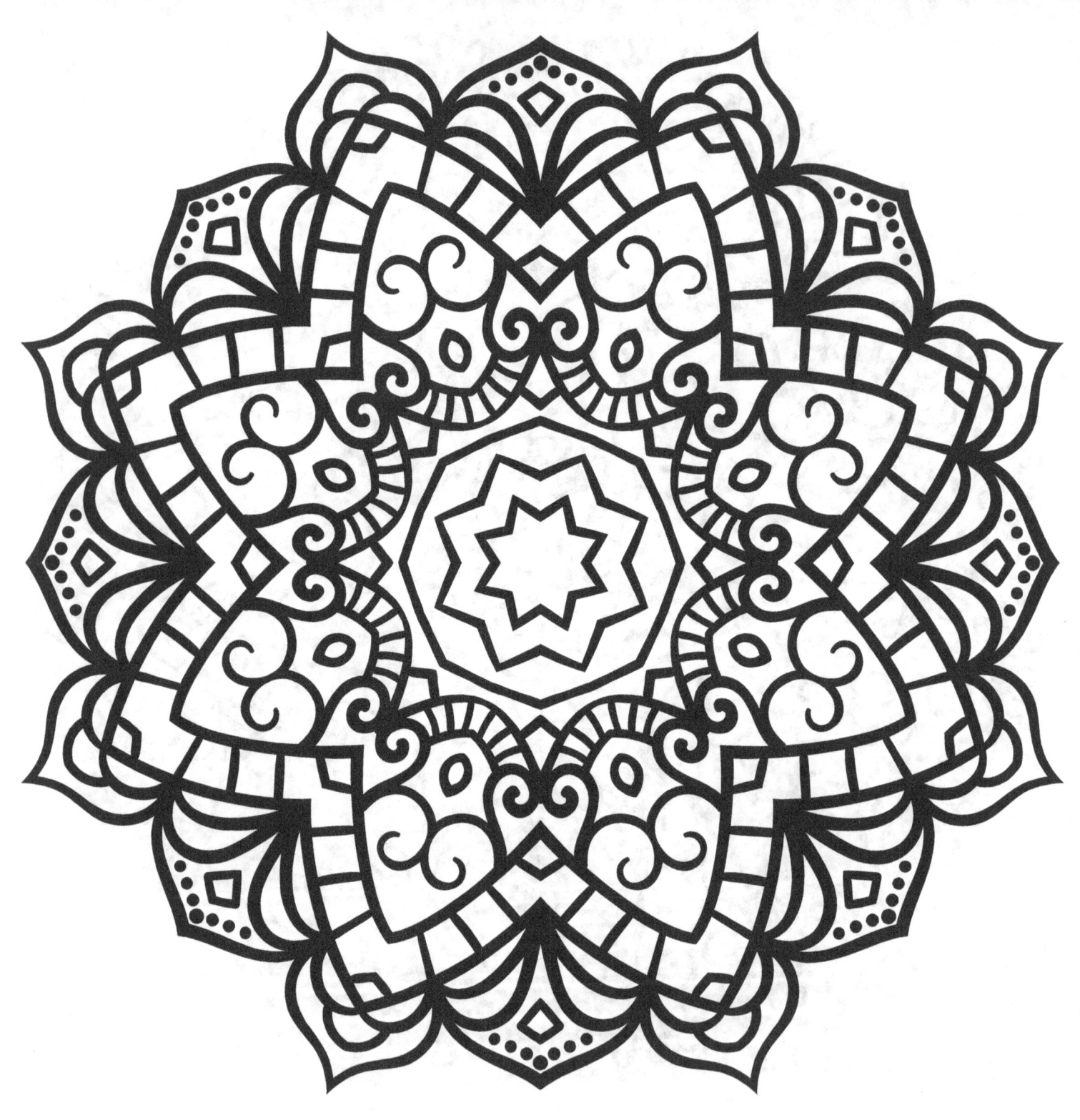

A happy person is not a person in a certain set of circumstances, but rather a person with a certain set of attitudes.
– Hugh Downs

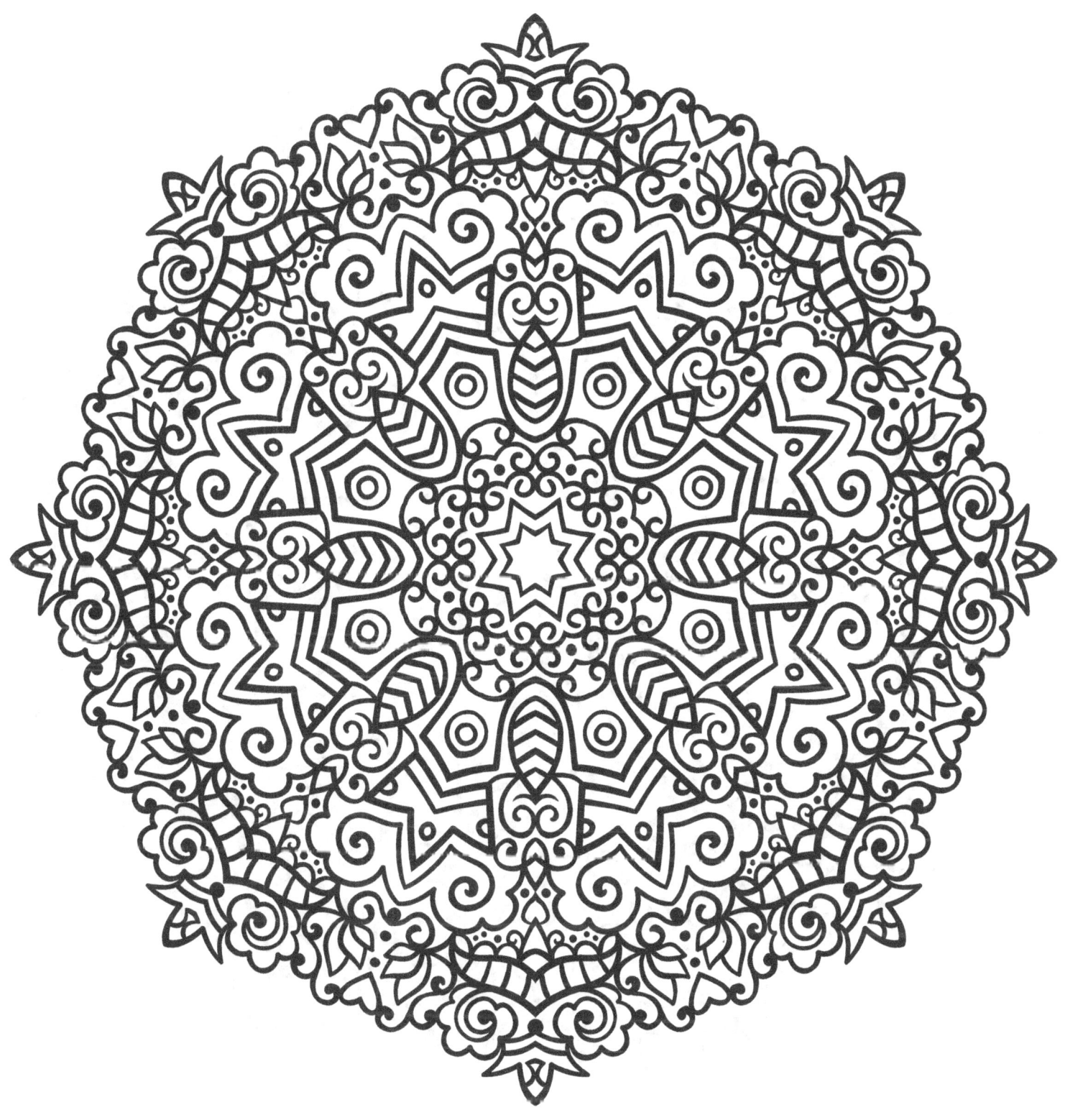

*If you're going to be able to look back
on something and laugh about it,
you might as well laugh about it
now.
– Marie Osmond*

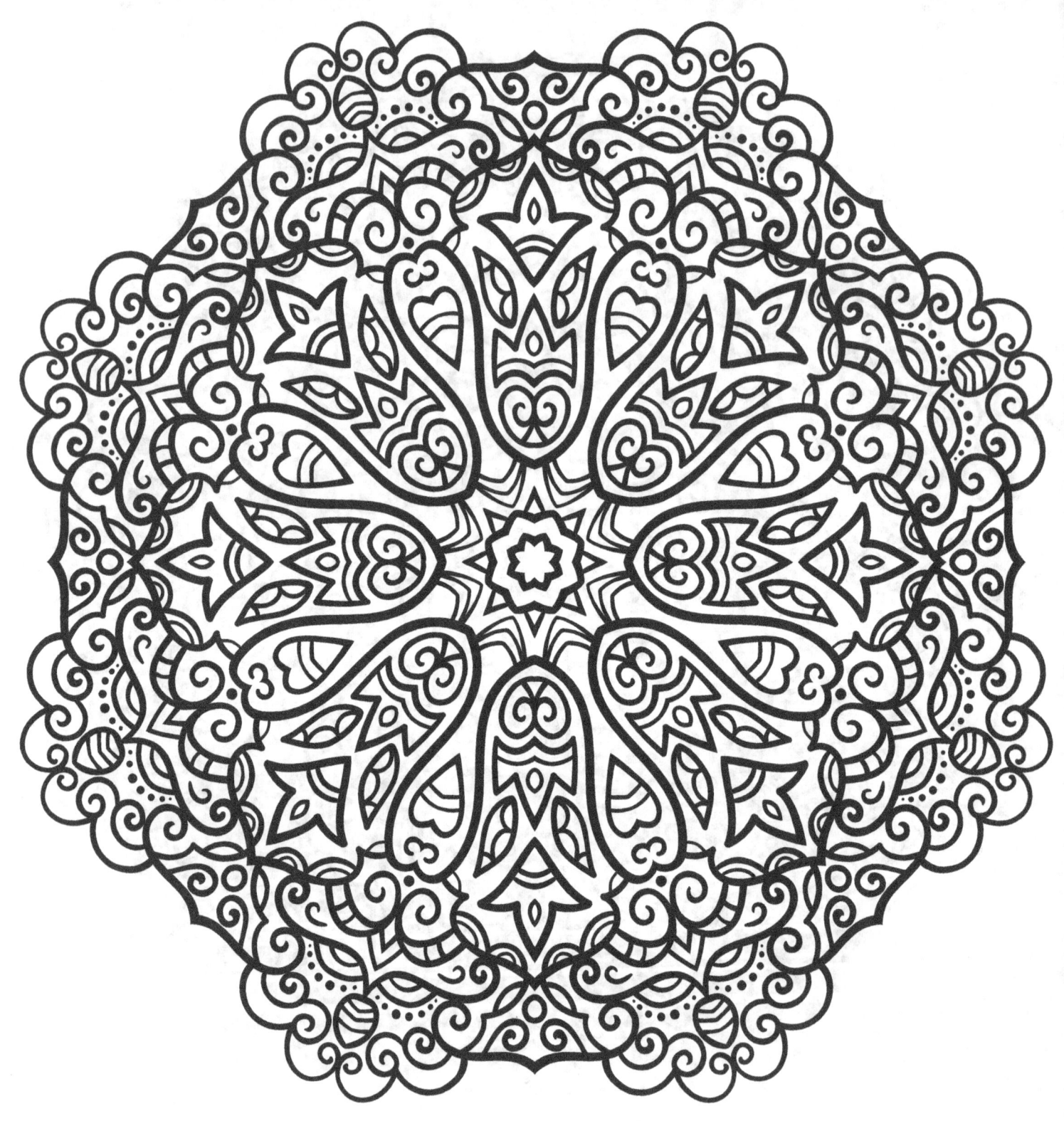

Some succeed because they are destined.
Some succeed because they are determined.
— Unknown

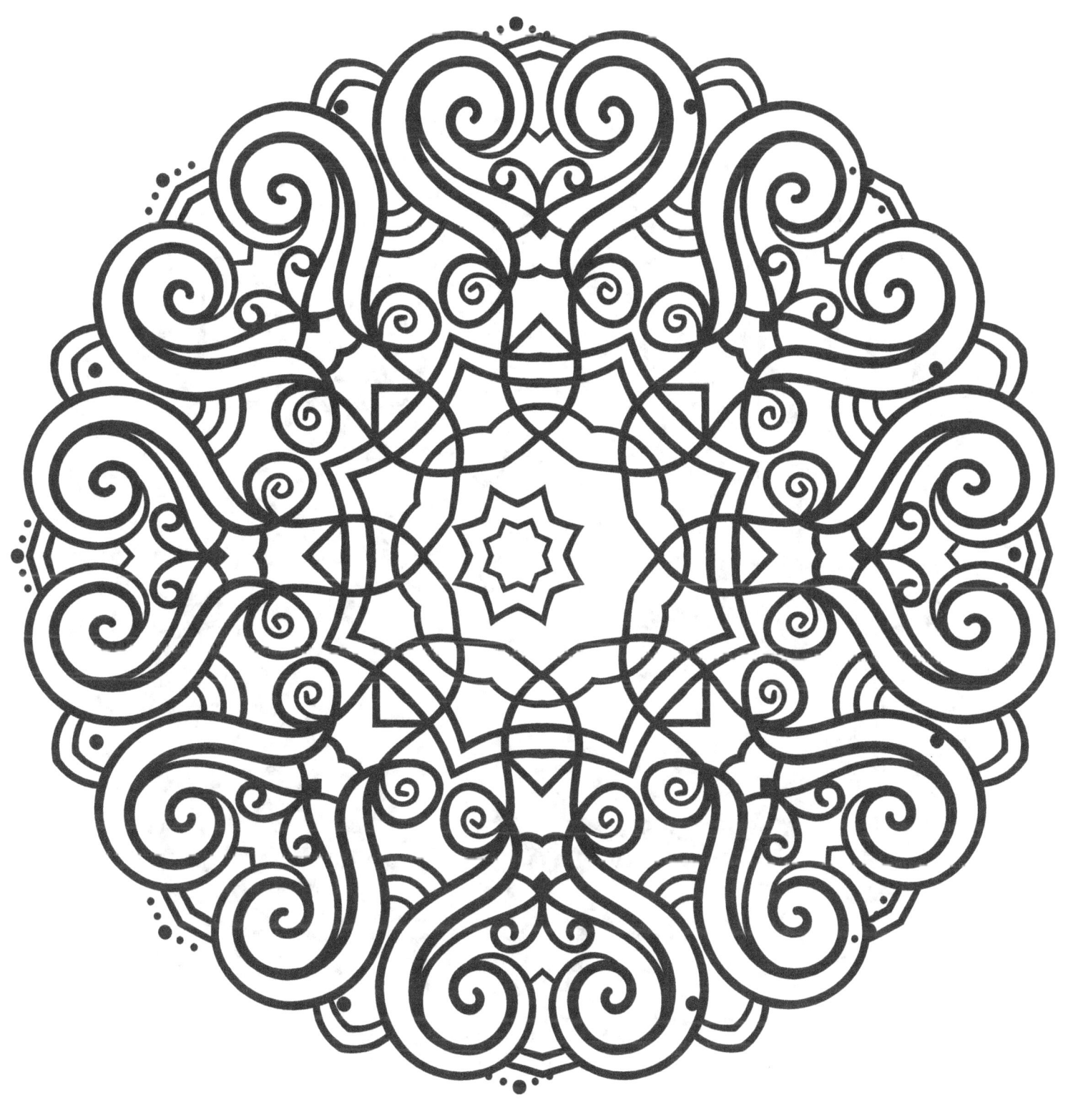

If you want to test your memory, try to recall what you were worrying about one year ago today.
— E. Joseph Cossman

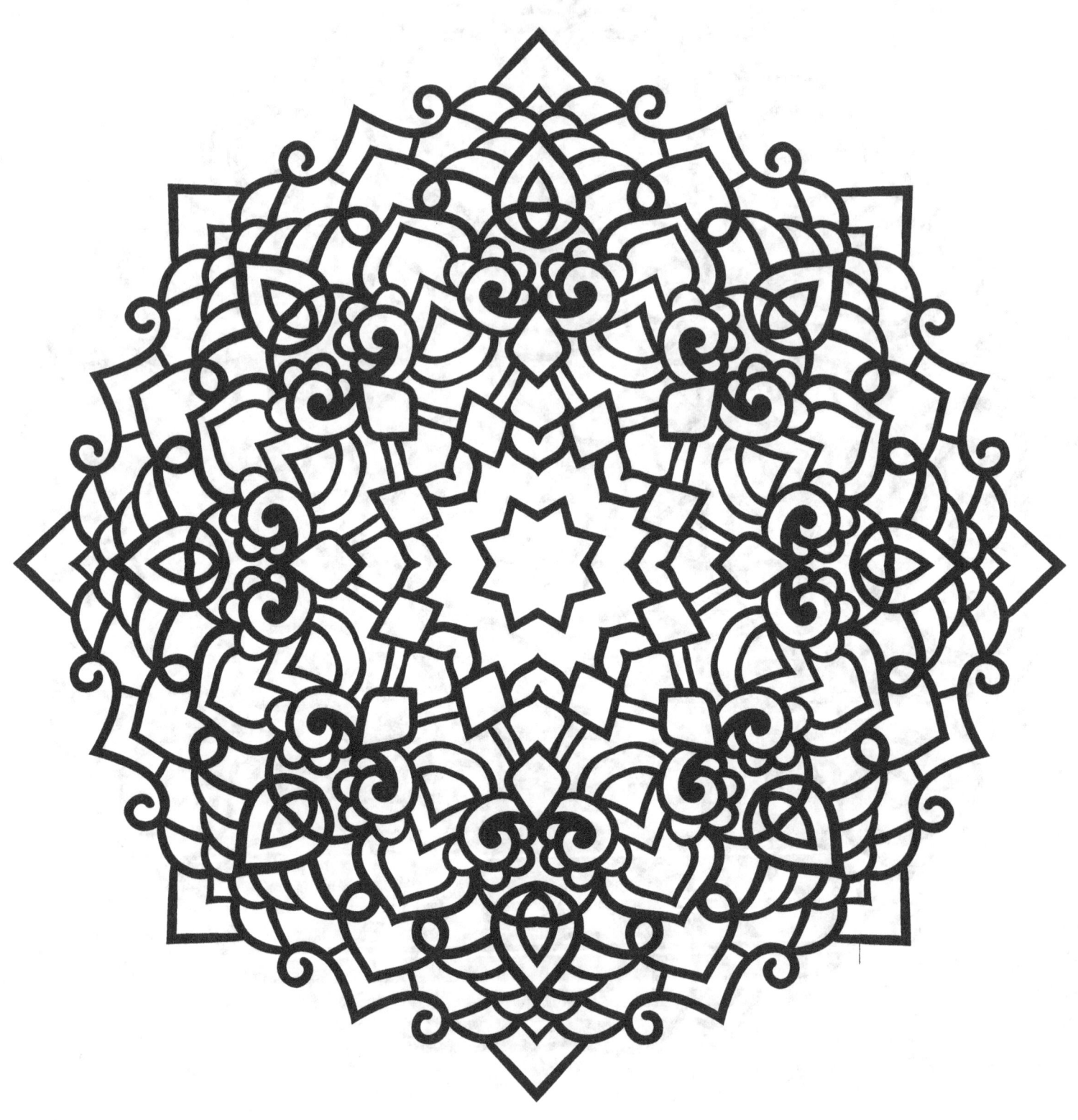

The best way to cheer yourself up is to try to cheer somebody else up.
– Mark Twain

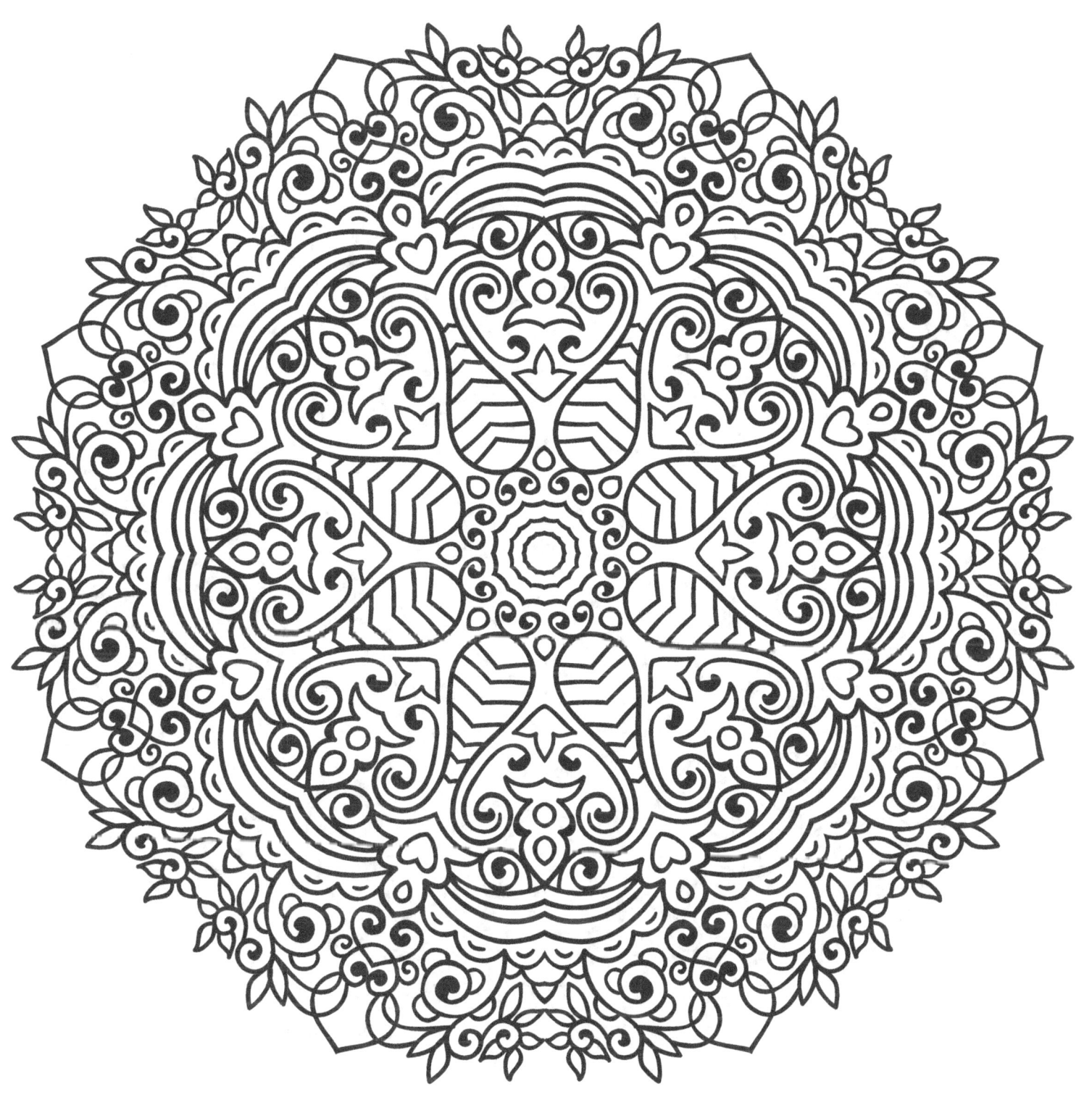

In any situation, the best thing you can do is the right thing; the next best thing you can do is the wrong thing; the worst thing you can do is nothing.
– Theodore Roosevelt

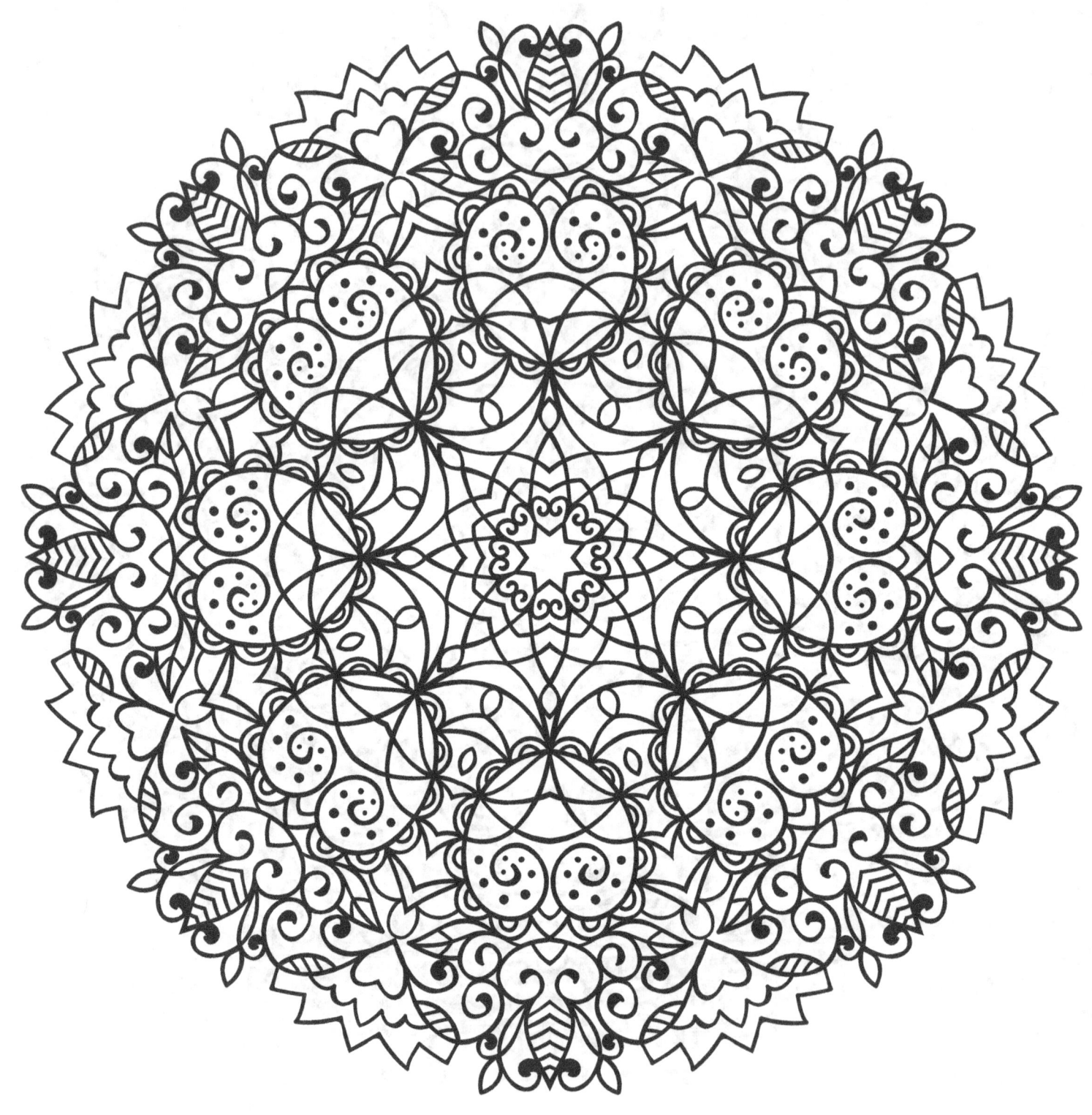

*Success consists of doing the common
things of life uncommonly well.*
— Unknown

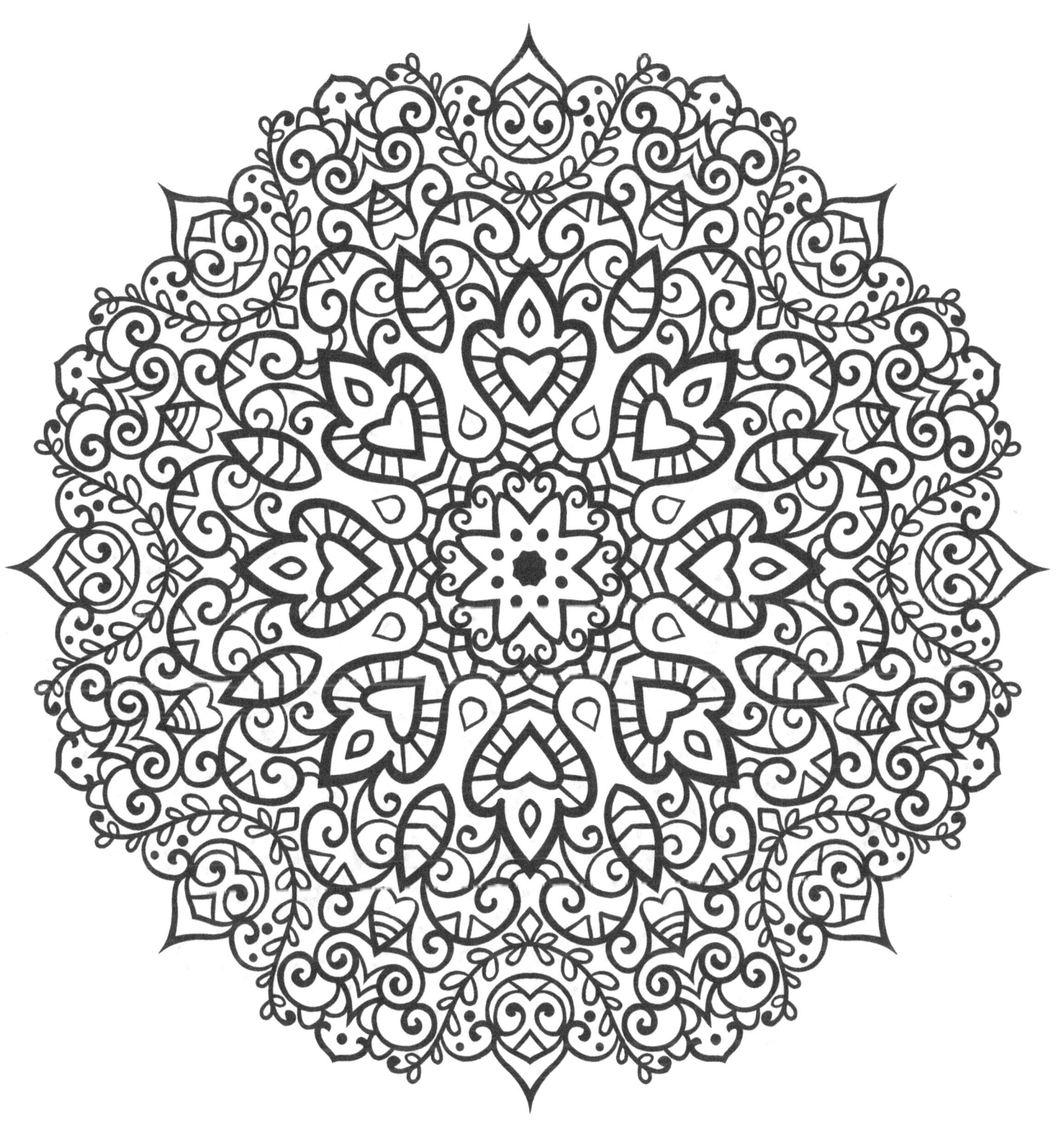

Keep on going and the chances are you will stumble on
something, perhaps when you are least expecting it.
I have never heard of anyone stumbling on
something sitting down.
– Charles F. Kettering, Engineer and Inventor

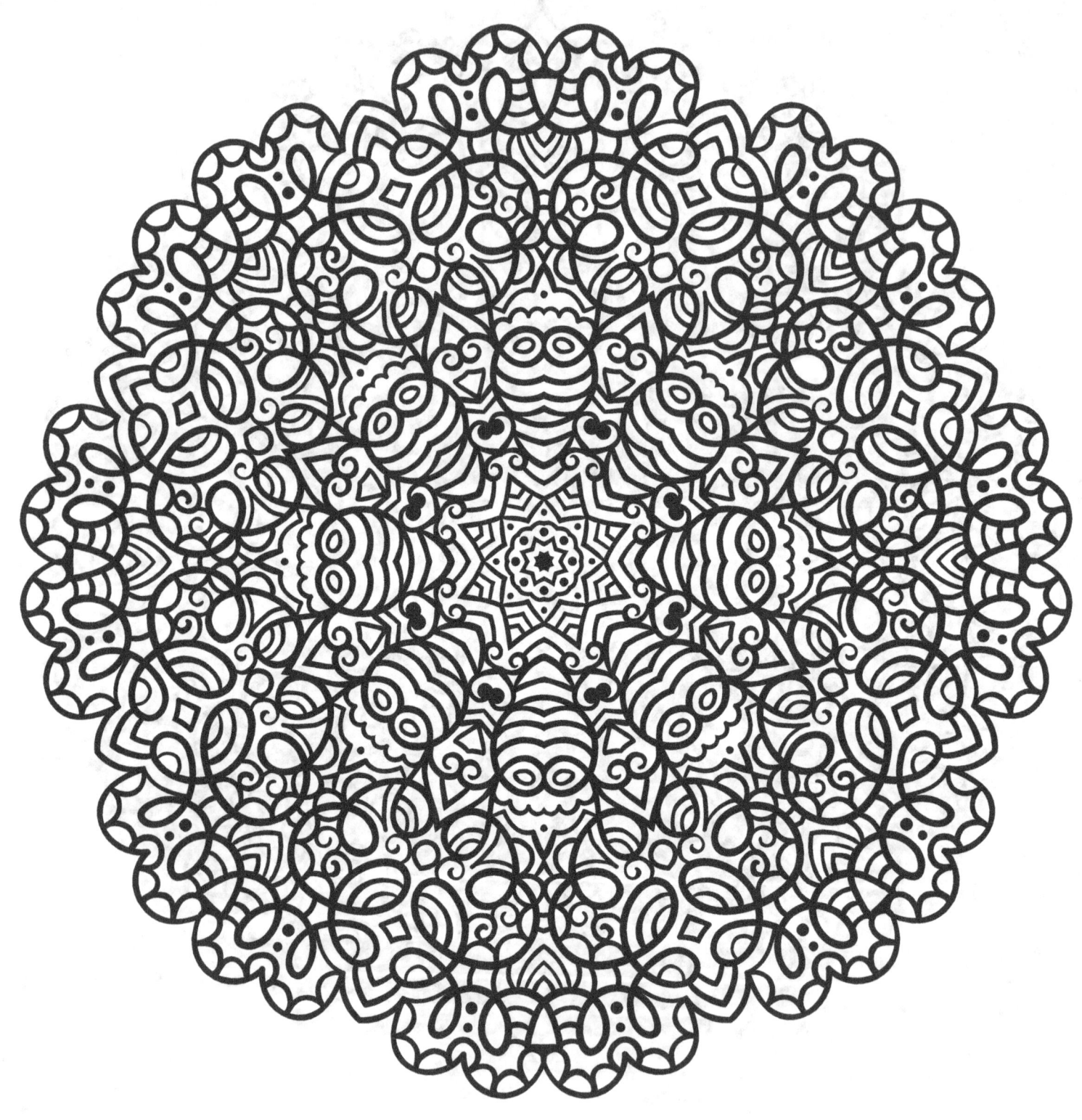

*Desire is the starting point of all achievement,
not a hope, not a wish, but a keen pulsating desire which
transcends everything.*
– Napoleon Hill

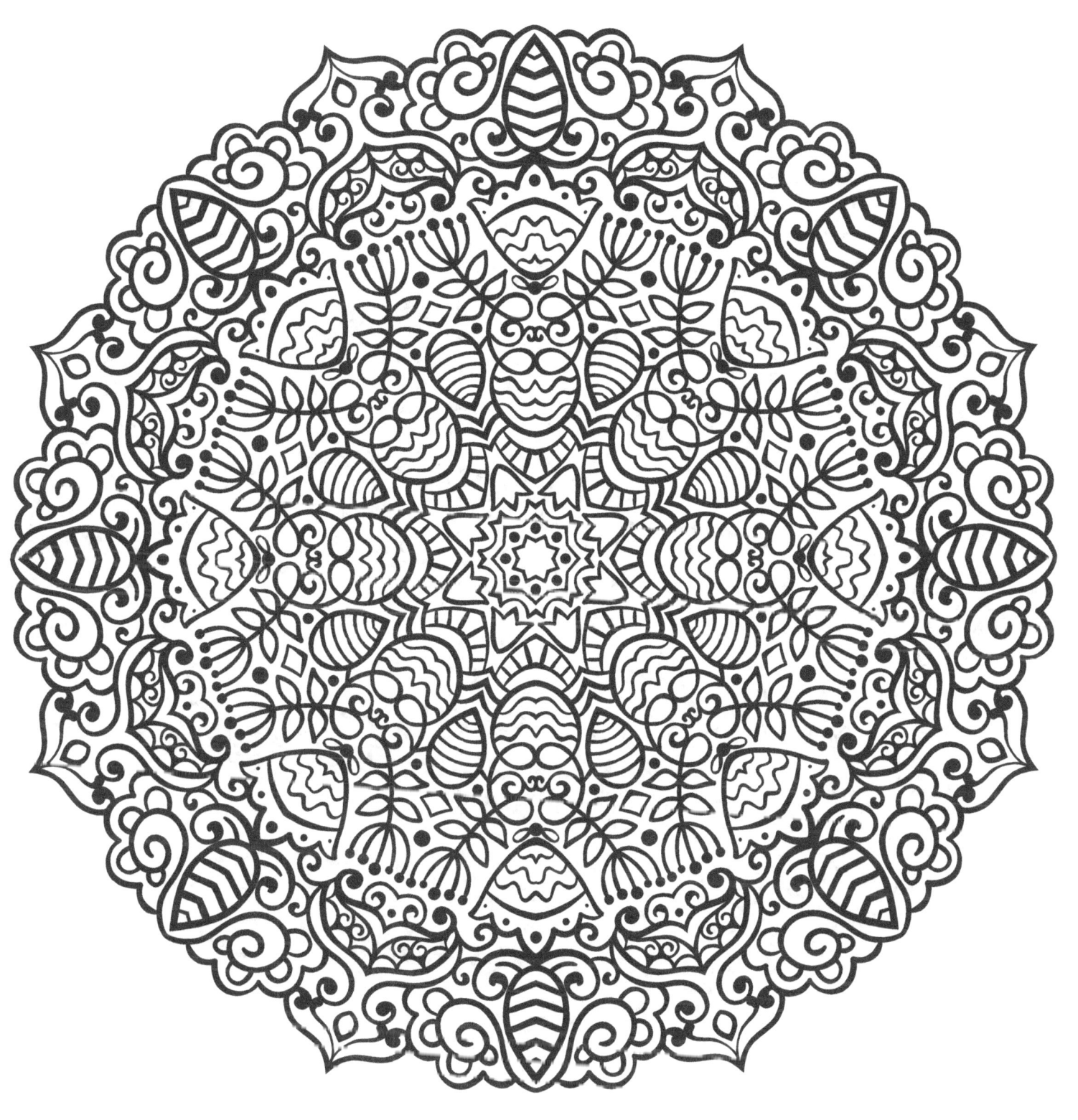

*Whatever you do will be insignificant,
but it is very important that you do it.
– Mahatma Gandhi*

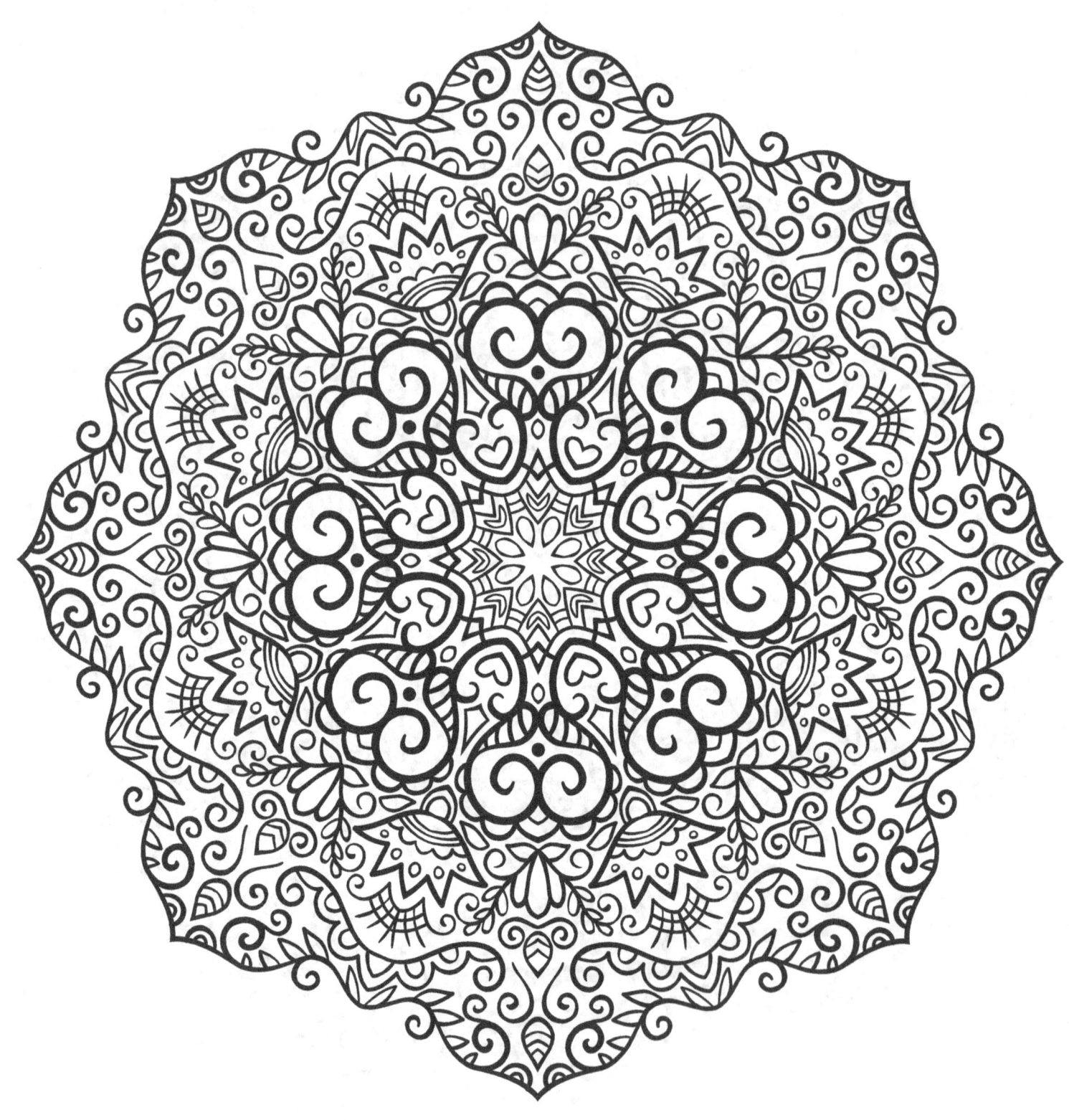

Vision without action is daydream.
Action without vision is nightmare.
— Japanese Proverb

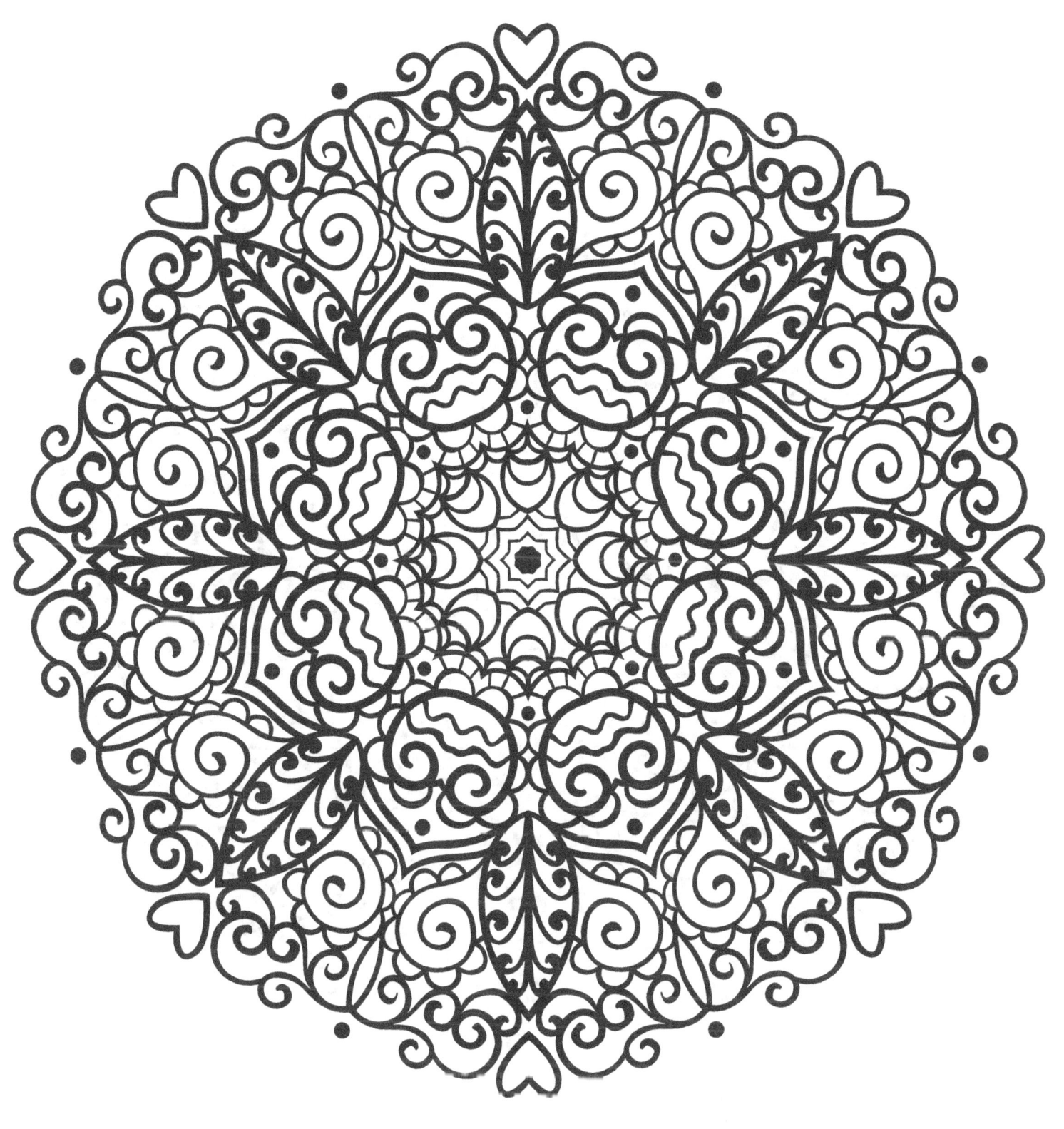

*"And, when you want something, all the universe
conspires in helping you to achieve it."
– Paulo Coelho, The Alchemist*

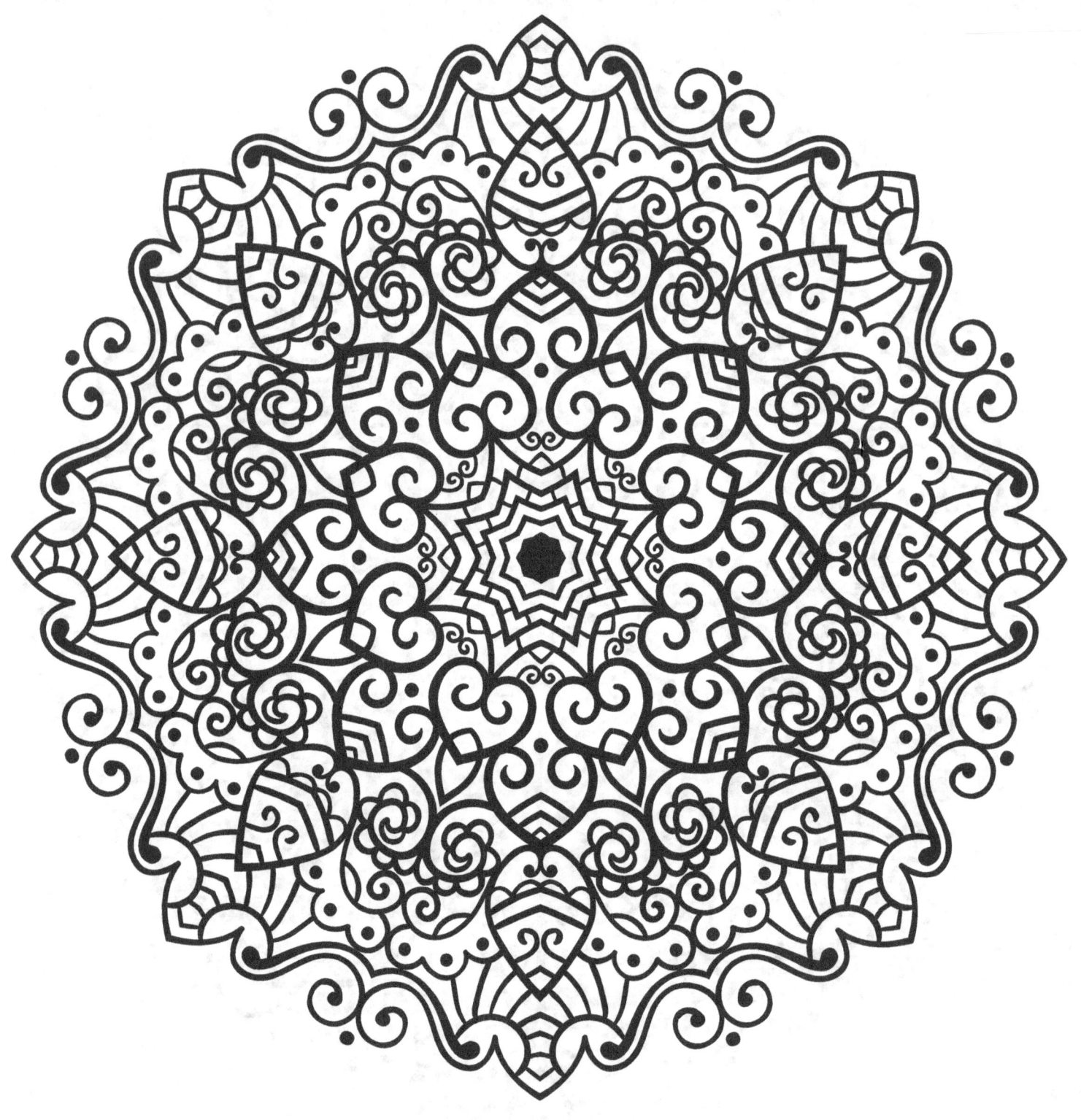

"Meditate. Live purely. Be quiet.
Do your work with mastery.
Like the moon, come outfrom behind the clouds!
Shine."
– Siddhrtha Gautama

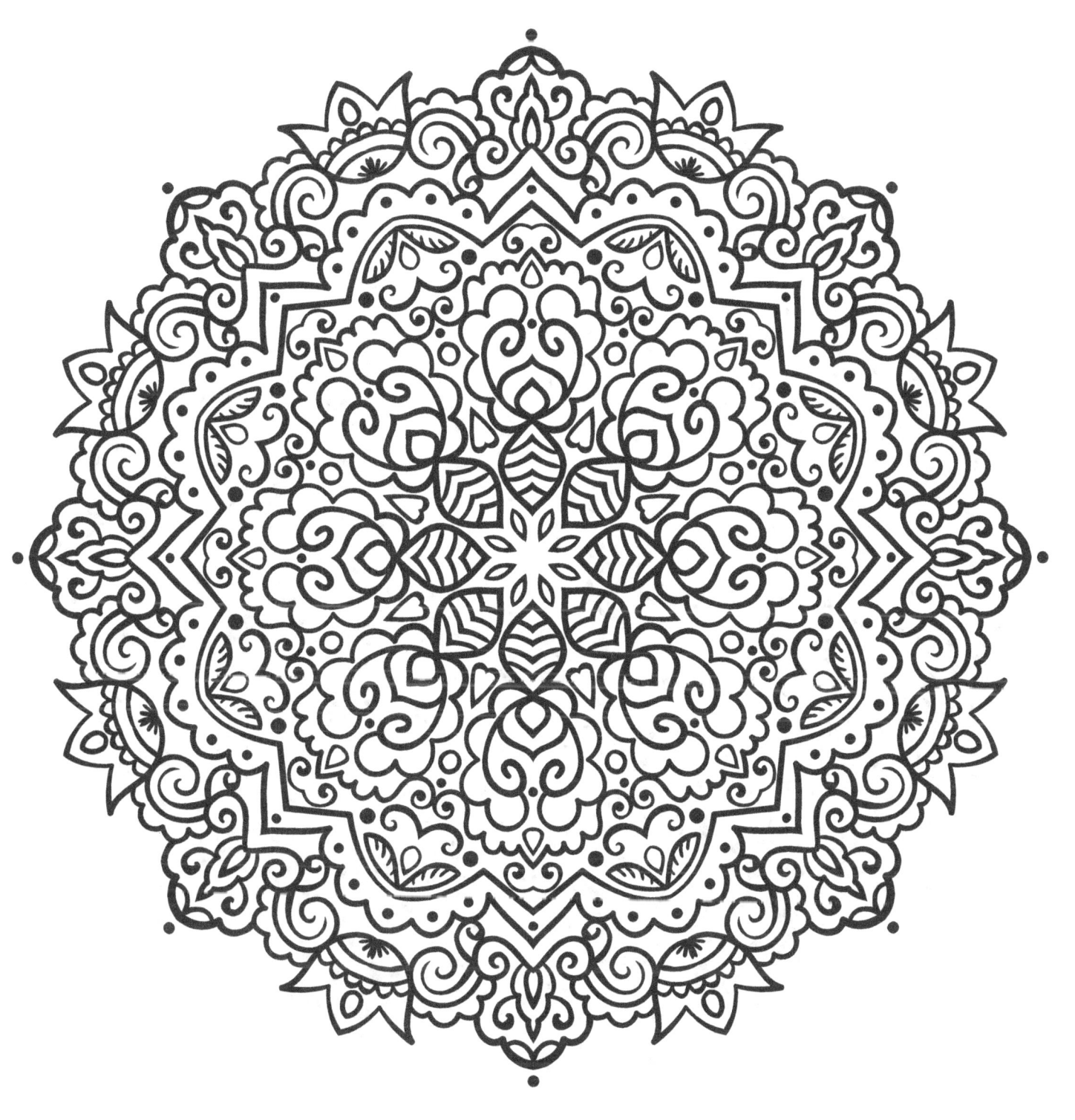

"*None but ourselves can free our minds.*"
— *Bob Marley*

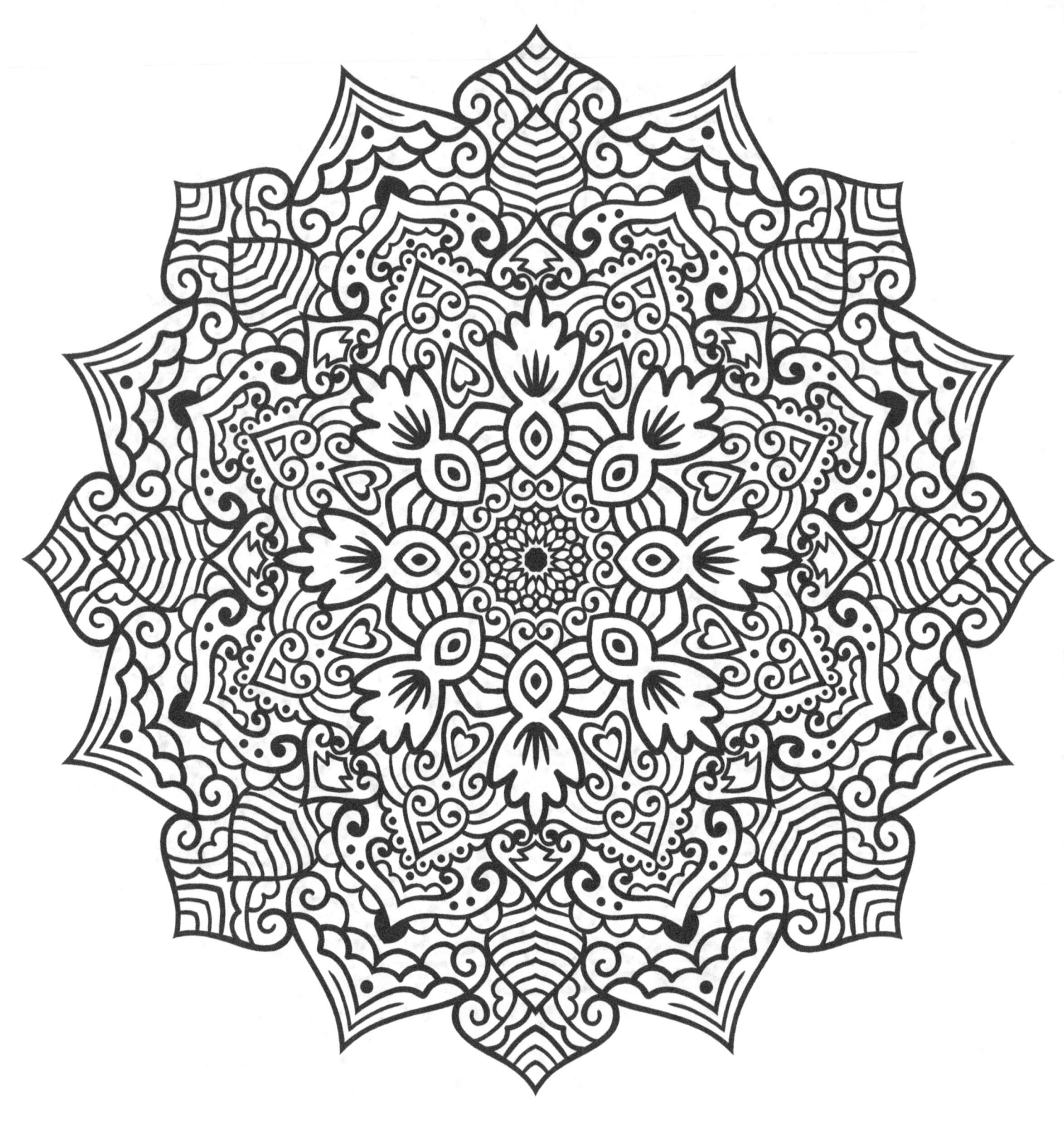

"All we have is all we need. All we need is the awareness of how blessed we really are."
— Sarah Ban Breathnach

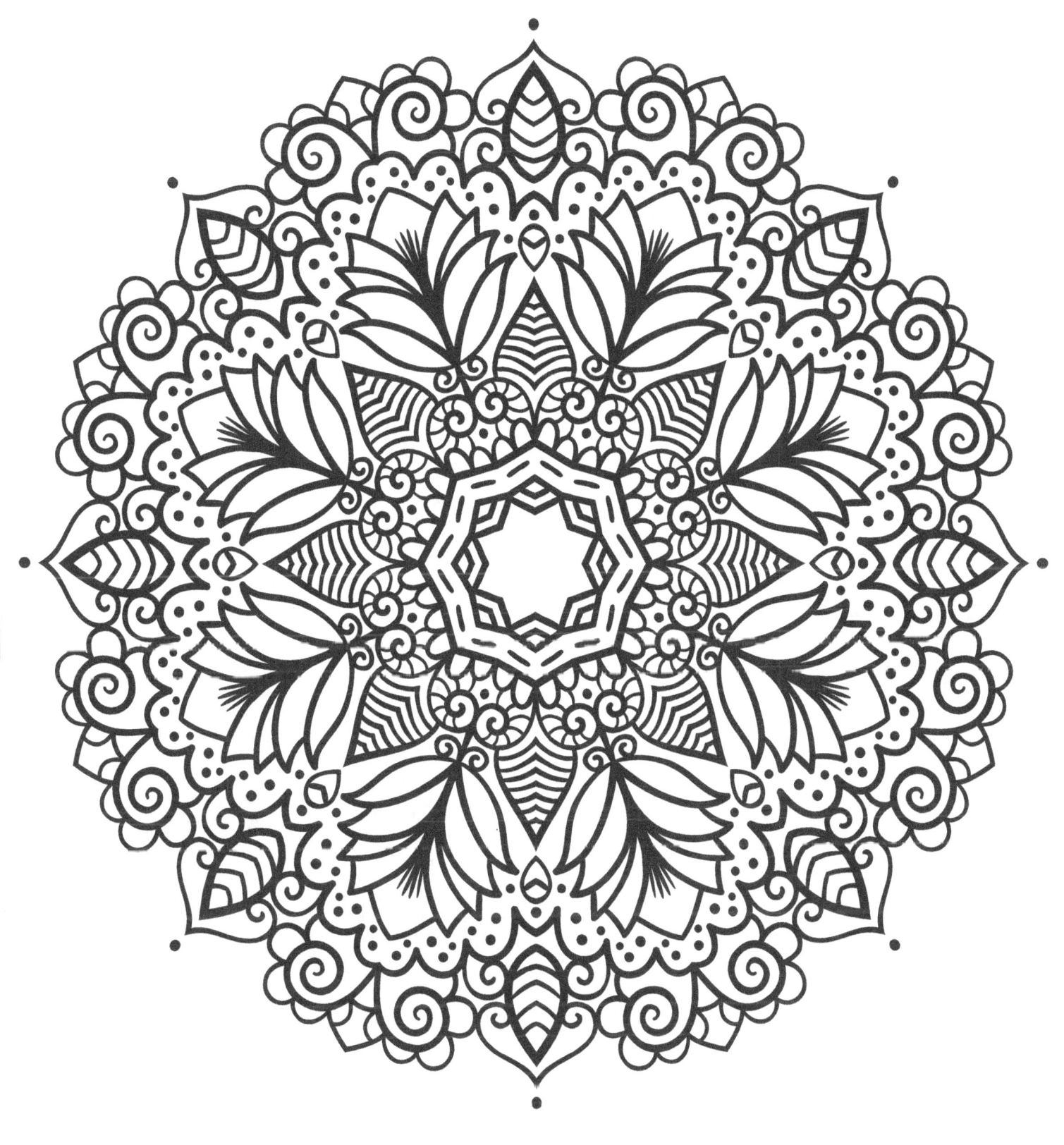

"Do not feel lonely, the entire universe is within you."
– Rumi